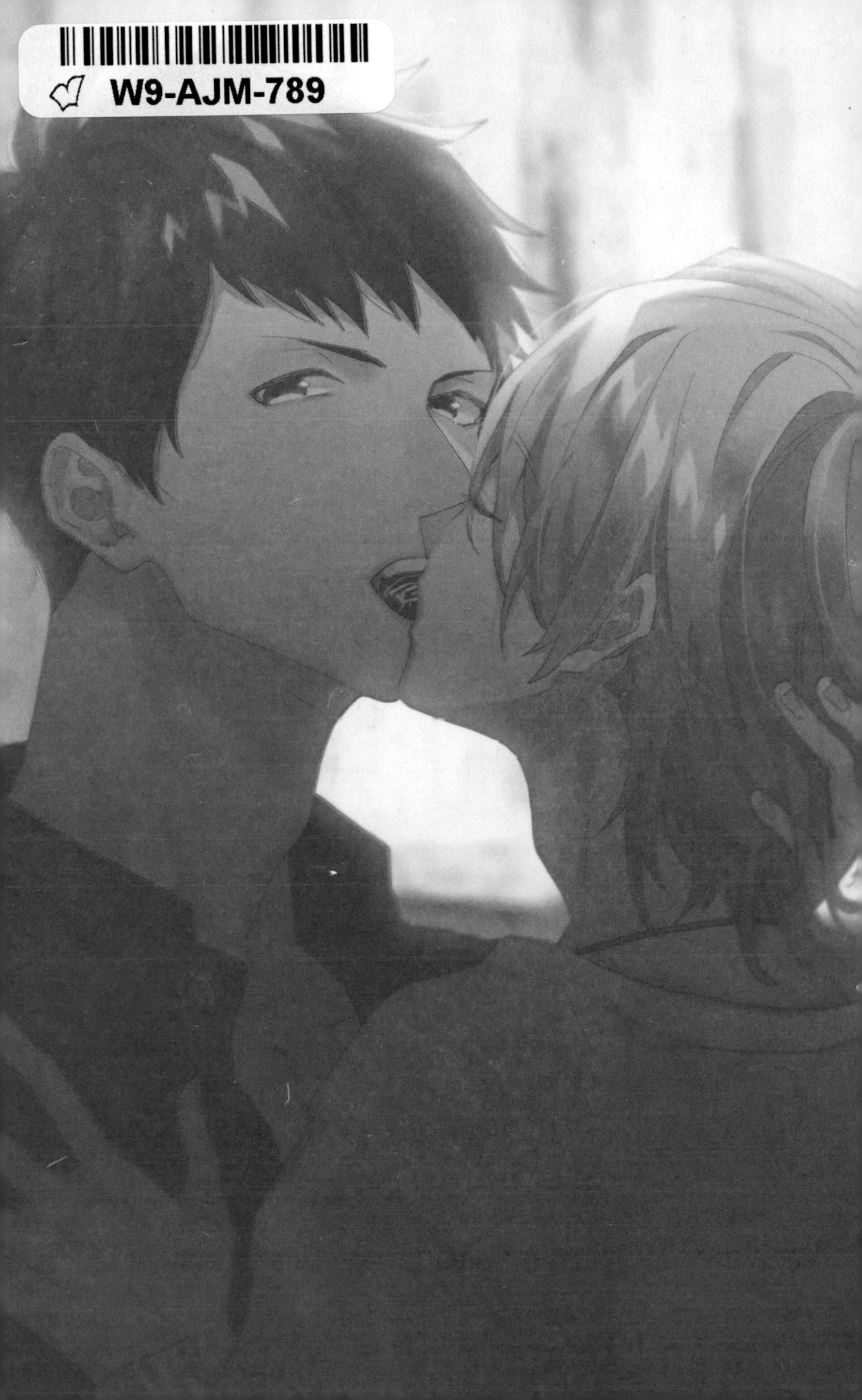

Chéri, my beloved déyainp

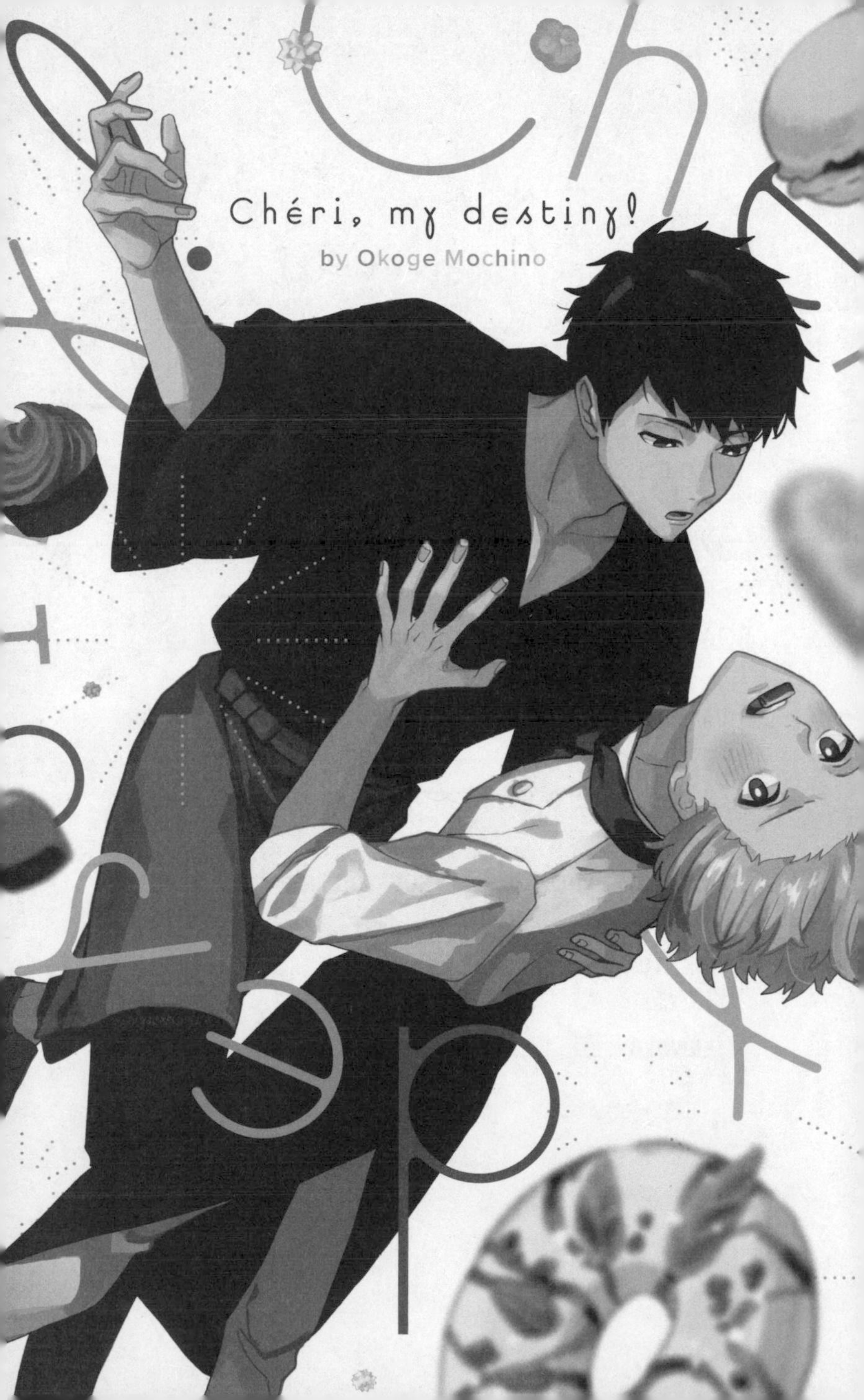
Chéri, my destiny!
by Okoge Mochino

Chéri, my destiny!

CONTENTS

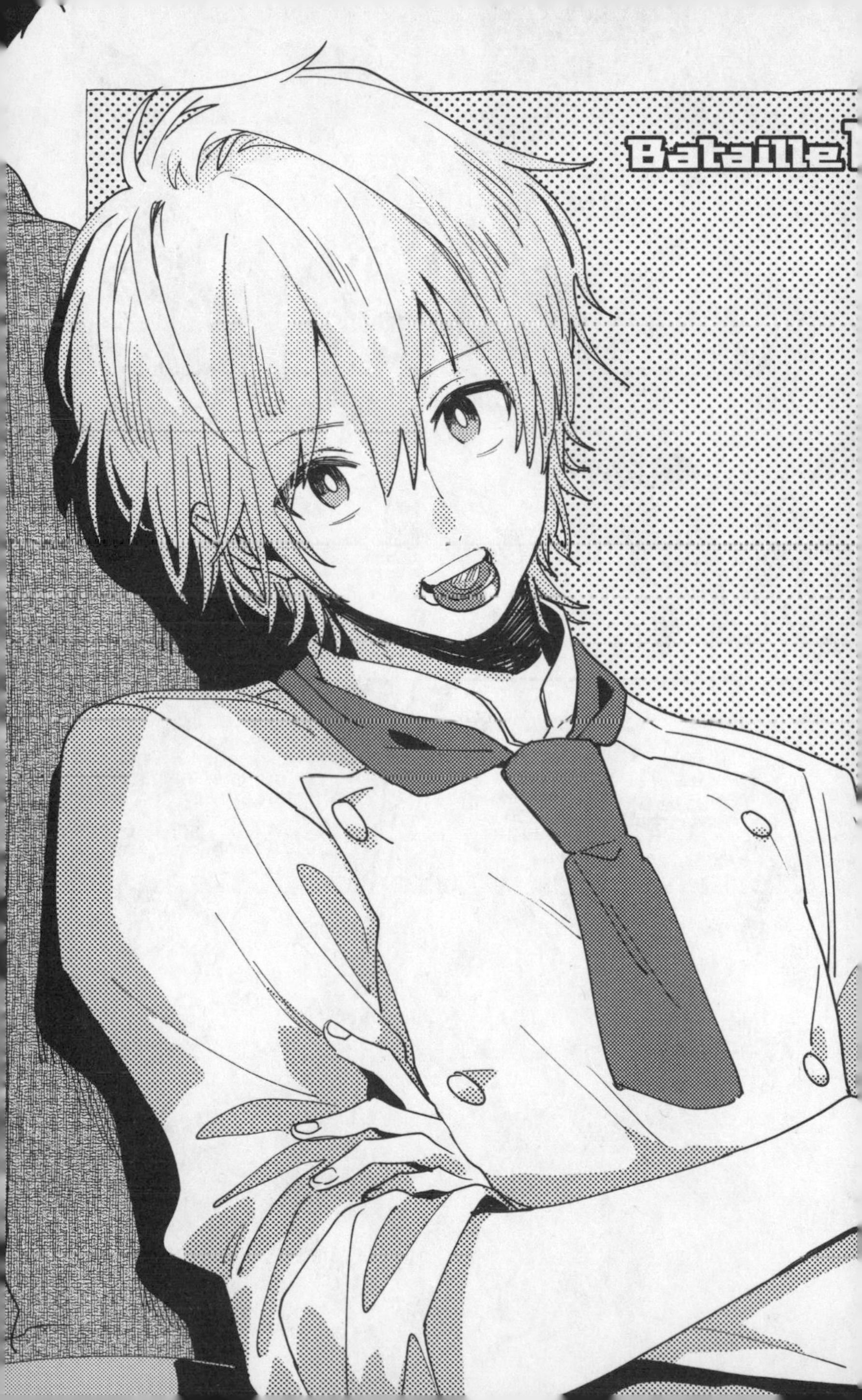
Bataille

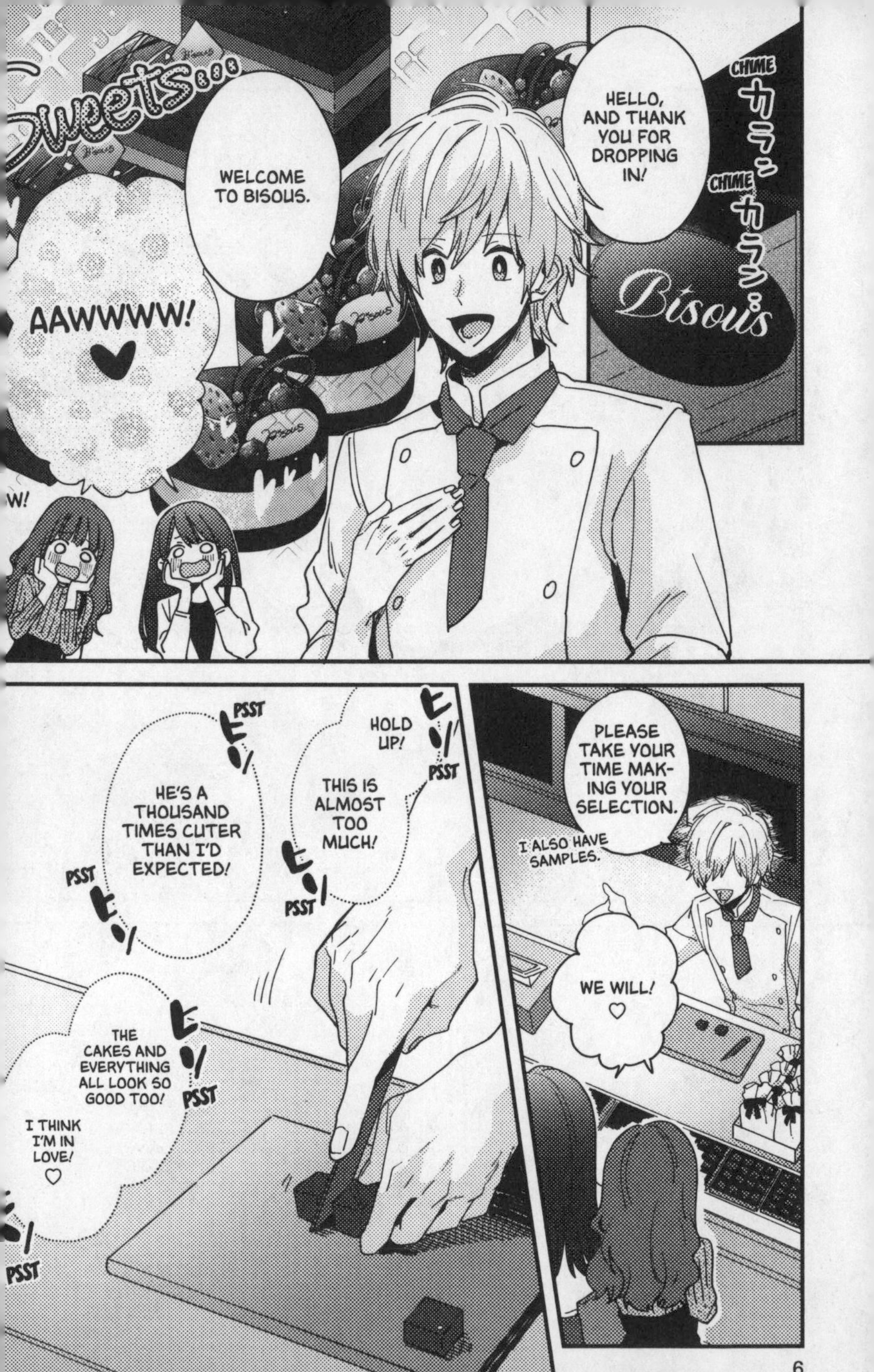
CHIME
カラン
CHIME
カラン
HELLO, AND THANK YOU FOR DROPPING IN!
Bisous
WELCOME TO BISOUS.
Sweets
AAWWWW!
W!
PLEASE TAKE YOUR TIME MAKING YOUR SELECTION.
I ALSO HAVE SAMPLES.
WE WILL!
HOLD UP!
THIS IS ALMOST TOO MUCH!
PSST
PSST
HE'S A THOUSAND TIMES CUTER THAN I'D EXPECTED!
PSST
PSST
THE CAKES AND EVERYTHING ALL LOOK SO GOOD TOO!
PSST
I THINK I'M IN LOVE!
PSST

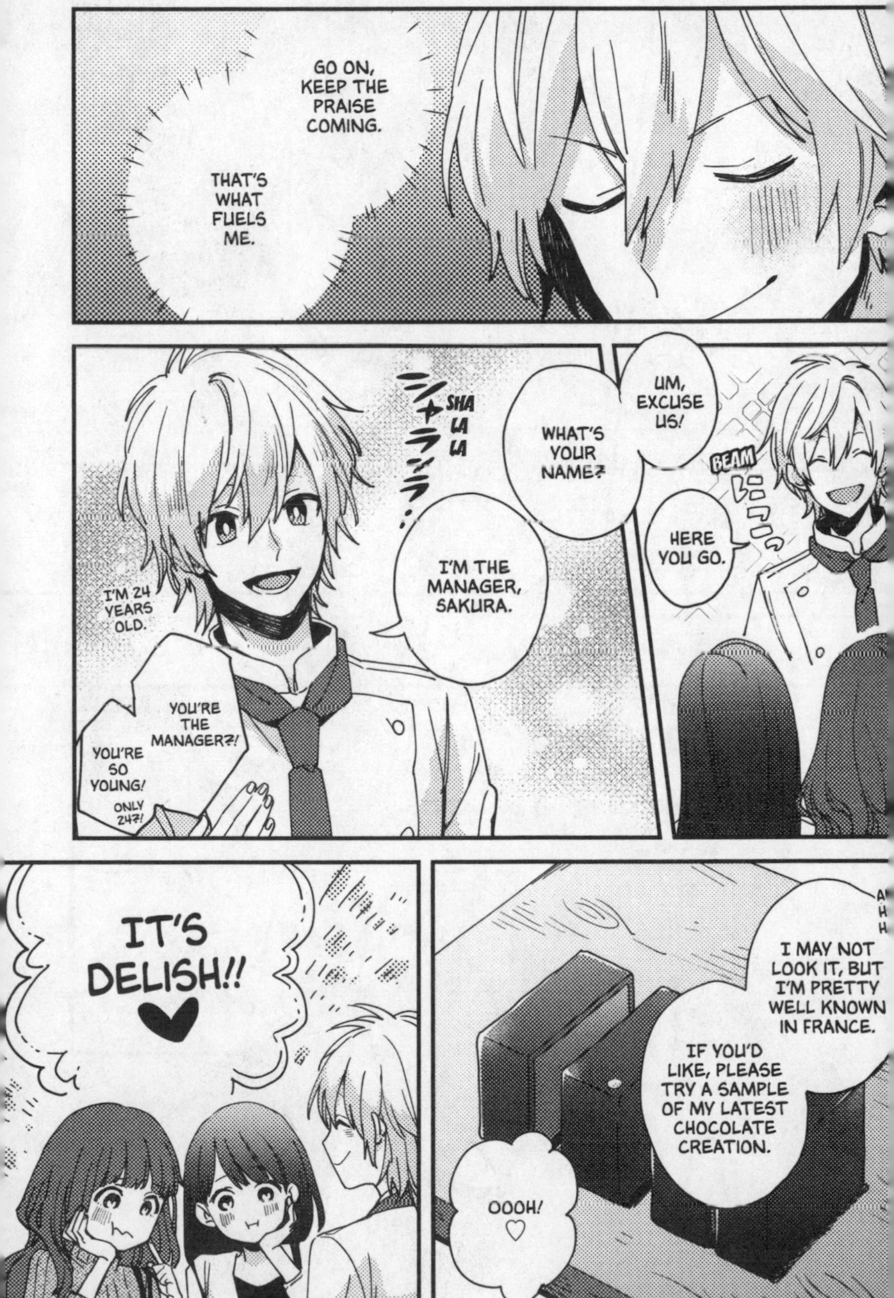
GO ON, KEEP THE PRAISE COMING.
THAT'S WHAT FUELS ME.
UM, EXCUSE US!
WHAT'S YOUR NAME?
BEAM
HERE YOU GO.
SHA LA LA
I'M THE MANAGER, SAKURA.
I'M 24 YEARS OLD.
YOU'RE THE MANAGER?!
YOU'RE SO YOUNG!
ONLY 24?!
AHH
I MAY NOT LOOK IT, BUT I'M PRETTY WELL KNOWN IN FRANCE.
IF YOU'D LIKE, PLEASE TRY A SAMPLE OF MY LATEST CHOCOLATE CREATION.
OOOH! ♡
IT'S DELISH!! ♥

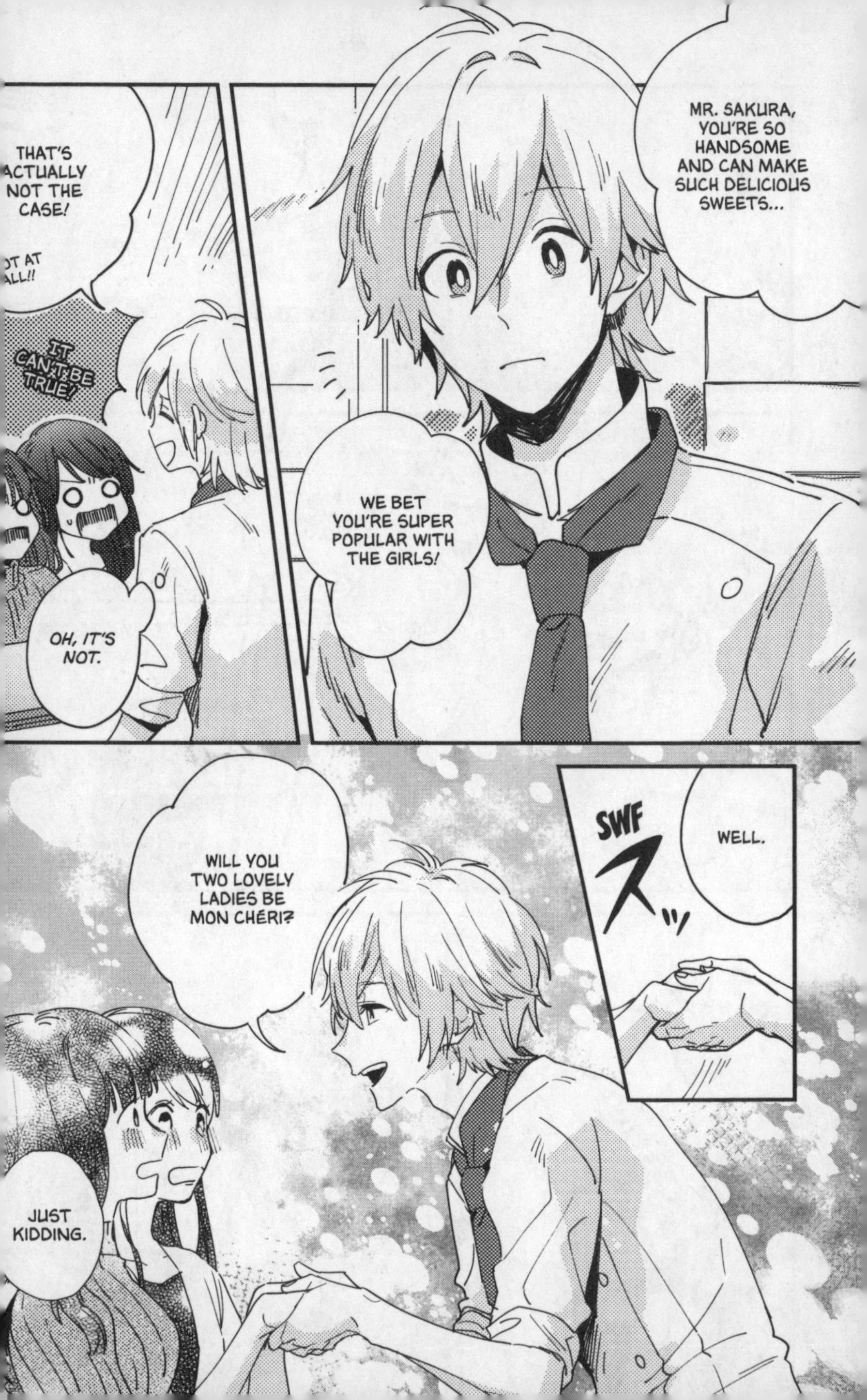
MR. SAKURA, YOU'RE SO HANDSOME AND CAN MAKE SUCH DELICIOUS SWEETS...
WE BET YOU'RE SUPER POPULAR WITH THE GIRLS!
THAT'S ACTUALLY NOT THE CASE!
OT AT ALL!!
IT CAN'T BE TRUE!
OH, IT'S NOT.
SWF
WELL.
WILL YOU TWO LOVELY LADIES BE MON CHÉRI?
JUST KIDDING.

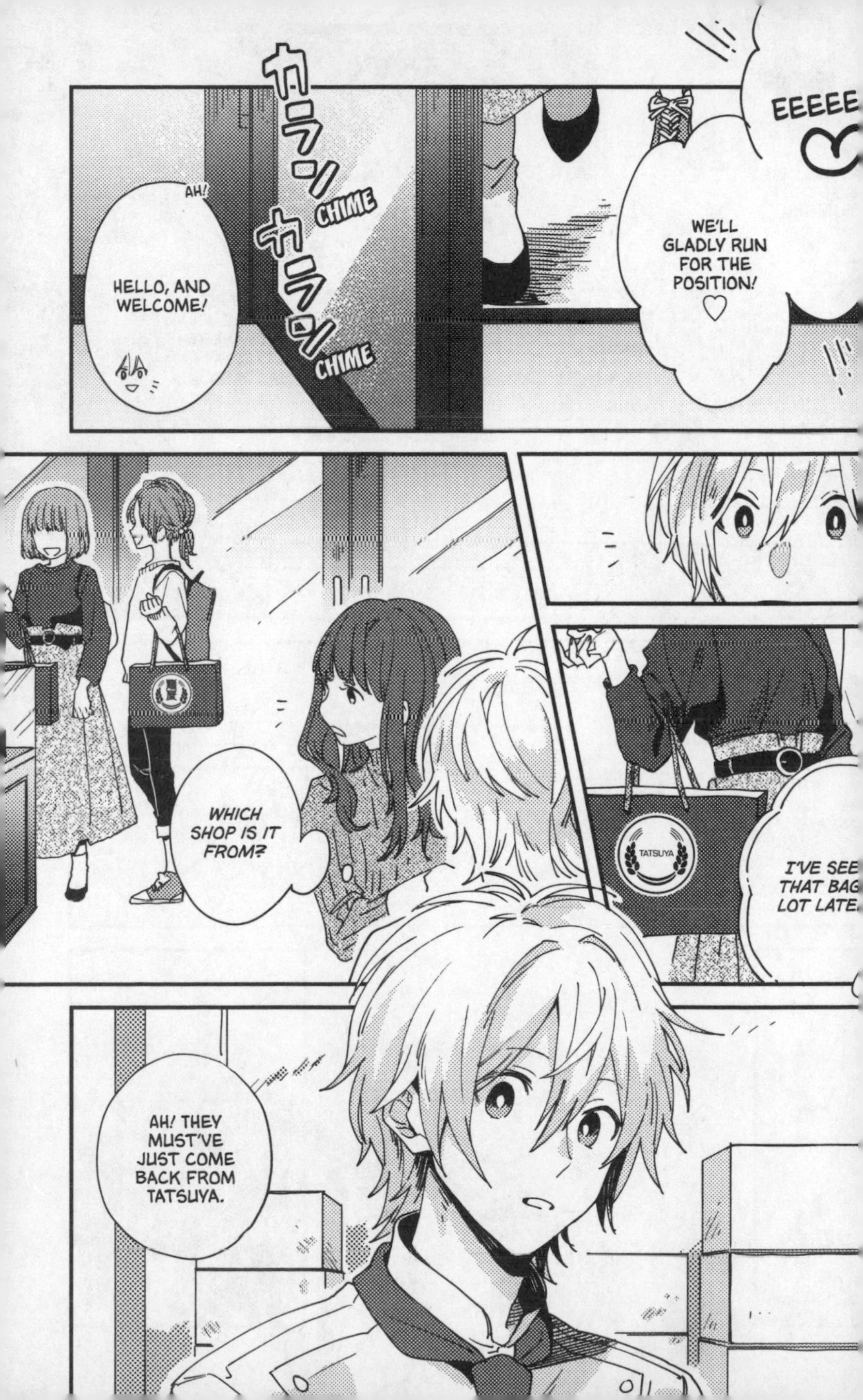
EEEEE
WE'LL GLADLY RUN FOR THE POSITION! ♡
カラン CHIME
カラン CHIME
AH!
HELLO, AND WELCOME!
TATSUYA
I'VE SEE THAT BAG LOT LATE
WHICH SHOP IS IT FROM?
AH! THEY MUST'VE JUST COME BACK FROM TATSUYA.
...

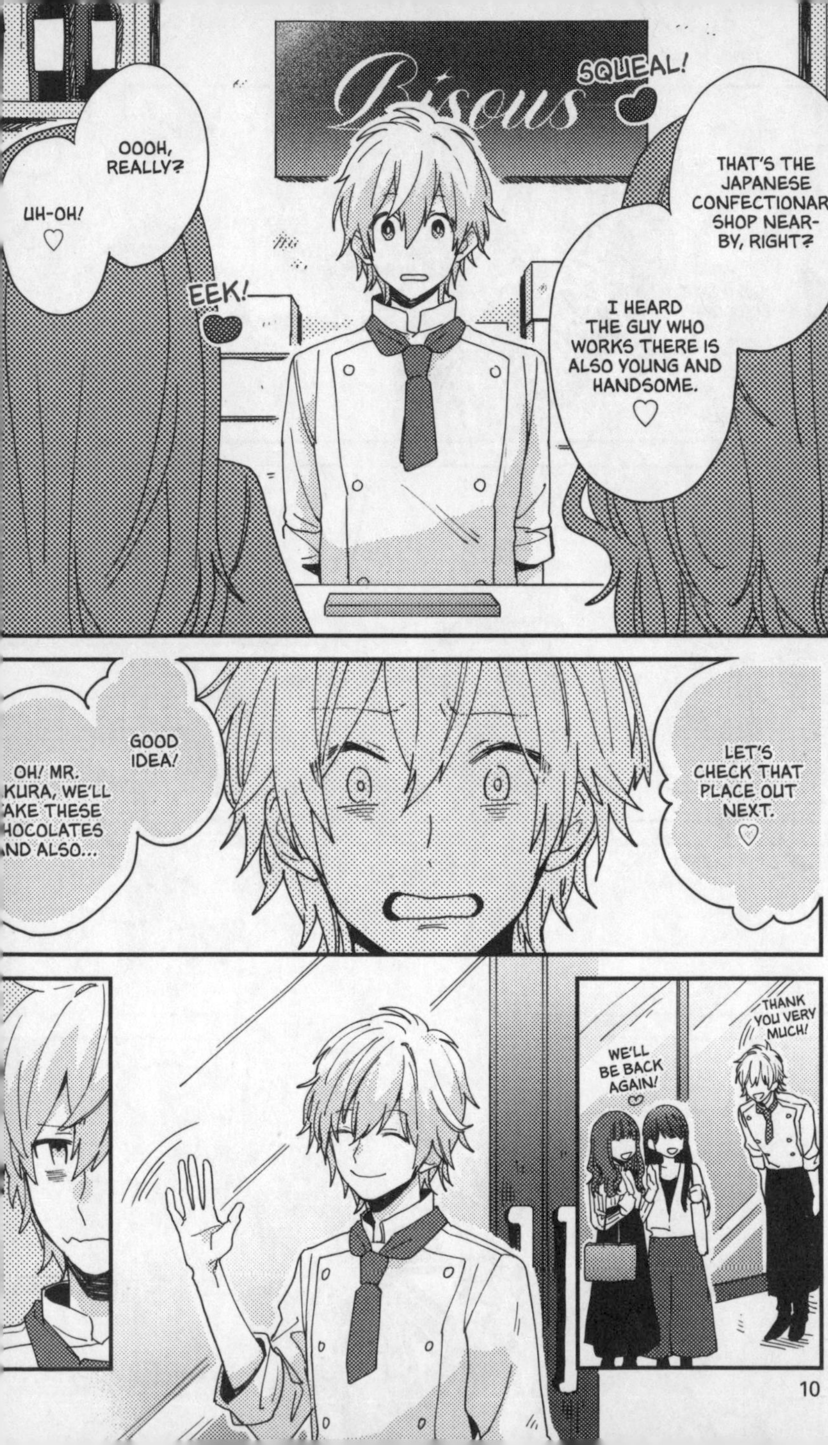
THAT'S THE JAPANESE CONFECTIONARY SHOP NEAR-BY, RIGHT?
I HEARD THE GUY WHO WORKS THERE IS ALSO YOUNG AND HANDSOME. ♡
SQUEAL! ♡
Bisous
OOOH, REALLY?
UH-OH! ♡
EEK! ♡
LET'S CHECK THAT PLACE OUT NEXT. ♡
GOOD IDEA!
OH! MR. KURA, WE'LL AKE THESE HOCOLATES ND ALSO...
THANK YOU VERY MUCH!
WE'LL BE BACK AGAIN! ♡

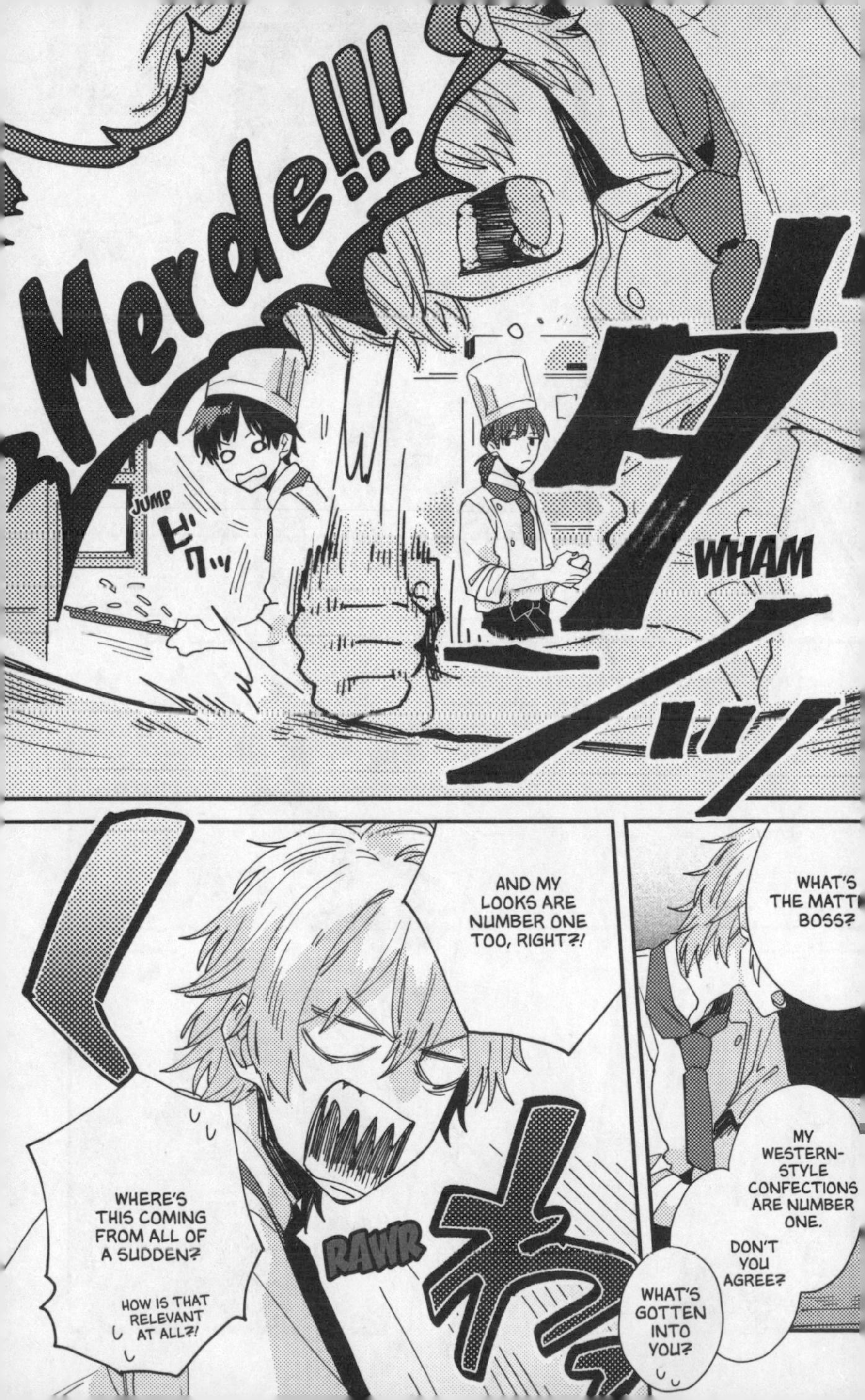
Merde!!!
WHAM
JUMP
ビクッ
WHAT'S THE MATT BOSS?
MY WESTERN-STYLE CONFECTIONS ARE NUMBER ONE.
DON'T YOU AGREE?
WHAT'S GOTTEN INTO YOU?
AND MY LOOKS ARE NUMBER ONE TOO, RIGHT?!
RAWR
WHERE'S THIS COMING FROM ALL OF A SUDDEN?
HOW IS THAT RELEVANT AT ALL?!

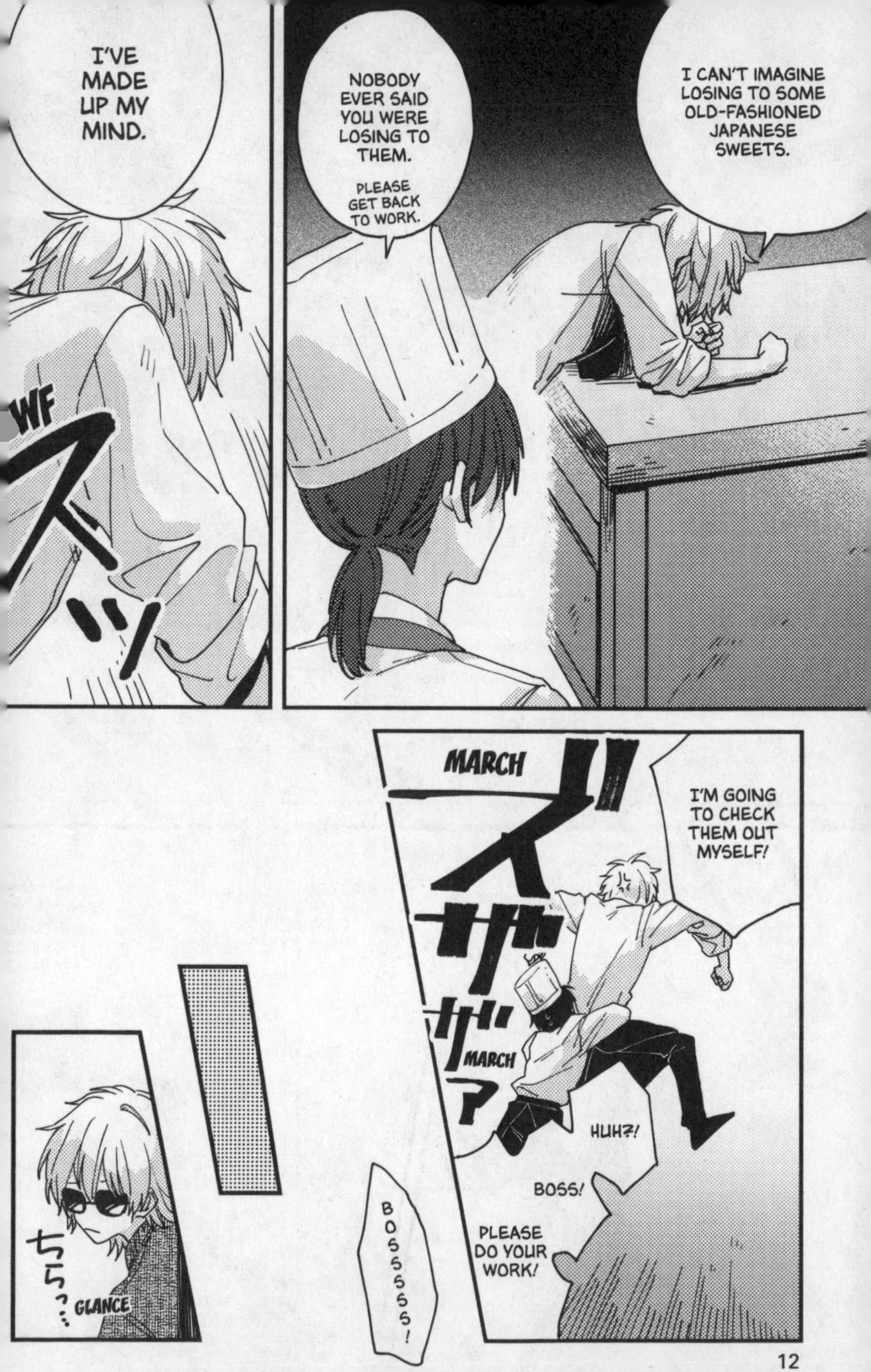

I CAN'T IMAGINE LOSING TO SOME OLD-FASHIONED JAPANESE SWEETS.
NOBODY EVER SAID YOU WERE LOSING TO THEM.
PLEASE GET BACK TO WORK.
I'VE MADE UP MY MIND.
MARCH
I'M GOING TO CHECK THEM OUT MYSELF!
MARCH
HUH?!
BOSS!
PLEASE DO YOUR WORK!
BOSSSSS!
ちら…
GLANCE

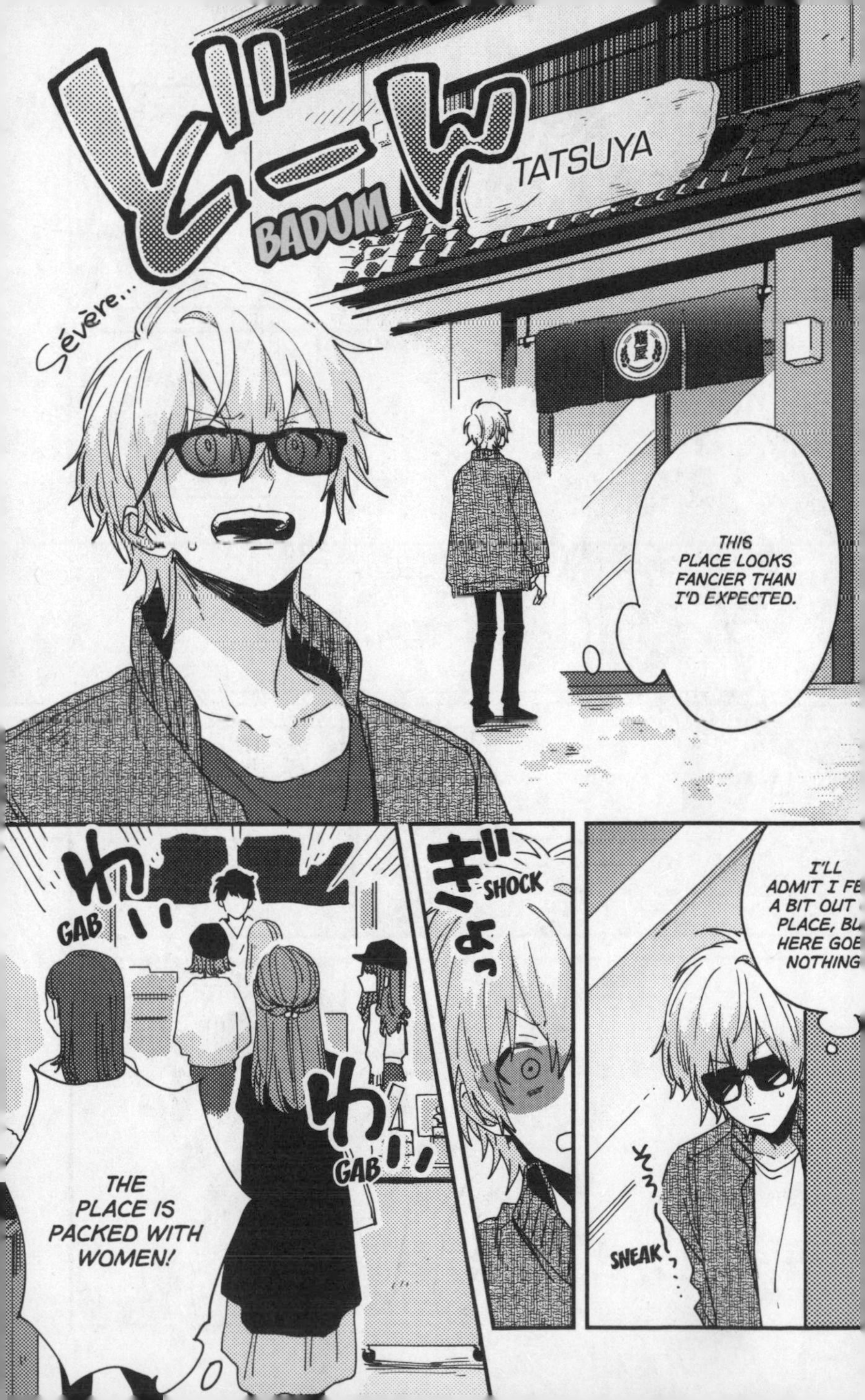
TATSUYA
どーん
BADUM
THIS PLACE LOOKS FANCIER THAN I'D EXPECTED.
Sévère...
I'LL ADMIT I FE
A BIT OUT
PLACE, BU
HERE GOE
NOTHING
そろ〜
SNEAK
ぎょっ
SHOCK
わい
GAB
わい
GAB
THE PLACE IS PACKED WITH WOMEN!

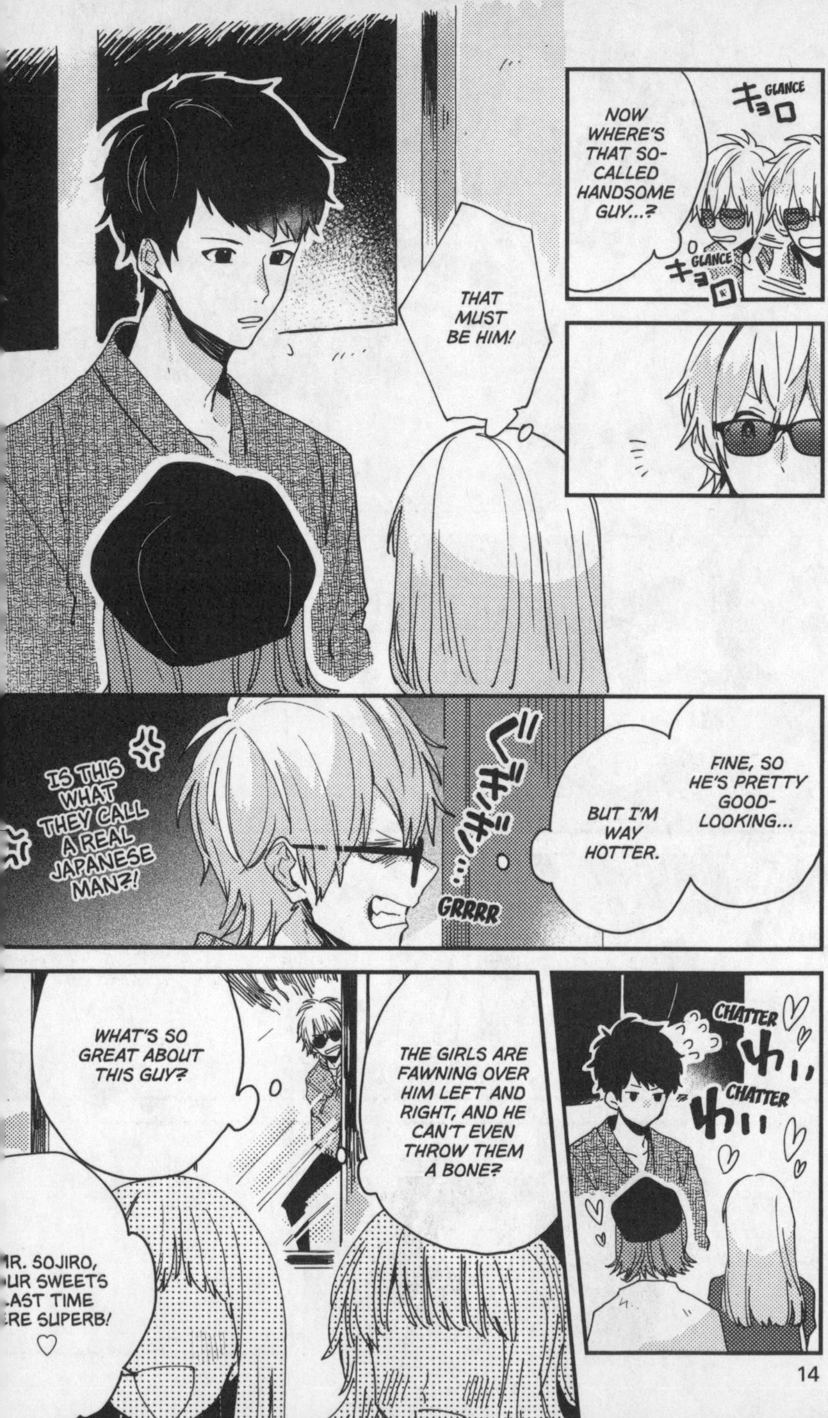
GLANCE キョロ
NOW WHERE'S THAT SO-CALLED HANDSOME GUY...?
GLANCE キョロ
THAT MUST BE HIM!
FINE, SO HE'S PRETTY GOOD-LOOKING...
BUT I'M WAY HOTTER.
ギギギ...
GRRRR
IS THIS WHAT THEY CALL A REAL JAPANESE MAN?!
CHATTER わい
CHATTER わい
THE GIRLS ARE FAWNING OVER HIM LEFT AND RIGHT, AND HE CAN'T EVEN THROW THEM A BONE?
WHAT'S SO GREAT ABOUT THIS GUY?
R. SOJIRO, UR SWEETS AST TIME ERE SUPERB! ♡

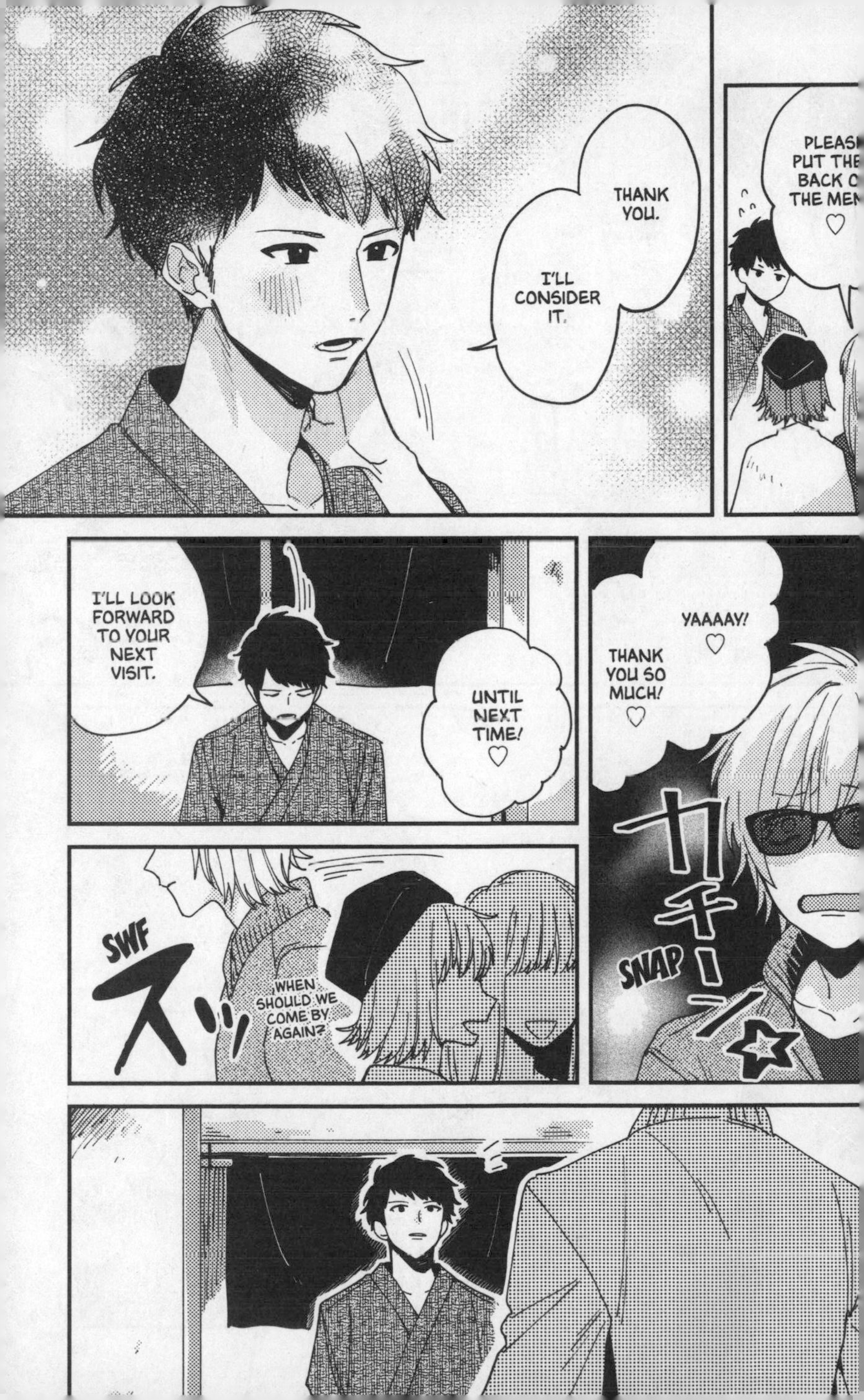
PLEAS PUT THE BACK O THE MEN ♡
THANK YOU.
I'LL CONSIDER IT.
YAAAAY! ♡
THANK YOU SO MUCH! ♡
SNAP
UNTIL NEXT TIME! ♡
I'LL LOOK FORWARD TO YOUR NEXT VISIT.
WHEN SHOULD WE COME BY AGAIN?
SWF

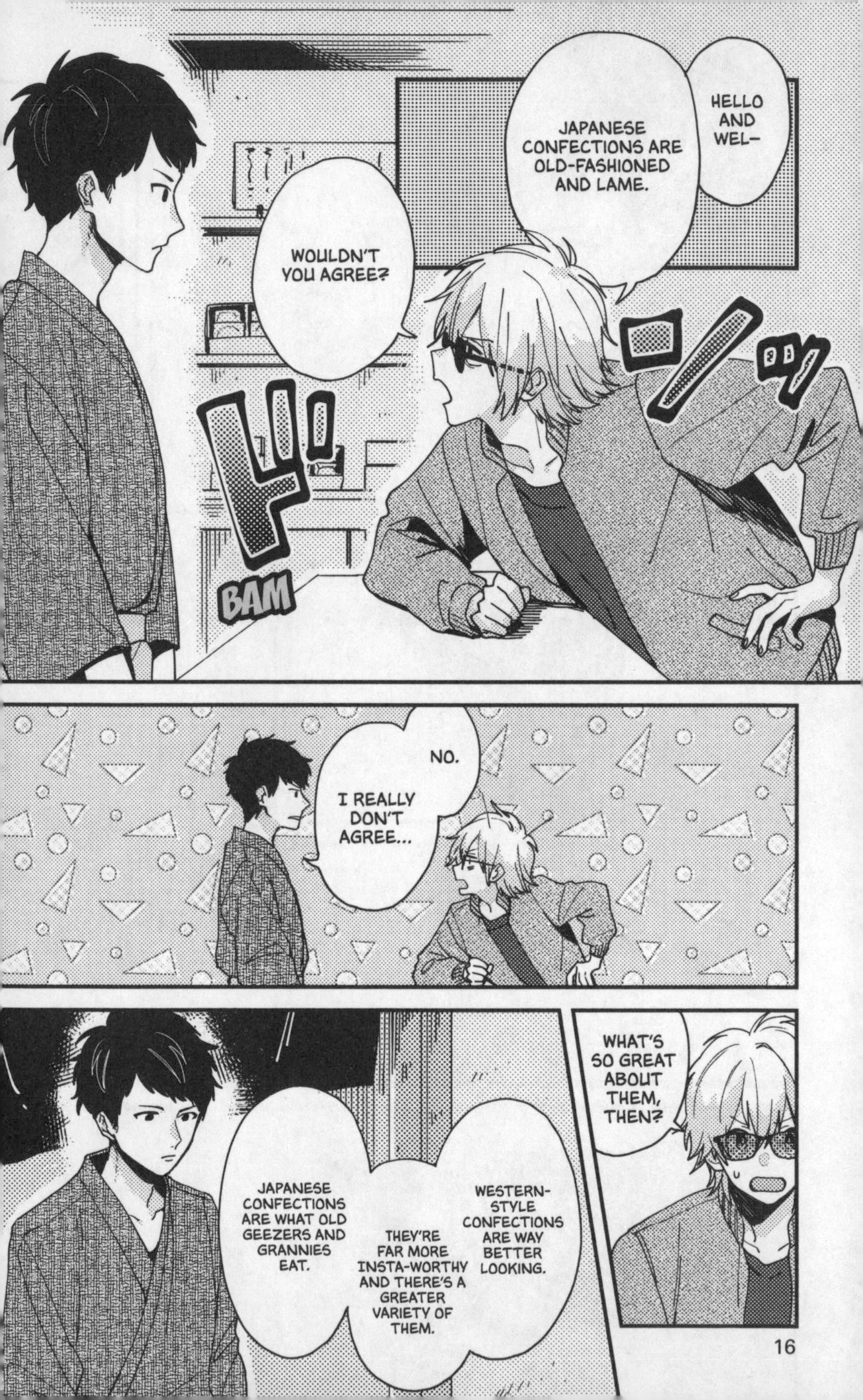

HELLO AND WEL—
JAPANESE CONFECTIONS ARE OLD-FASHIONED AND LAME.
WOULDN'T YOU AGREE?
BAM
NO.
I REALLY DON'T AGREE...
WHAT'S SO GREAT ABOUT THEM, THEN?
WESTERN-STYLE CONFECTIONS ARE WAY BETTER LOOKING.
THEY'RE FAR MORE INSTA-WORTHY AND THERE'S A GREATER VARIETY OF THEM.
JAPANESE CONFECTIONS ARE WHAT OLD GEEZERS AND GRANNIES EAT.

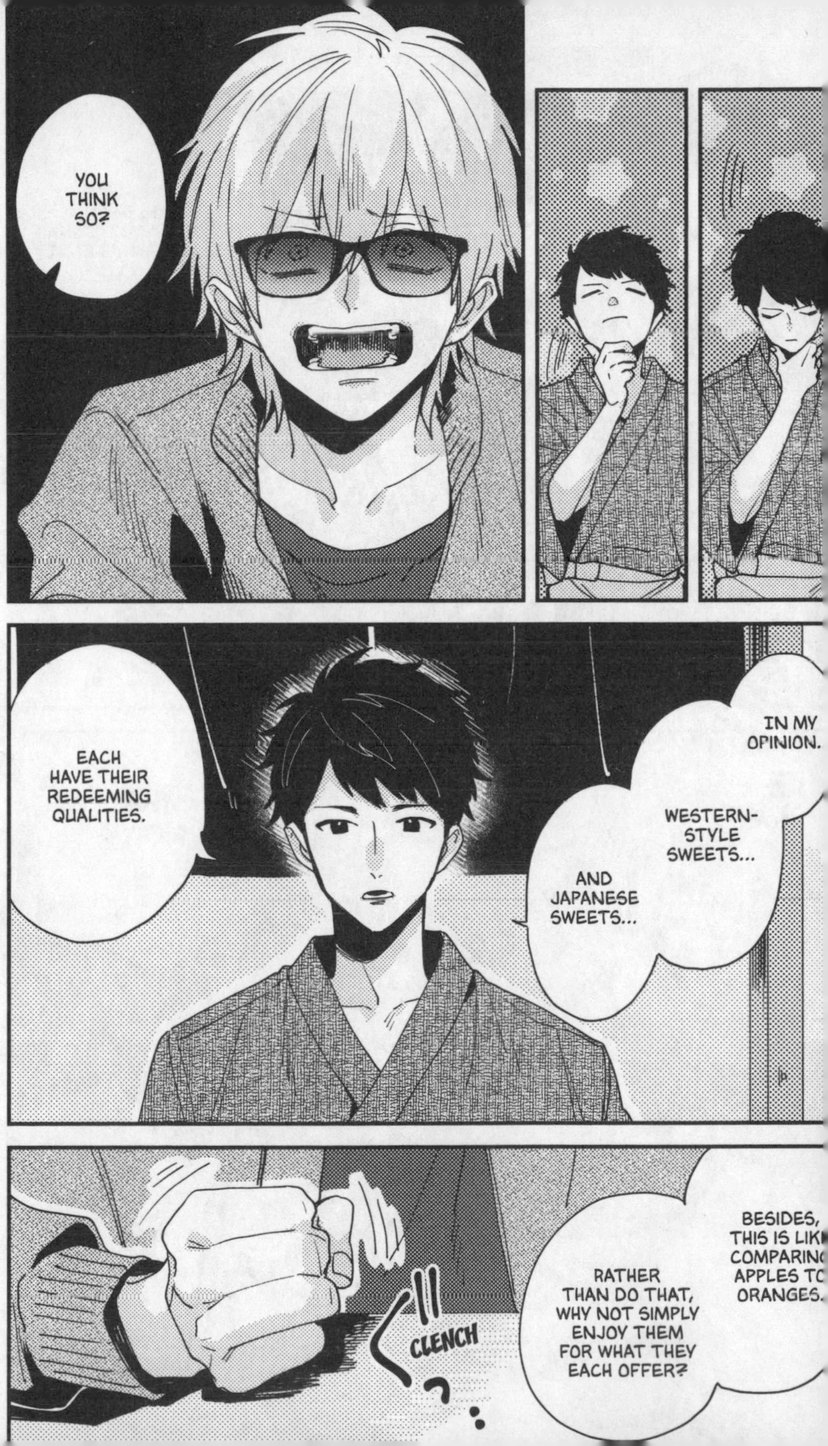
YOU THINK SO?
IN MY OPINION.
WESTERN-STYLE SWEETS...
AND JAPANESE SWEETS...
EACH HAVE THEIR REDEEMING QUALITIES.
BESIDES, THIS IS LIK COMPARIN APPLES T ORANGES.
RATHER THAN DO THAT, WHY NOT SIMPLY ENJOY THEM FOR WHAT THEY EACH OFFER?
CLENCH

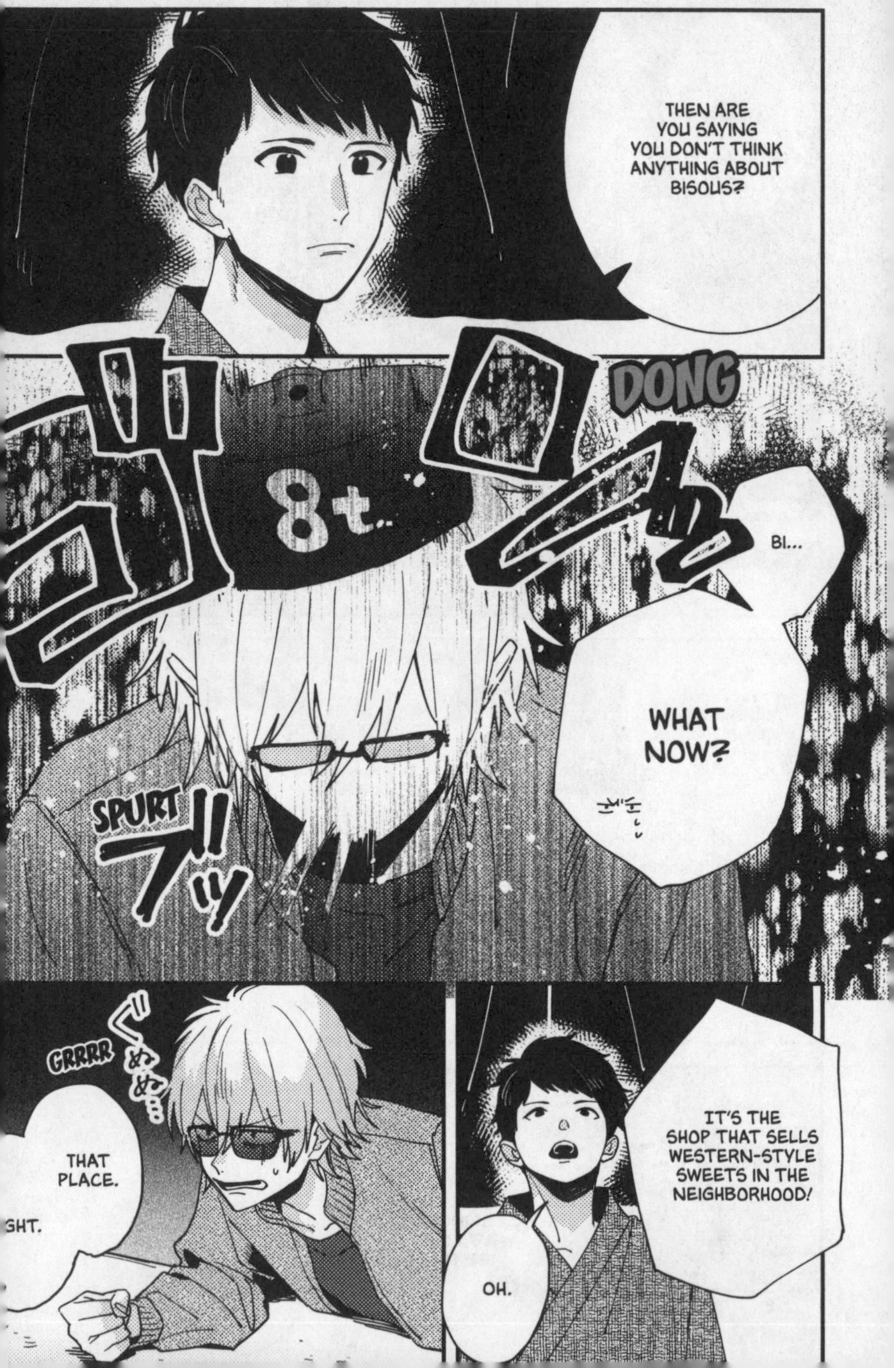
THEN ARE YOU SAYING YOU DON'T THINK ANYTHING ABOUT BISOUS?
DONG
BI...
WHAT NOW?
SPURT
IT'S THE SHOP THAT SELLS WESTERN-STYLE SWEETS IN THE NEIGHBORHOOD!
OH.
GRRRR
THAT PLACE.
GHT.

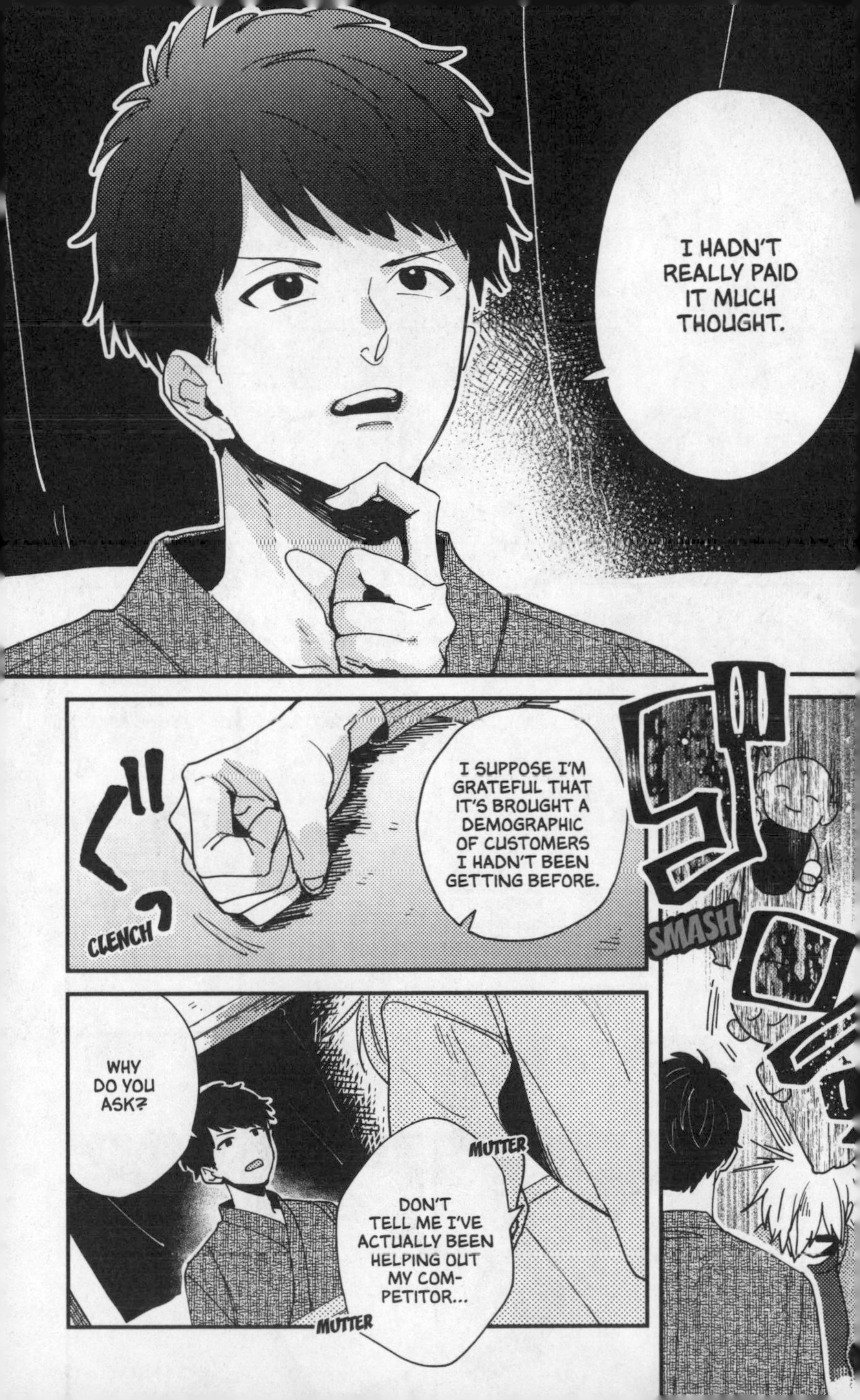

I HADN'T REALLY PAID IT MUCH THOUGHT.
SMASH
I SUPPOSE I'M GRATEFUL THAT IT'S BROUGHT A DEMOGRAPHIC OF CUSTOMERS I HADN'T BEEN GETTING BEFORE.
CLENCH
WHY DO YOU ASK?
MUTTER
DON'T TELL ME I'VE ACTUALLY BEEN HELPING OUT MY COM-PETITOR...
MUTTER

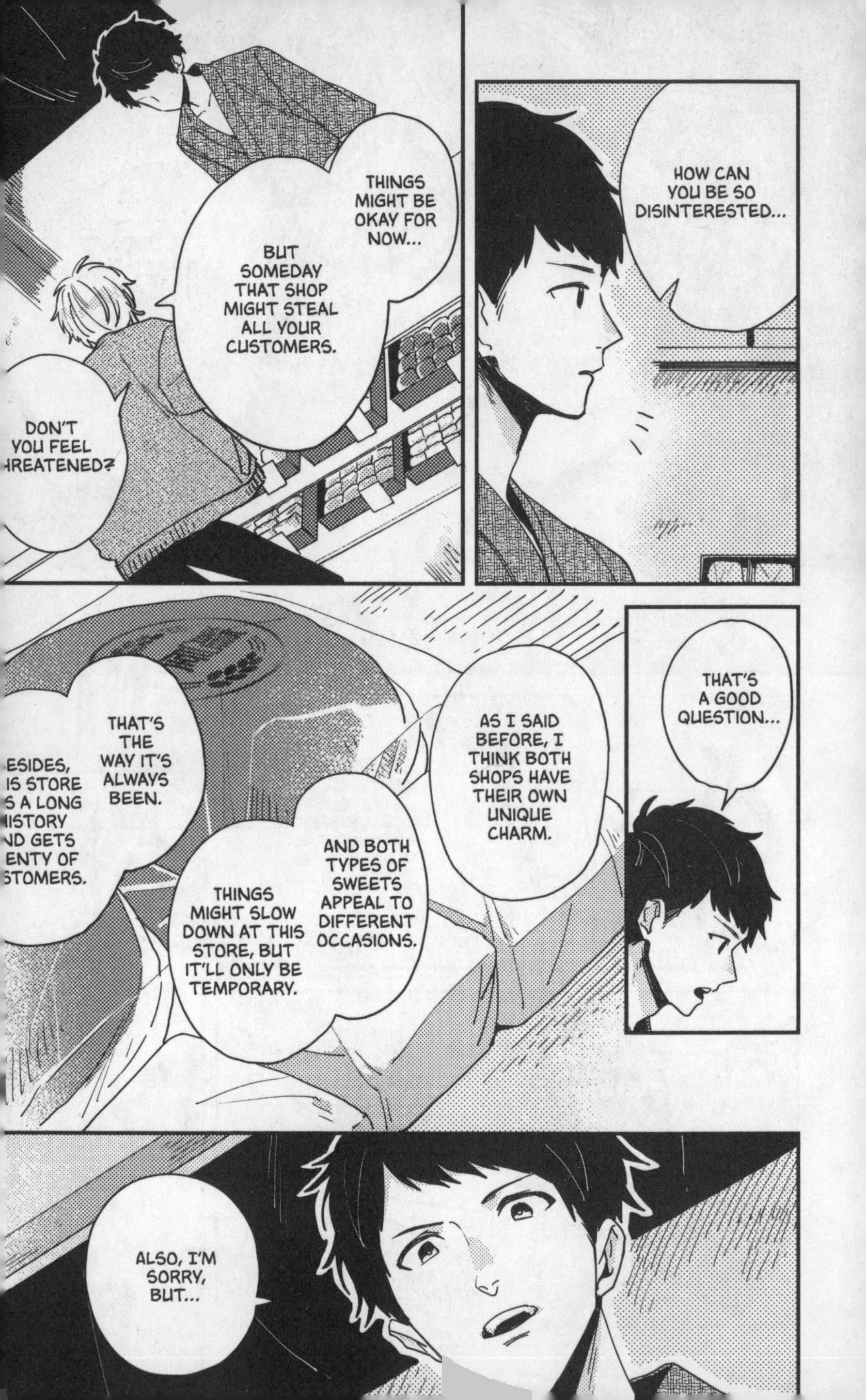
HOW CAN YOU BE SO DISINTERESTED...
THINGS MIGHT BE OKAY FOR NOW...
BUT SOMEDAY THAT SHOP MIGHT STEAL ALL YOUR CUSTOMERS.
DON'T YOU FEEL HREATENED?
THAT'S A GOOD QUESTION...
AS I SAID BEFORE, I THINK BOTH SHOPS HAVE THEIR OWN UNIQUE CHARM.
AND BOTH TYPES OF SWEETS APPEAL TO DIFFERENT OCCASIONS.
THINGS MIGHT SLOW DOWN AT THIS STORE, BUT IT'LL ONLY BE TEMPORARY.
THAT'S THE WAY IT'S ALWAYS BEEN.
ESIDES, IS STORE S A LONG ISTORY ND GETS ENTY OF STOMERS.
ALSO, I'M SORRY, BUT...

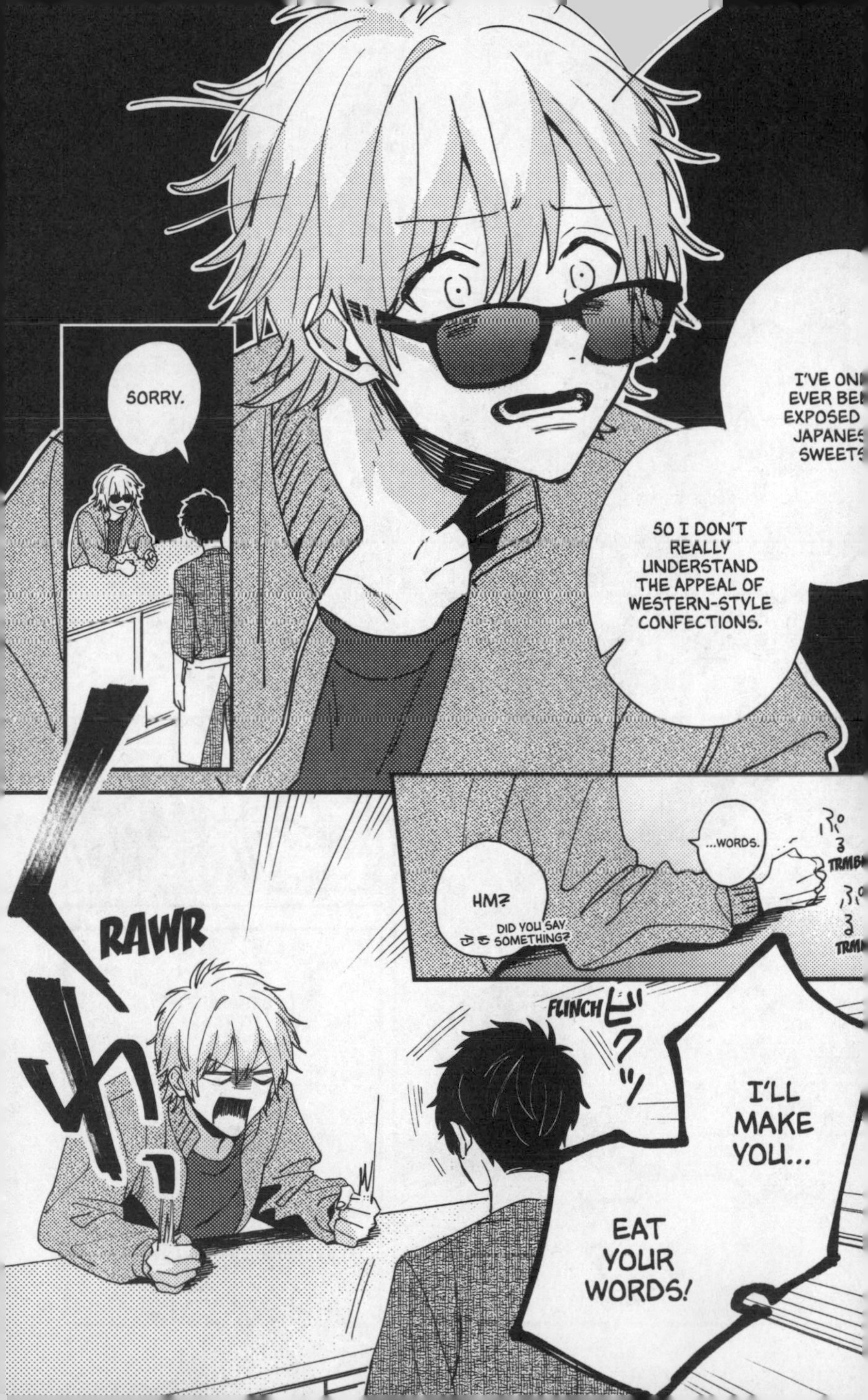
I'VE ONL EVER BE EXPOSED JAPANES SWEETS
SO I DON'T REALLY UNDERSTAND THE APPEAL OF WESTERN-STYLE CONFECTIONS.
SORRY.
TRMB
TRM
...WORDS.
HM?
DID YOU SAY SOMETHING?
FLINCH
ビクッ
RAWR
I'LL MAKE YOU...
EAT YOUR WORDS!

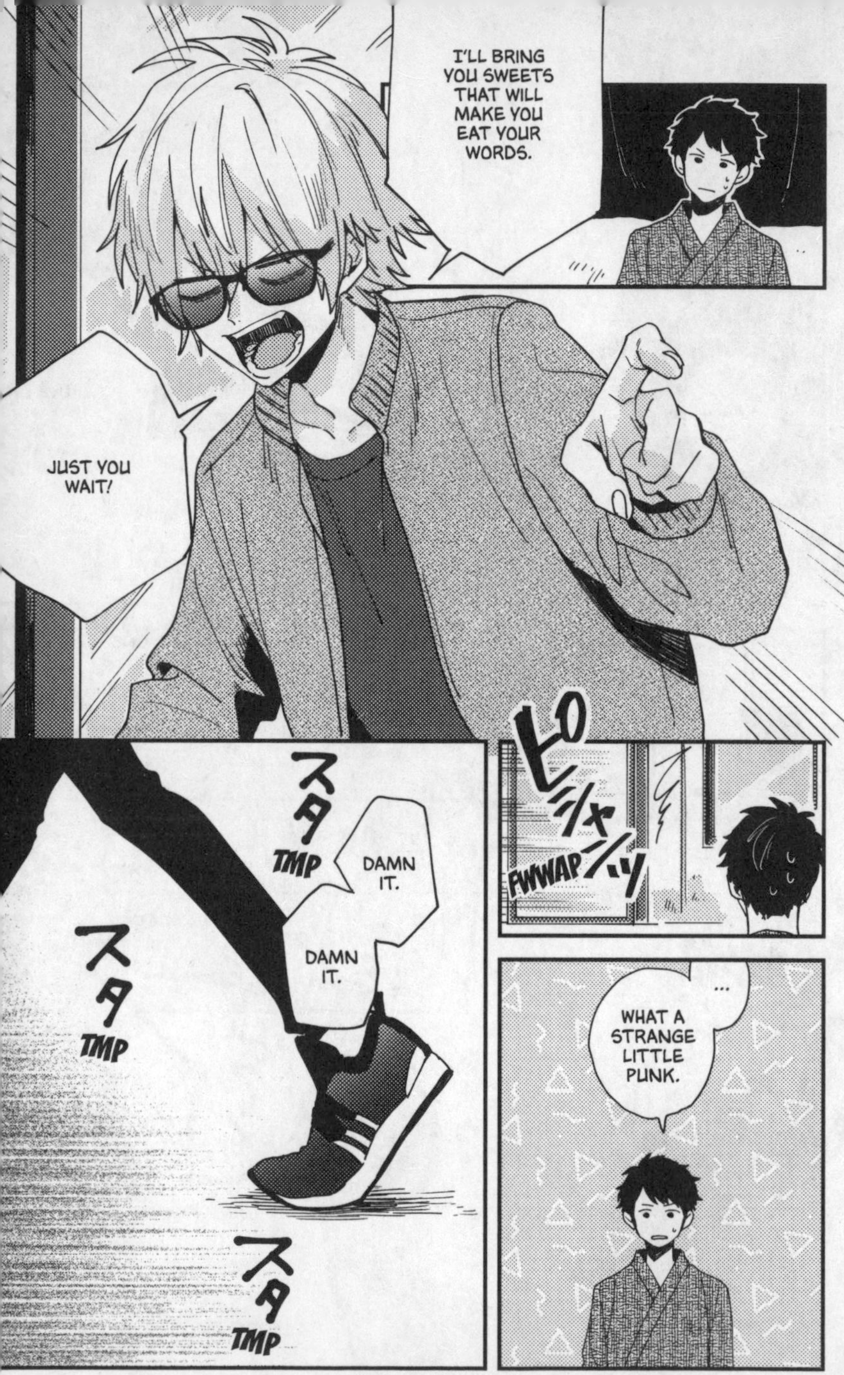
I'LL BRING YOU SWEETS THAT WILL MAKE YOU EAT YOUR WORDS.
JUST YOU WAIT!
ピシャッ
FWWAP
...
WHAT A STRANGE LITTLE PUNK.
スタ
TMP
DAMN IT.
DAMN IT.
スタ
TMP
スタ
TMP

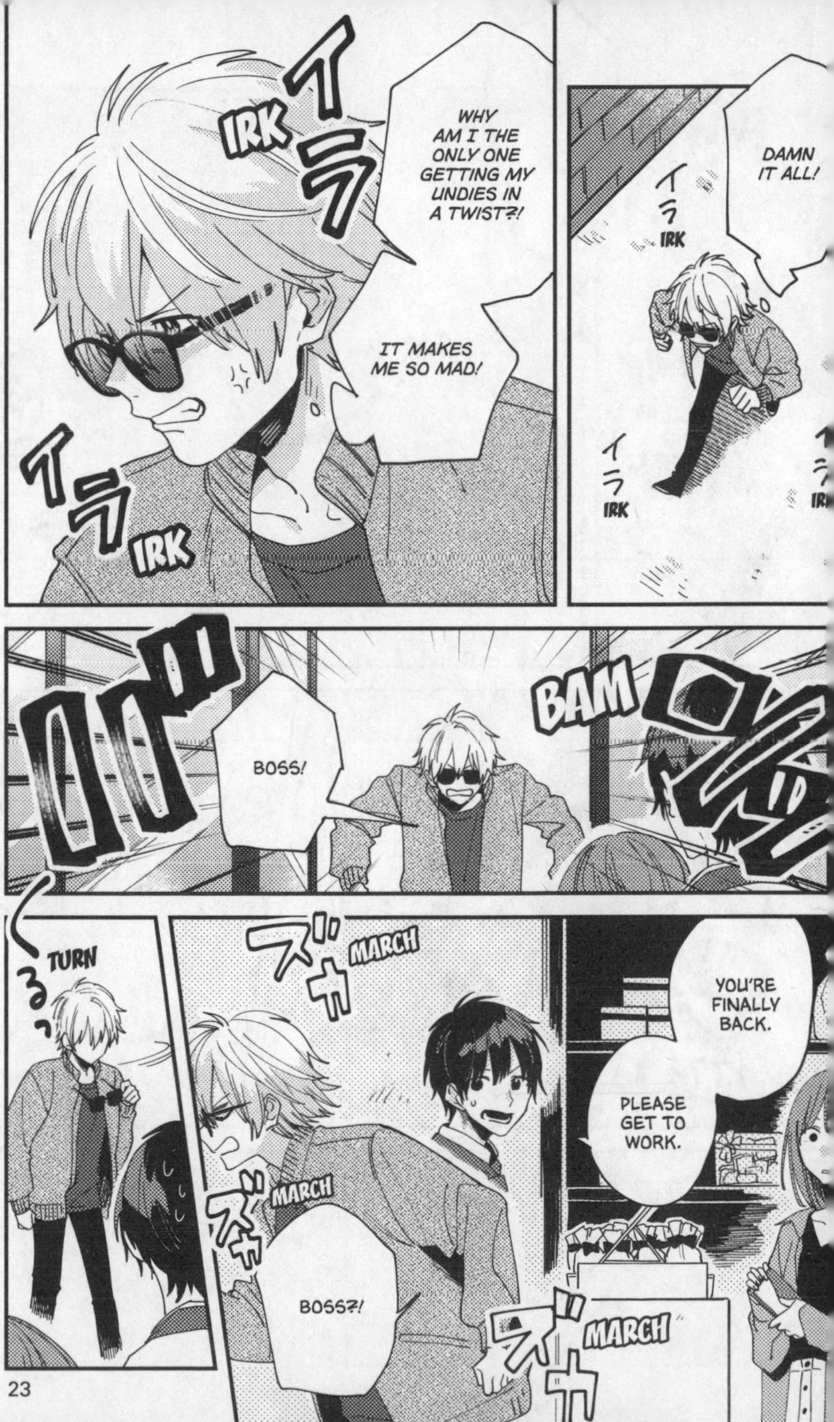
DAMN IT ALL!
イラ IRK
イラ IRK
WHY AM I THE ONLY ONE GETTING MY UNDIES IN A TWIST?!
イラ IRK
IT MAKES ME SO MAD!
イラ IRK
BAM
BOSS!
YOU'RE FINALLY BACK.
PLEASE GET TO WORK.
MARCH
MARCH
BOSS?!
MARCH
TURN

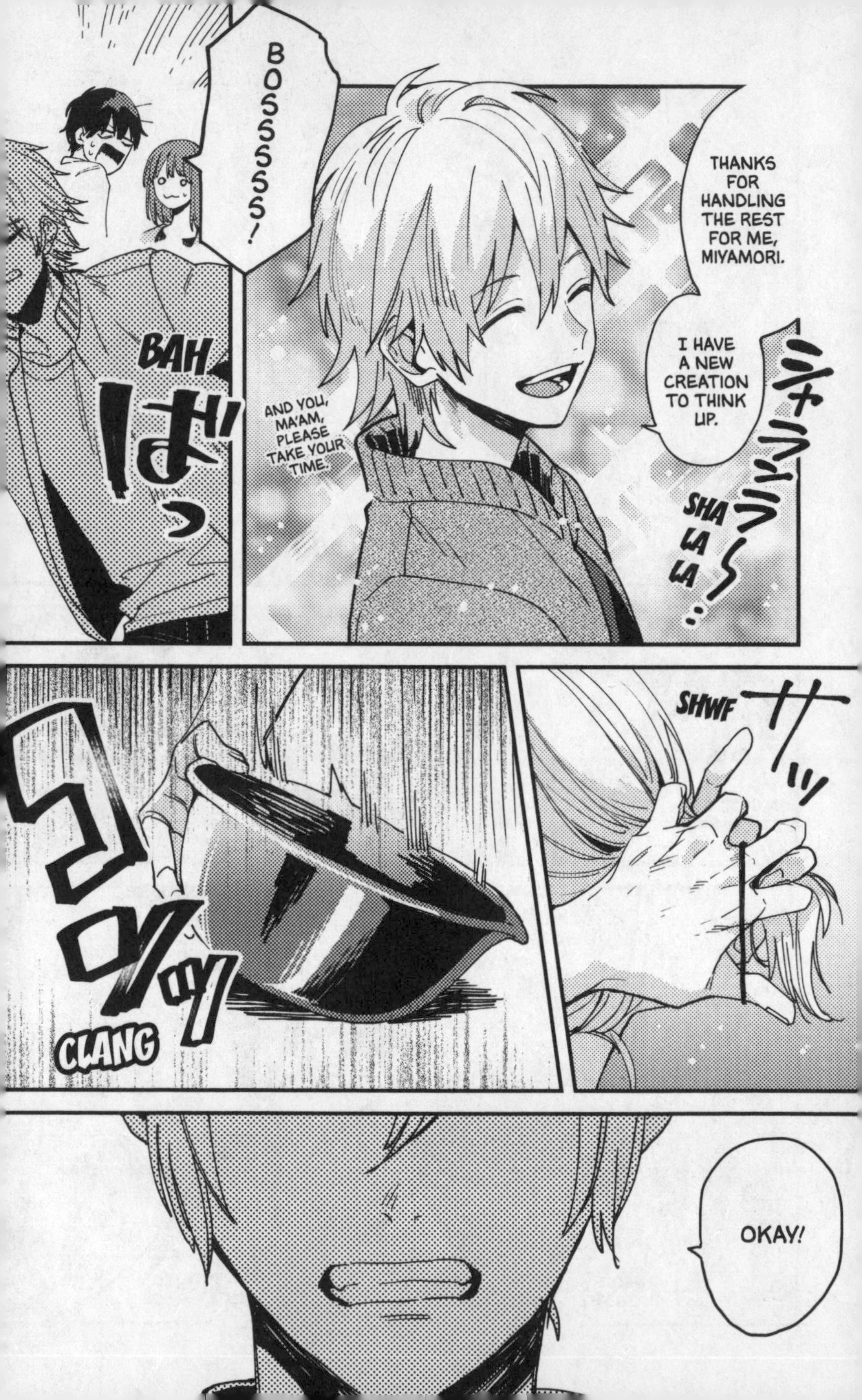
THANKS FOR HANDLING THE REST FOR ME, MIYAMORI.
I HAVE A NEW CREATION TO THINK UP.
SHA LA LA
AND YOU, MA'AM, PLEASE TAKE YOUR TIME.
BOSSSSSS!
BAH
SHWF
CLANG
OKAY!

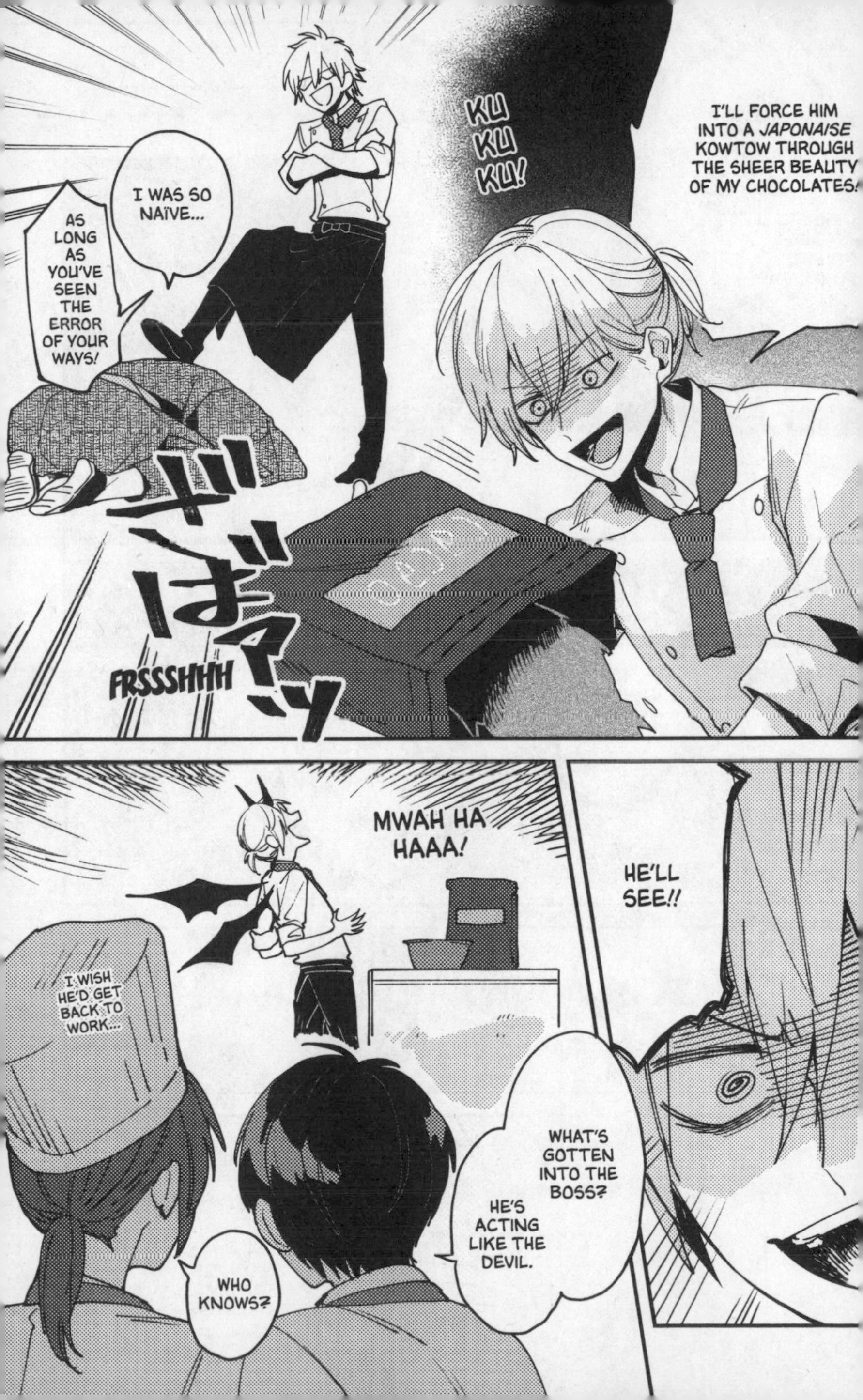
I'LL FORCE HIM INTO A *JAPONAISE* KOWTOW THROUGH THE SHEER BEAUTY OF MY CHOCOLATES!
KU KU KU!
I WAS SO NAÏVE...
AS LONG AS YOU'VE SEEN THE ERROR OF YOUR WAYS!
FRSSSHHH
HE'LL SEE!!
MWAH HA HAAA!
WHAT'S GOTTEN INTO THE BOSS?
HE'S ACTING LIKE THE DEVIL.
WHO KNOWS?
I WISH HE'D GET BACK TO WORK...

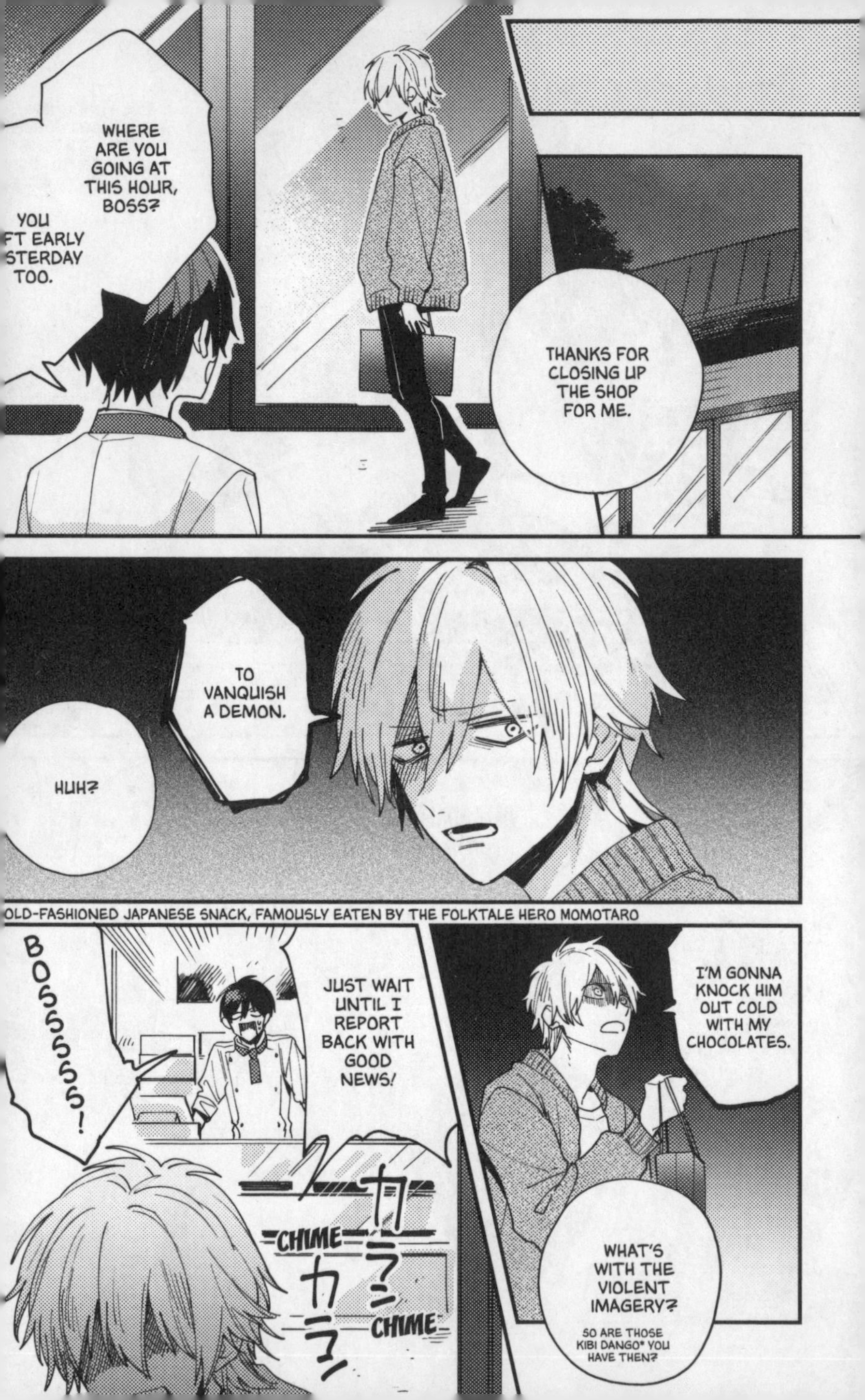
THANKS FOR CLOSING UP THE SHOP FOR ME.
WHERE ARE YOU GOING AT THIS HOUR, BOSS?
YOU
FT EARLY
STERDAY
TOO.
TO VANQUISH A DEMON.
HUH?
I'M GONNA KNOCK HIM OUT COLD WITH MY CHOCOLATES.
WHAT'S WITH THE VIOLENT IMAGERY?
SO ARE THOSE KIBI DANGO* YOU HAVE THEN?
JUST WAIT UNTIL I REPORT BACK WITH GOOD NEWS!
BOSSSSS!
CHIME
カラ
CHIME
カラ

OLD-FASHIONED JAPANESE SNACK, FAMOUSLY EATEN BY THE FOLKTALE HERO MOMOTARO

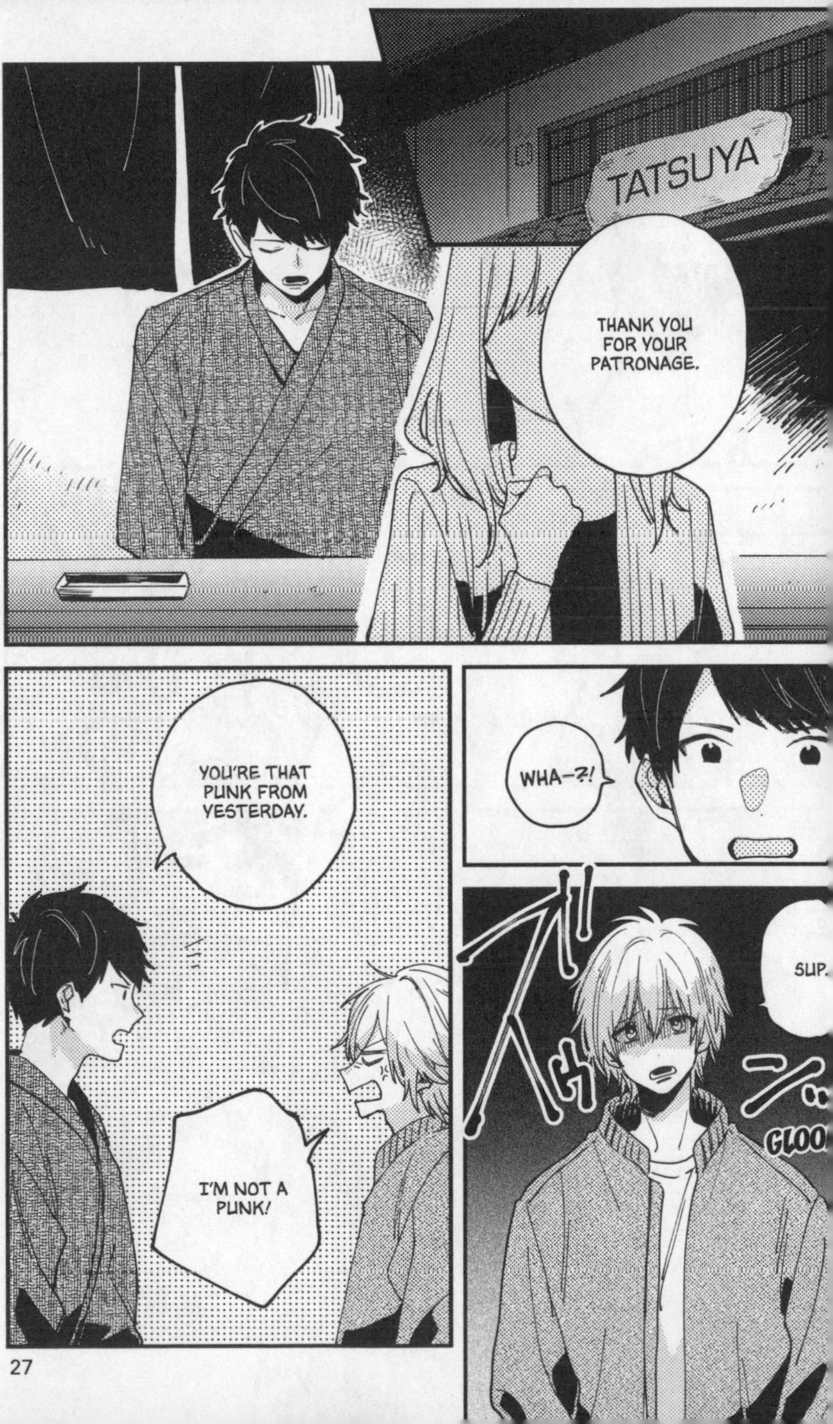
TATSUYA
THANK YOU FOR YOUR PATRONAGE.
WHA-?!
SUP.
GLOO
YOU'RE THAT PUNK FROM YESTERDAY.
I'M NOT A PUNK!

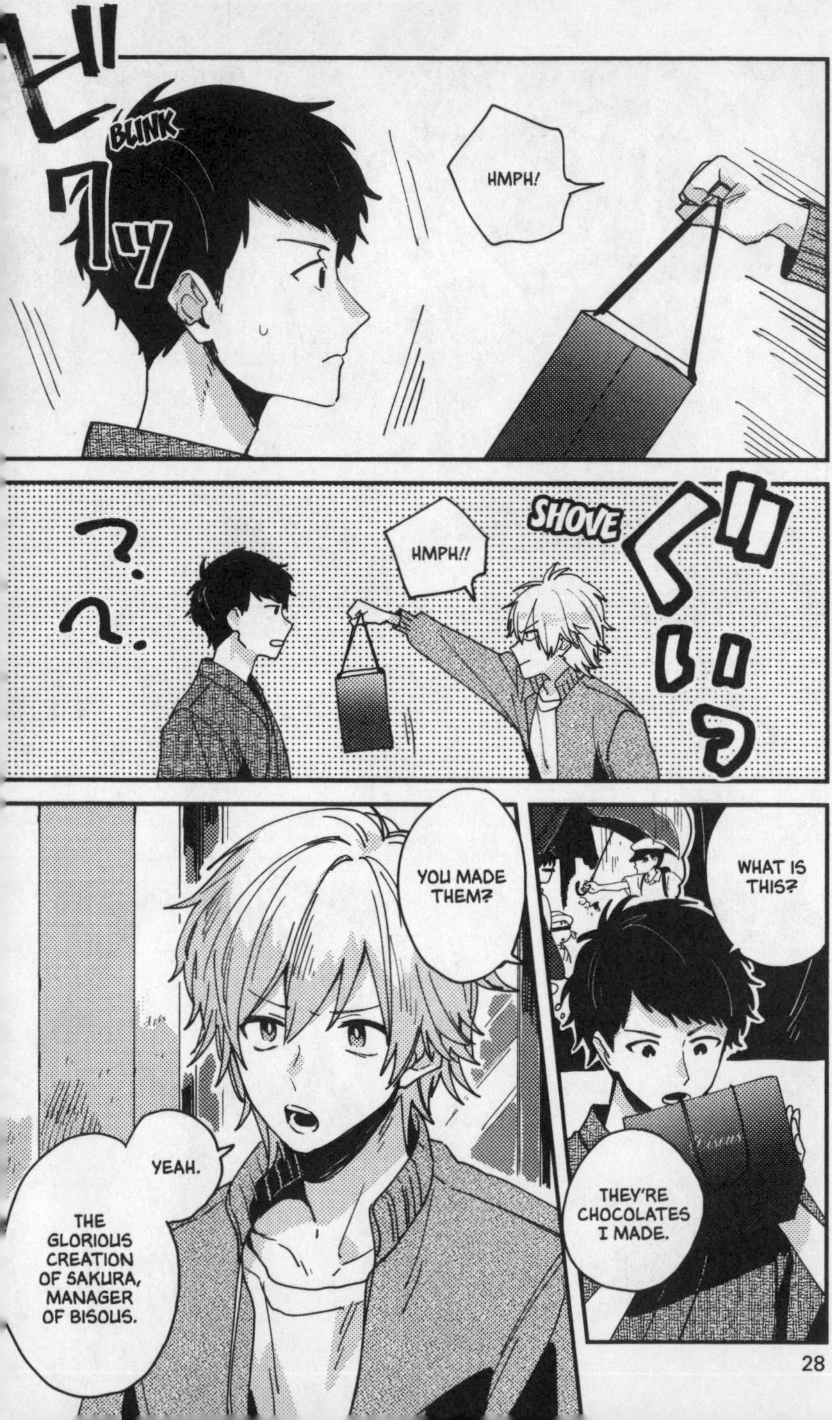
HMPH!
BLINK
SHOVE
HMPH!!
WHAT IS THIS?
THEY'RE CHOCOLATES I MADE.
YOU MADE THEM?
YEAH.
THE GLORIOUS CREATION OF SAKURA, MANAGER OF BISOUS.

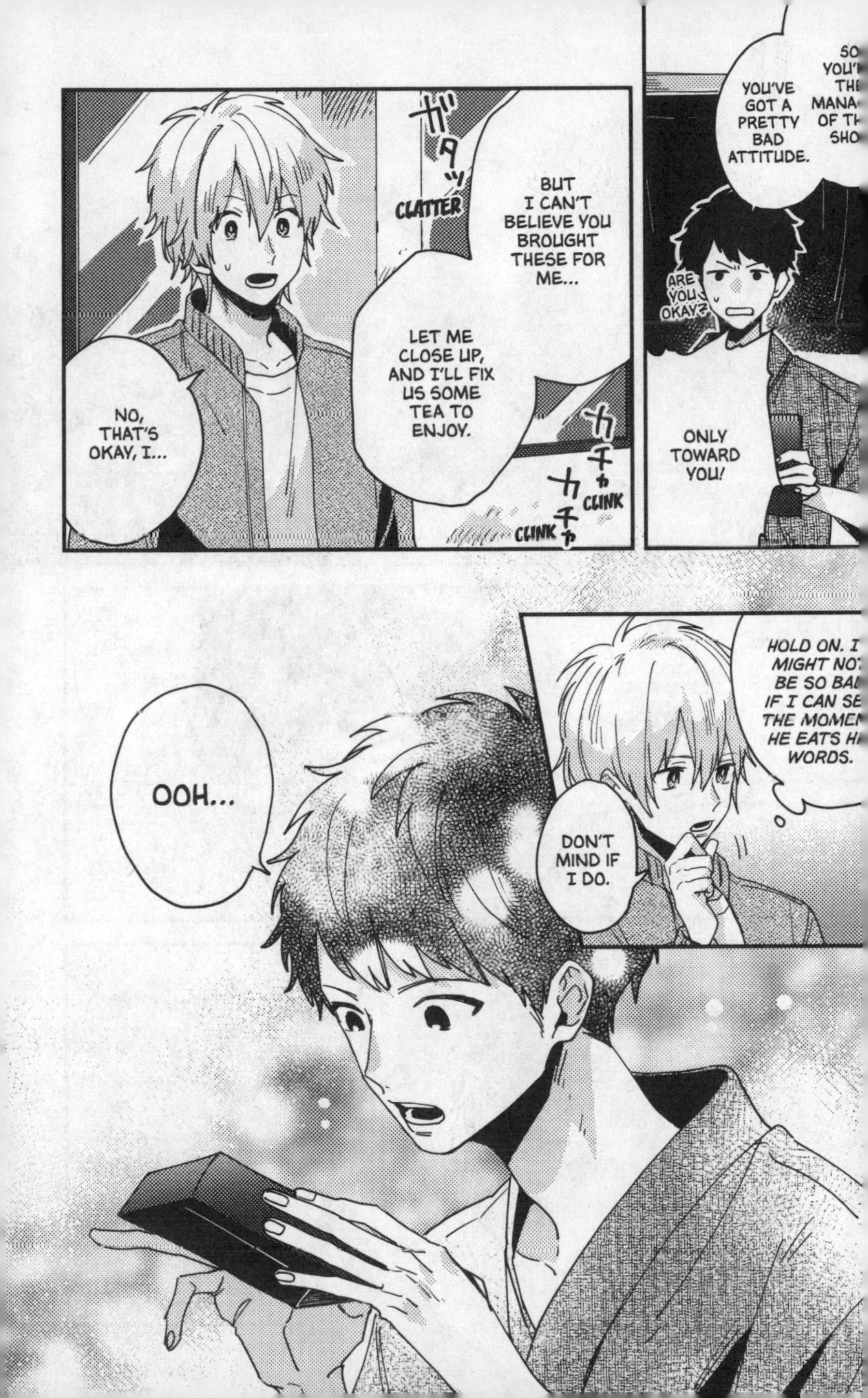
SO YOU' THE MANA OF TH SHO
YOU'VE GOT A PRETTY BAD ATTITUDE.
ARE YOU OKAY?
ONLY TOWARD YOU!
ガタッ
CLATTER
BUT I CAN'T BELIEVE YOU BROUGHT THESE FOR ME...
LET ME CLOSE UP, AND I'LL FIX US SOME TEA TO ENJOY.
カチャ カチャ
CLINK
CLINK
NO, THAT'S OKAY, I...
HOLD ON. I MIGHT NO BE SO BA IF I CAN SE THE MOMEN HE EATS HI WORDS.
DON'T MIND IF I DO.
OOH...

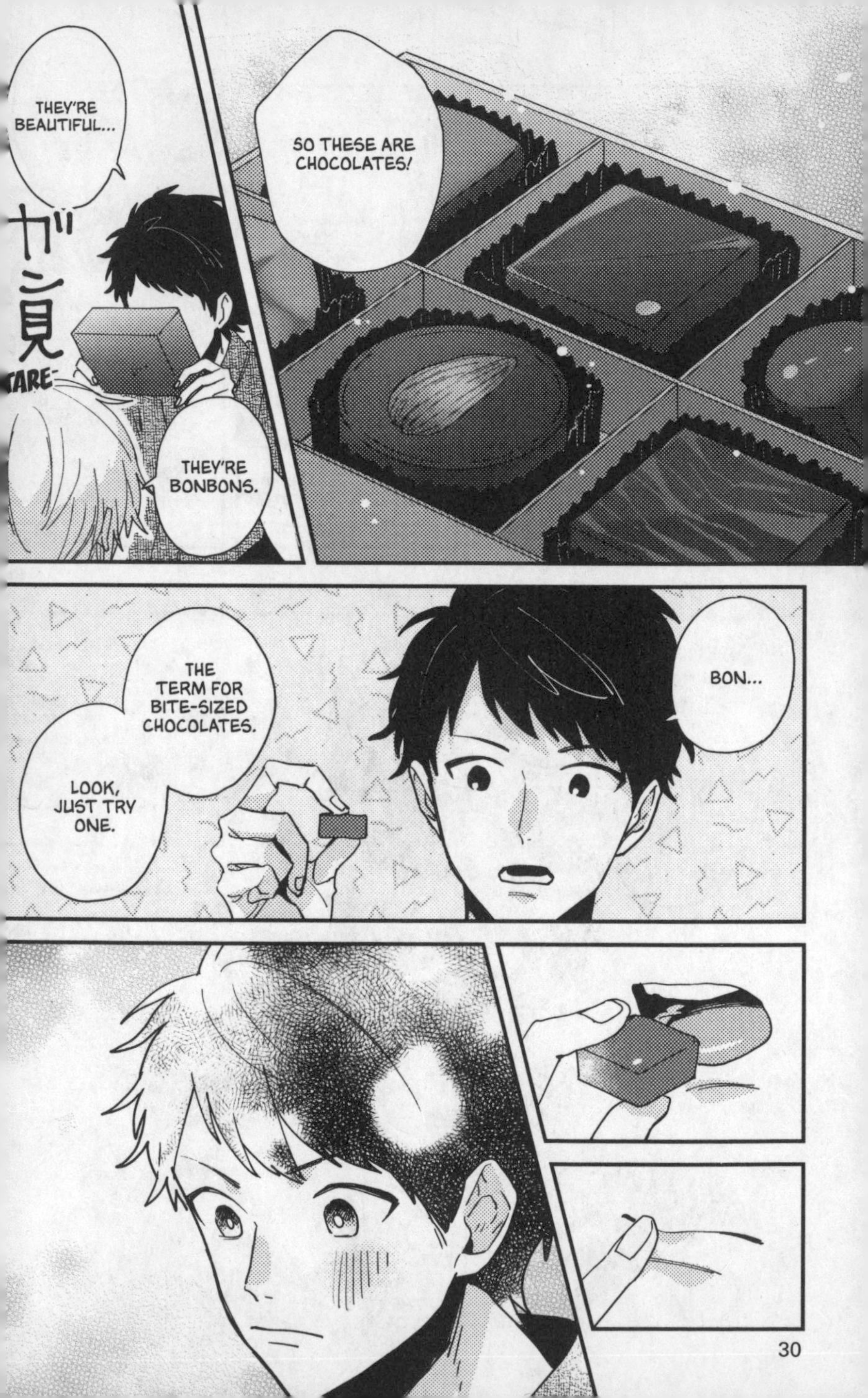
SO THESE ARE CHOCOLATES!
THEY'RE BEAUTIFUL...
ガン見
THEY'RE BONBONS.
BON...
THE TERM FOR BITE-SIZED CHOCOLATES.
LOOK, JUST TRY ONE.

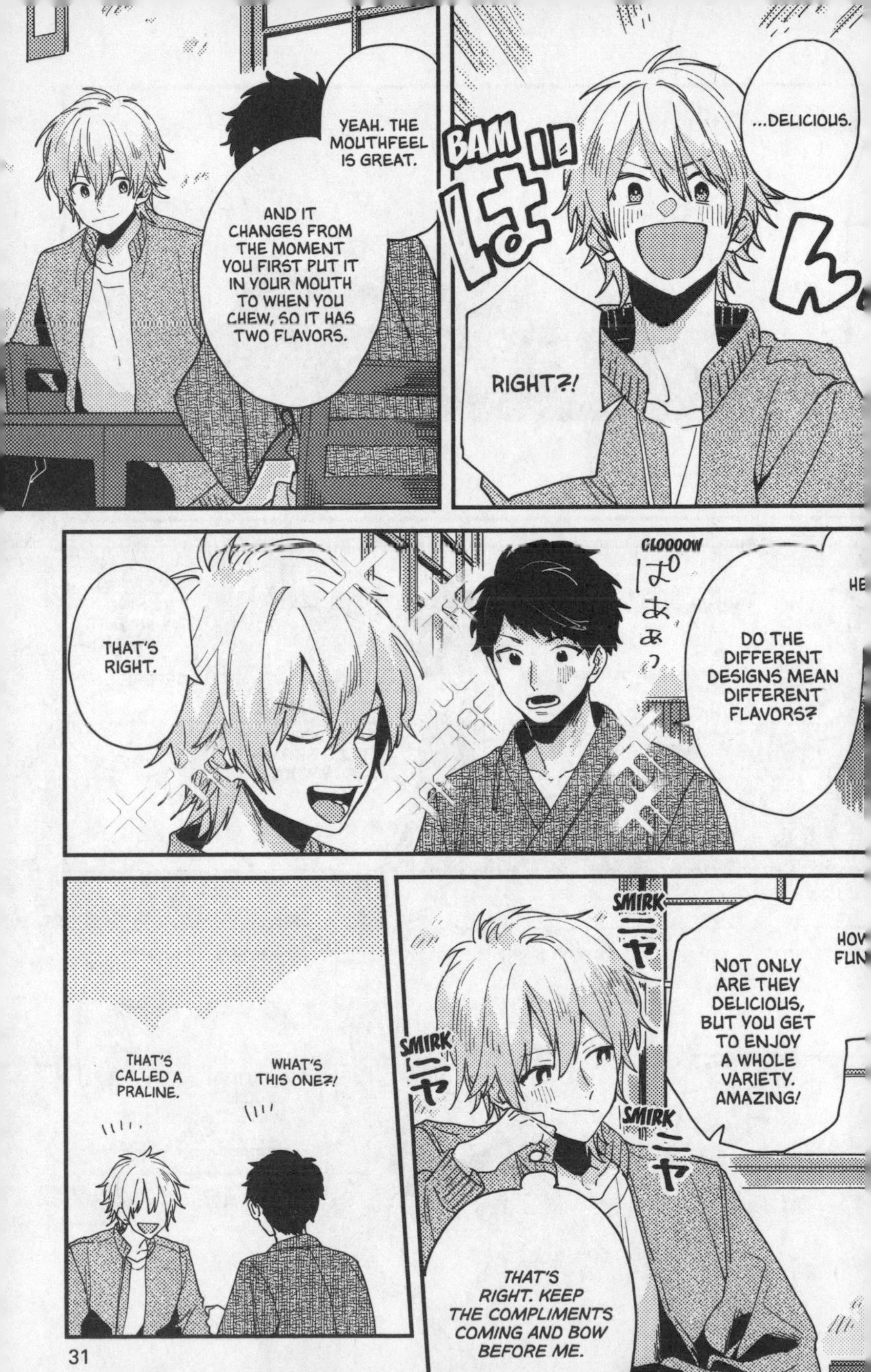
...DELICIOUS.
BAM
はっ
RIGHT?!
YEAH. THE MOUTHFEEL IS GREAT.
AND IT CHANGES FROM THE MOMENT YOU FIRST PUT IT IN YOUR MOUTH TO WHEN YOU CHEW, SO IT HAS TWO FLAVORS.
DO THE DIFFERENT DESIGNS MEAN DIFFERENT FLAVORS?
GLOOOOW
ぱぁぁっ
THAT'S RIGHT.
NOT ONLY ARE THEY DELICIOUS, BUT YOU GET TO ENJOY A WHOLE VARIETY. AMAZING!
SMIRK
ニヤ
SMIRK
ニヤ
SMIRK
ニヤ
THAT'S RIGHT. KEEP THE COMPLIMENTS COMING AND BOW BEFORE ME.
WHAT'S THIS ONE?!
THAT'S CALLED A PRALINE.

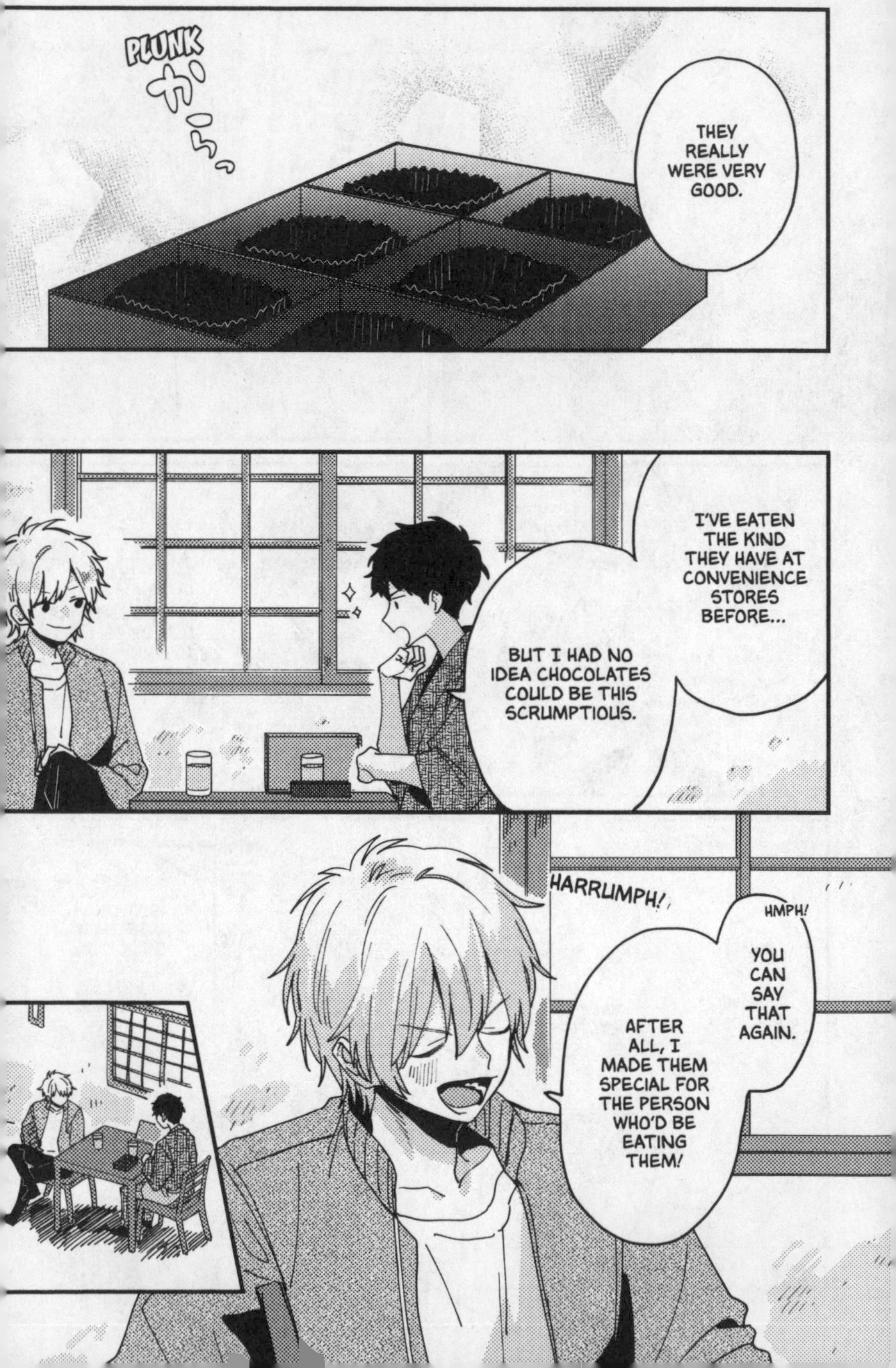
THEY REALLY WERE VERY GOOD.
PLUNK
I'VE EATEN THE KIND THEY HAVE AT CONVENIENCE STORES BEFORE...
BUT I HAD NO IDEA CHOCOLATES COULD BE THIS SCRUMPTIOUS.
HARRUMPH!
HMPH!
YOU CAN SAY THAT AGAIN.
AFTER ALL, I MADE THEM SPECIAL FOR THE PERSON WHO'D BE EATING THEM!

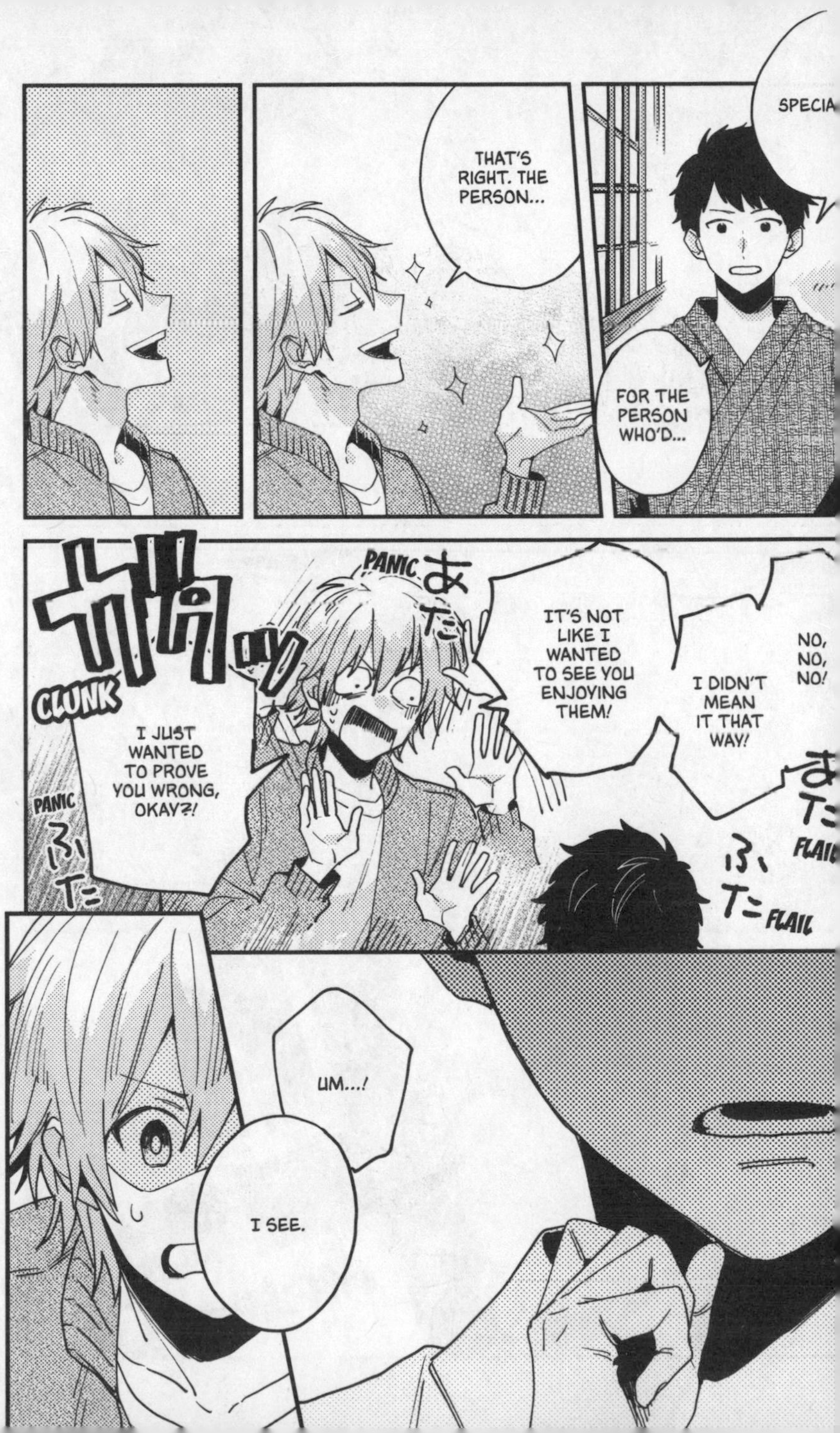
SPECIA
FOR THE PERSON WHO'D...
THAT'S RIGHT. THE PERSON...
NO, NO, NO!
I DIDN'T MEAN IT THAT WAY!
IT'S NOT LIKE I WANTED TO SEE YOU ENJOYING THEM!
PANIC あたふた
FLAIL すたふた FLAIL
I JUST WANTED TO PROVE YOU WRONG, OKAY?!
CLUNK
PANIC ふたふた
UM...!
I SEE.

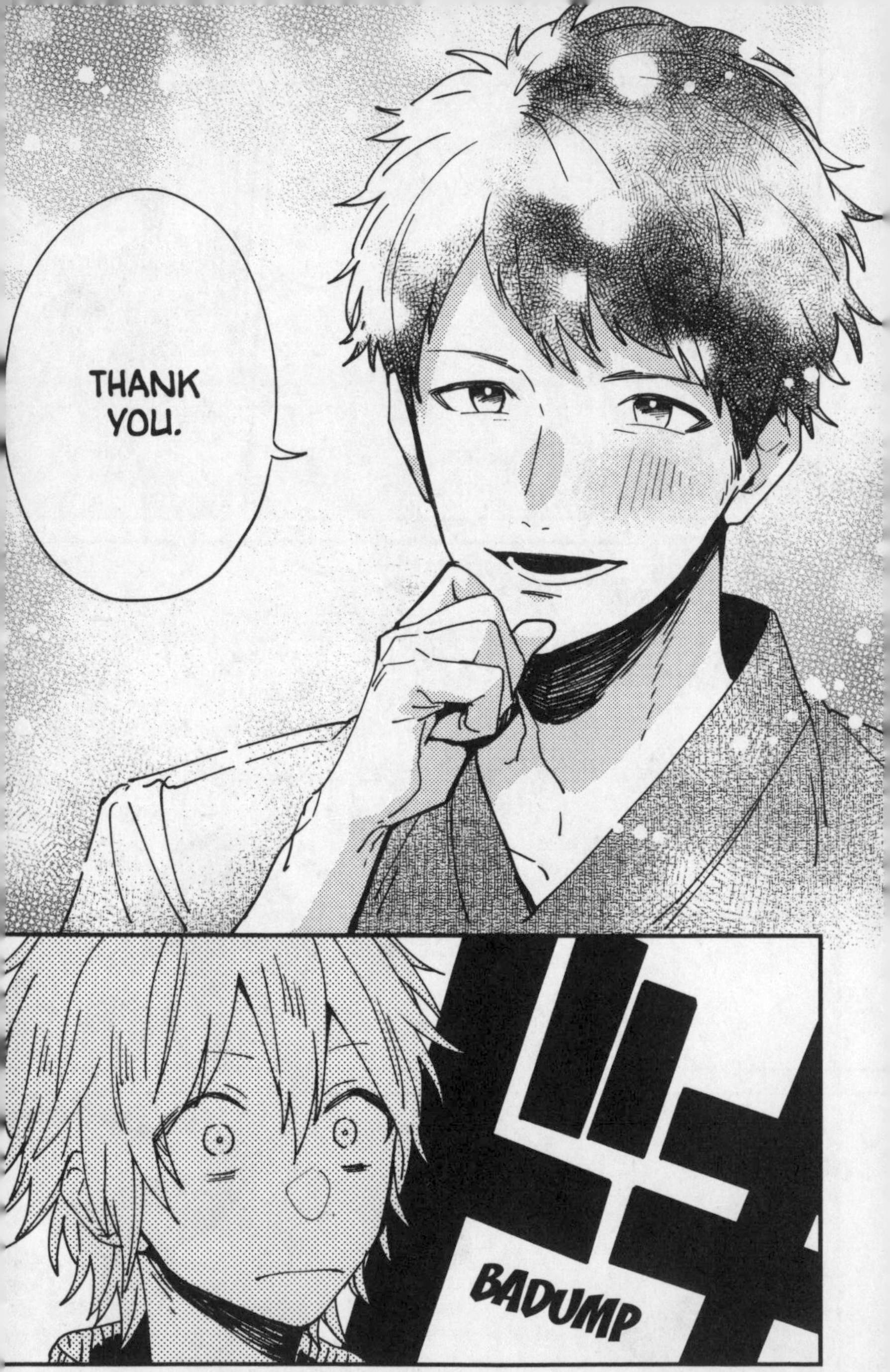
THANK YOU.
BADUMP

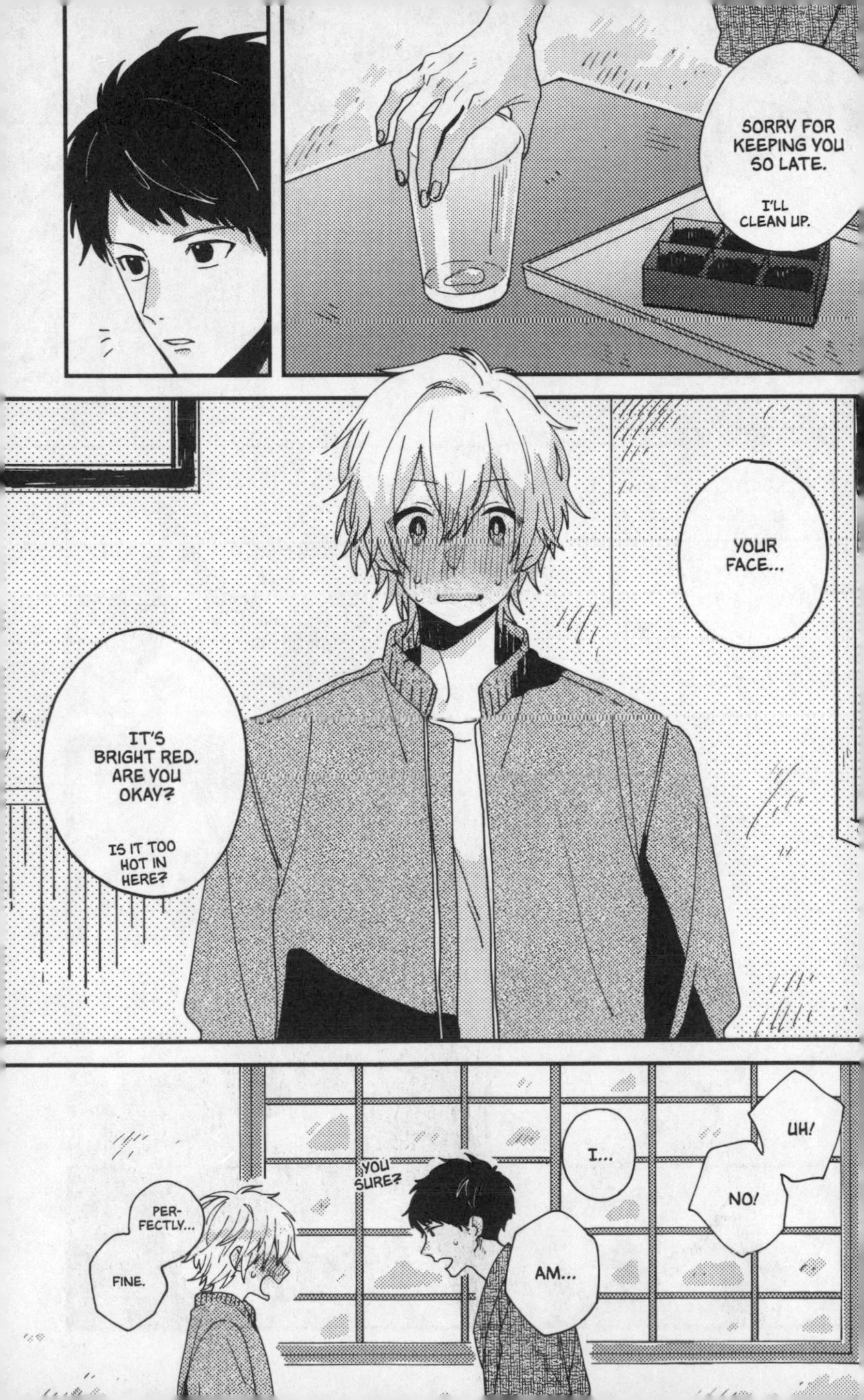
SORRY FOR KEEPING YOU SO LATE.
I'LL CLEAN UP.
YOUR FACE...
IT'S BRIGHT RED. ARE YOU OKAY?
IS IT TOO HOT IN HERE?
UH!
NO!
I...
AM...
YOU SURE?
PER-FECTLY...
FINE.

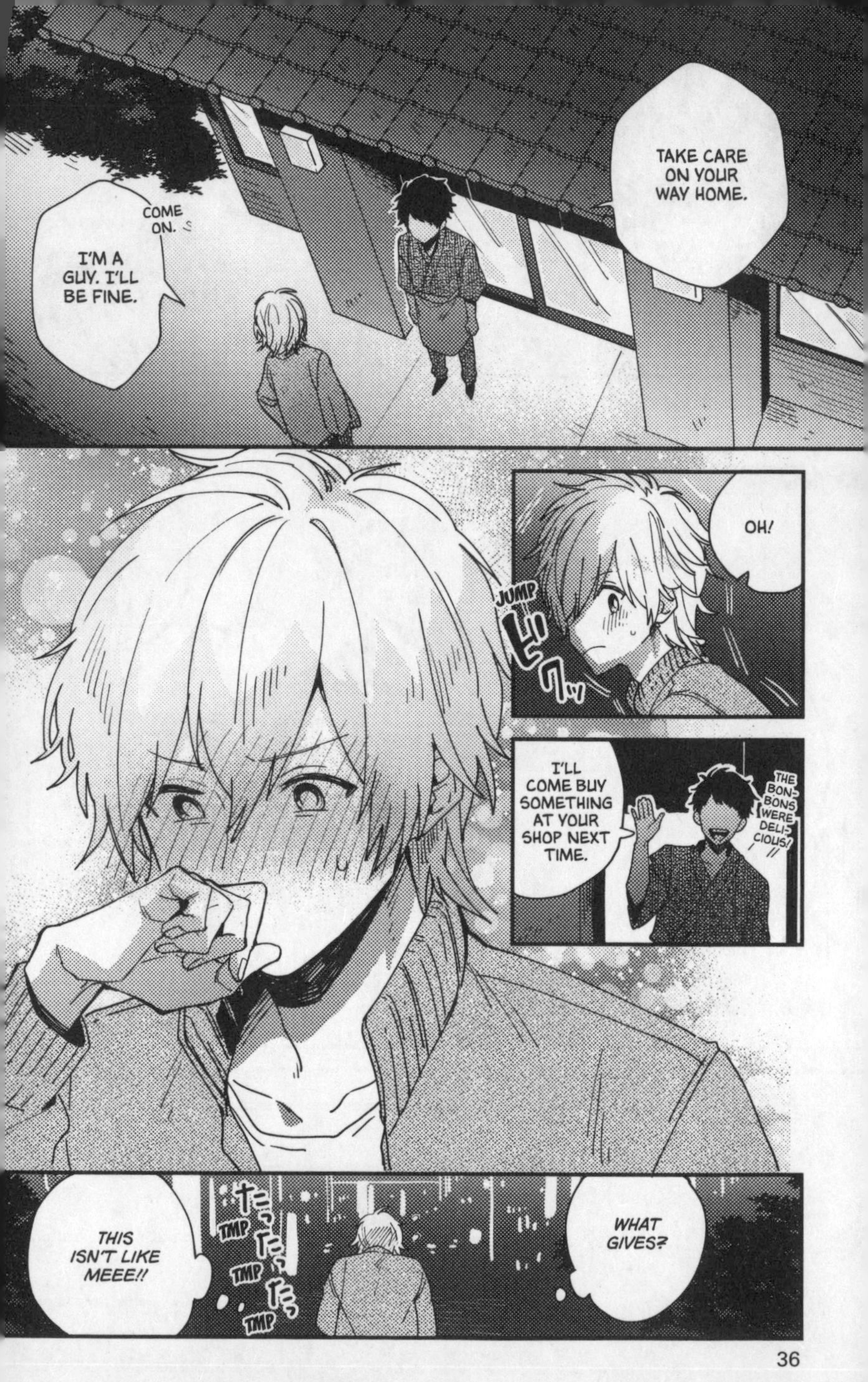
TAKE CARE ON YOUR WAY HOME.
COME ON.
I'M A GUY. I'LL BE FINE.
OH!
JUMP
I'LL COME BUY SOMETHING AT YOUR SHOP NEXT TIME.
THE BON-BONS WERE DELI-CIOUS!
WHAT GIVES?
TMP TMP TMP TMP
THIS ISN'T LIKE MEEE!!

Chéri, my destiny!

Chéri, my destiny!
Chéri, my destiny!

Chéri, my destiny!

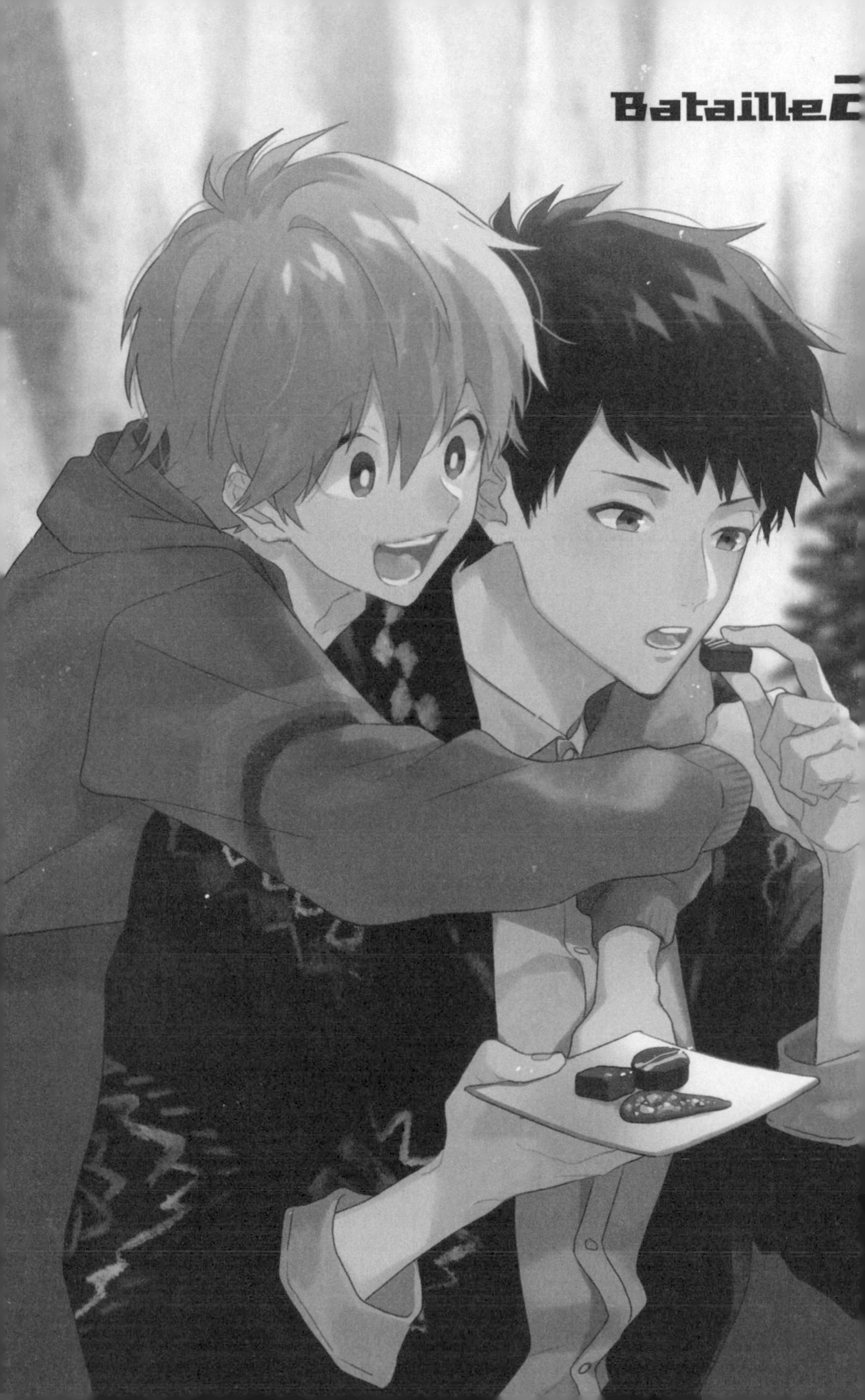
Bataille 2

Chéri, my destiny!

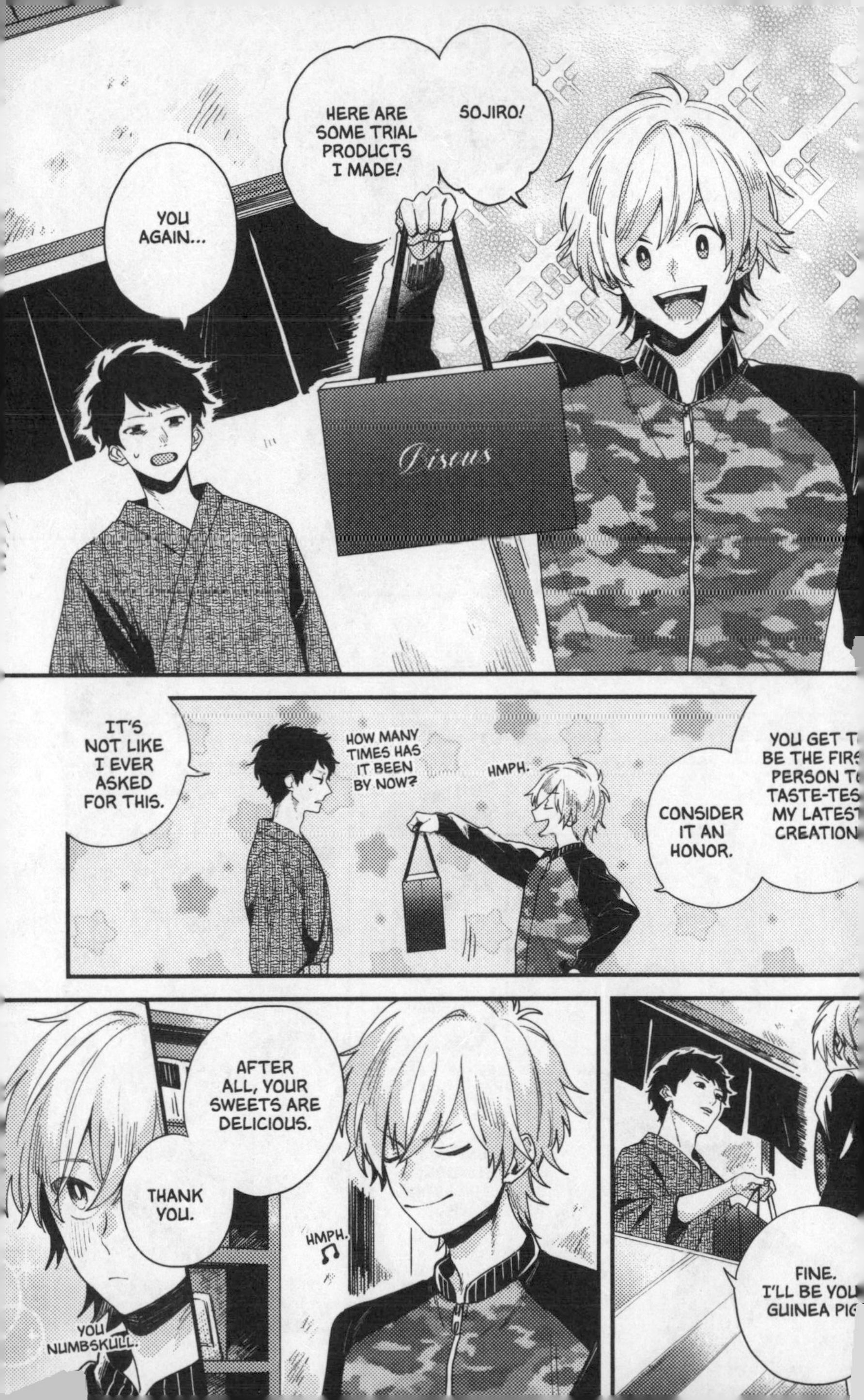
SOJIRO!
HERE ARE SOME TRIAL PRODUCTS I MADE!
YOU AGAIN...
YOU GET T BE THE FIRS PERSON T TASTE-TES MY LATEST CREATION
CONSIDER IT AN HONOR.
HMPH.
HOW MANY TIMES HAS IT BEEN BY NOW?
IT'S NOT LIKE I EVER ASKED FOR THIS.
FINE. I'LL BE YOU GUINEA PIG
AFTER ALL, YOUR SWEETS ARE DELICIOUS.
THANK YOU.
HMPH.
YOU NUMBSKULL.

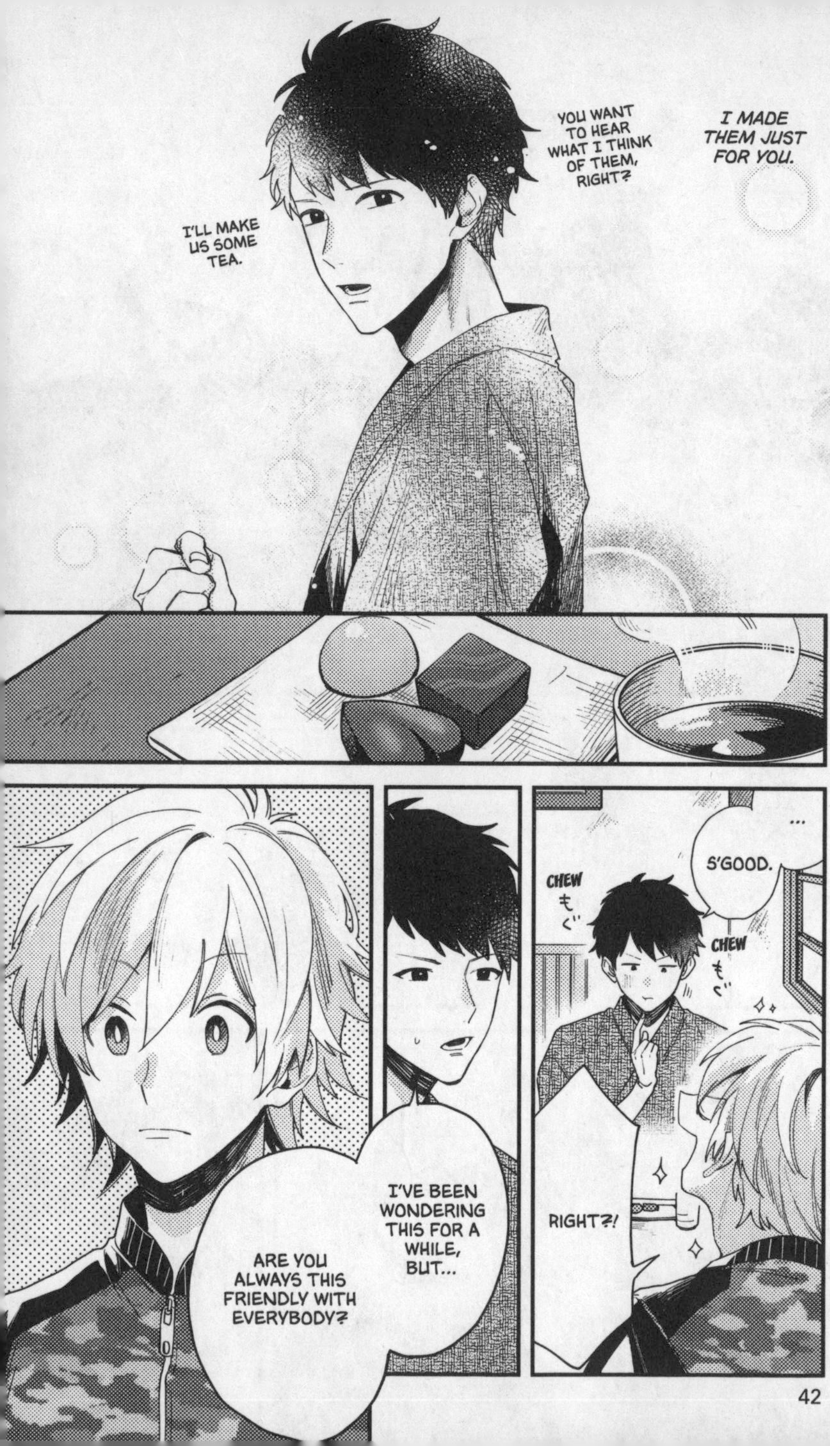
I MADE THEM JUST FOR YOU.
YOU WANT TO HEAR WHAT I THINK OF THEM, RIGHT?
I'LL MAKE US SOME TEA.
...
S'GOOD.
CHEW もぐ
CHEW もぐ
RIGHT?!
I'VE BEEN WONDERING THIS FOR A WHILE, BUT...
ARE YOU ALWAYS THIS FRIENDLY WITH EVERYBODY?

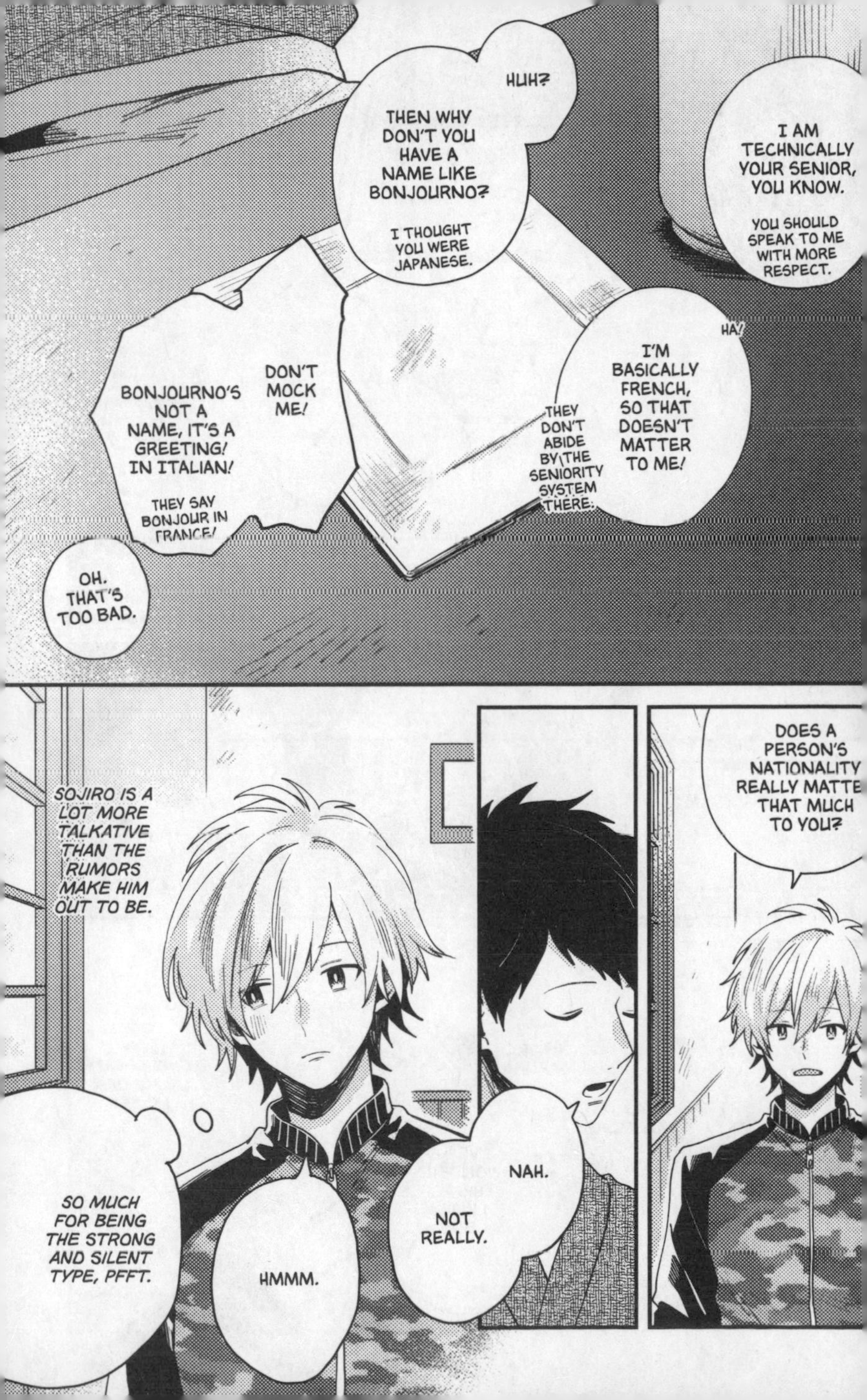
I AM TECHNICALLY YOUR SENIOR, YOU KNOW.
YOU SHOULD SPEAK TO ME WITH MORE RESPECT.
HA!
I'M BASICALLY FRENCH, SO THAT DOESN'T MATTER TO ME!
THEY DON'T ABIDE BY THE SENIORITY SYSTEM THERE.
HUH?
THEN WHY DON'T YOU HAVE A NAME LIKE BONJOURNO?
I THOUGHT YOU WERE JAPANESE.
DON'T MOCK ME!
BONJOURNO'S NOT A NAME, IT'S A GREETING! IN ITALIAN!
THEY SAY BONJOUR IN FRANCE!
OH. THAT'S TOO BAD.
DOES A PERSON'S NATIONALITY REALLY MATTE THAT MUCH TO YOU?
NAH.
NOT REALLY.
SOJIRO IS A LOT MORE TALKATIVE THAN THE RUMORS MAKE HIM OUT TO BE.
HMMM.
SO MUCH FOR BEING THE STRONG AND SILENT TYPE, PFFT.

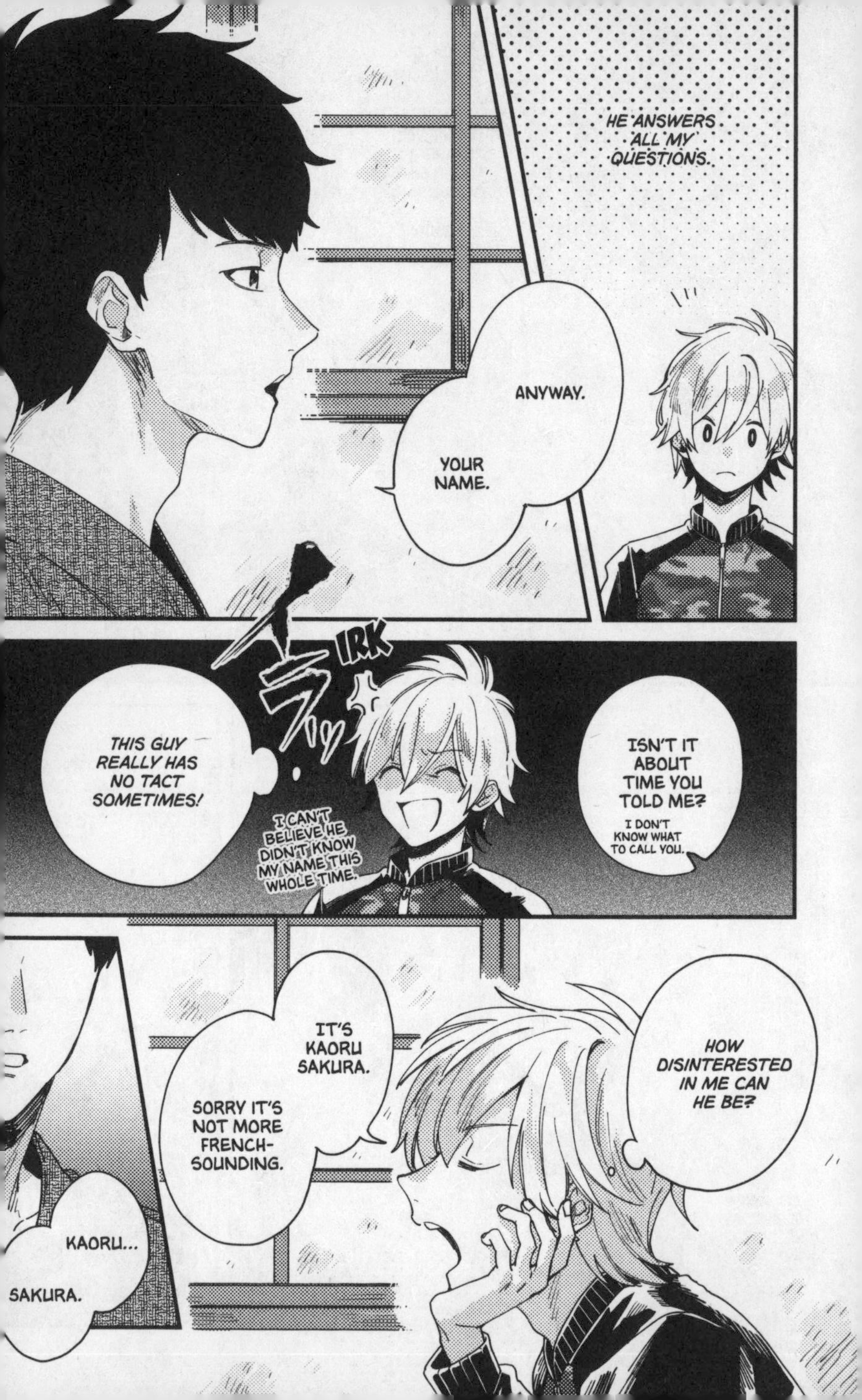
HE ANSWERS ALL MY QUESTIONS.
ANYWAY.
YOUR NAME.
ISN'T IT ABOUT TIME YOU TOLD ME?
I DON'T KNOW WHAT TO CALL YOU.
IRK
I CAN'T BELIEVE HE DIDN'T KNOW MY NAME THIS WHOLE TIME.
THIS GUY REALLY HAS NO TACT SOMETIMES!
HOW DISINTERESTED IN ME CAN HE BE?
IT'S KAORU SAKURA.
SORRY IT'S NOT MORE FRENCH-SOUNDING.
KAORU...
SAKURA.

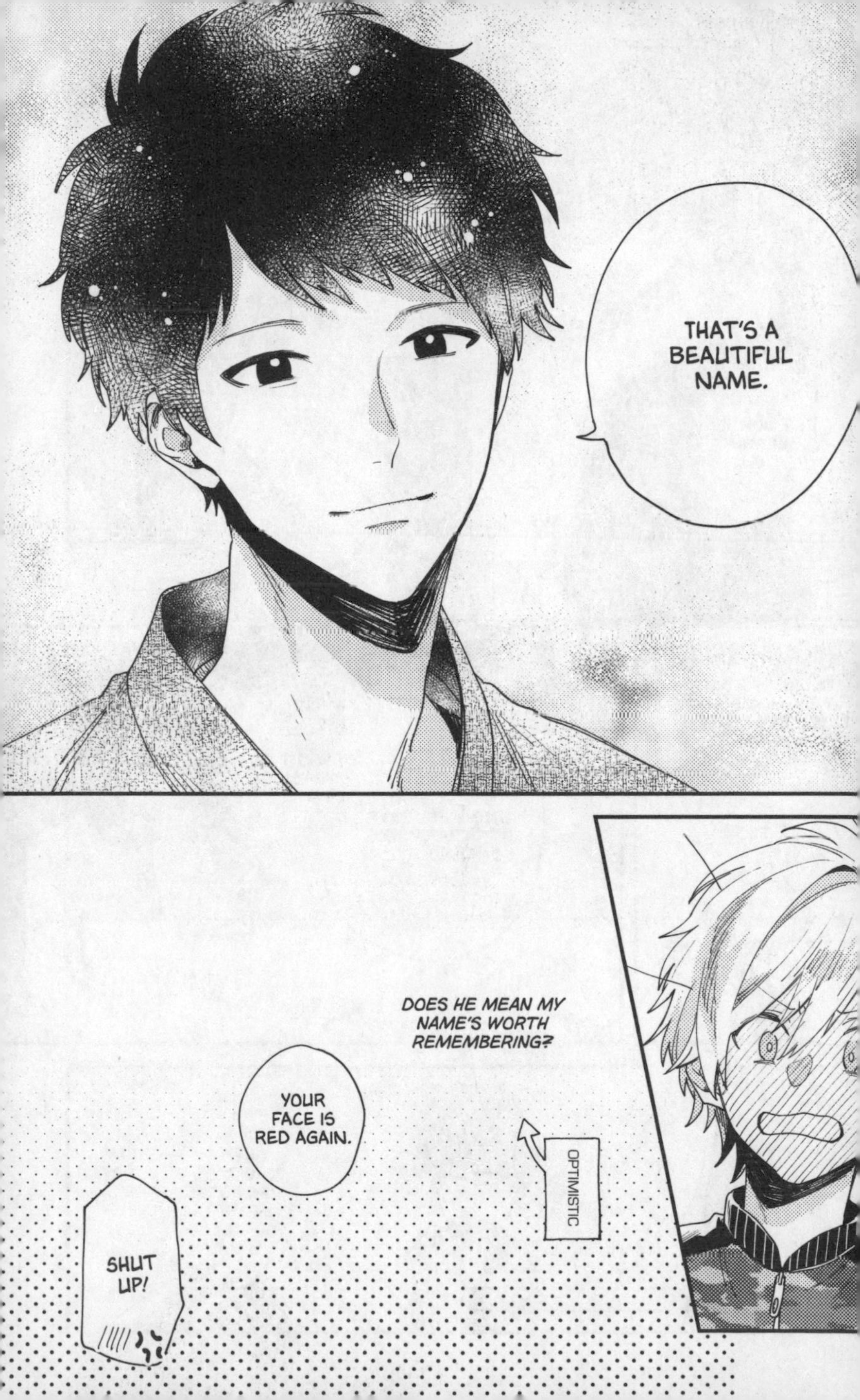
THAT'S A BEAUTIFUL NAME.
DOES HE MEAN MY NAME'S WORTH REMEMBERING?
OPTIMISTIC
YOUR FACE IS RED AGAIN.
SHUT UP!

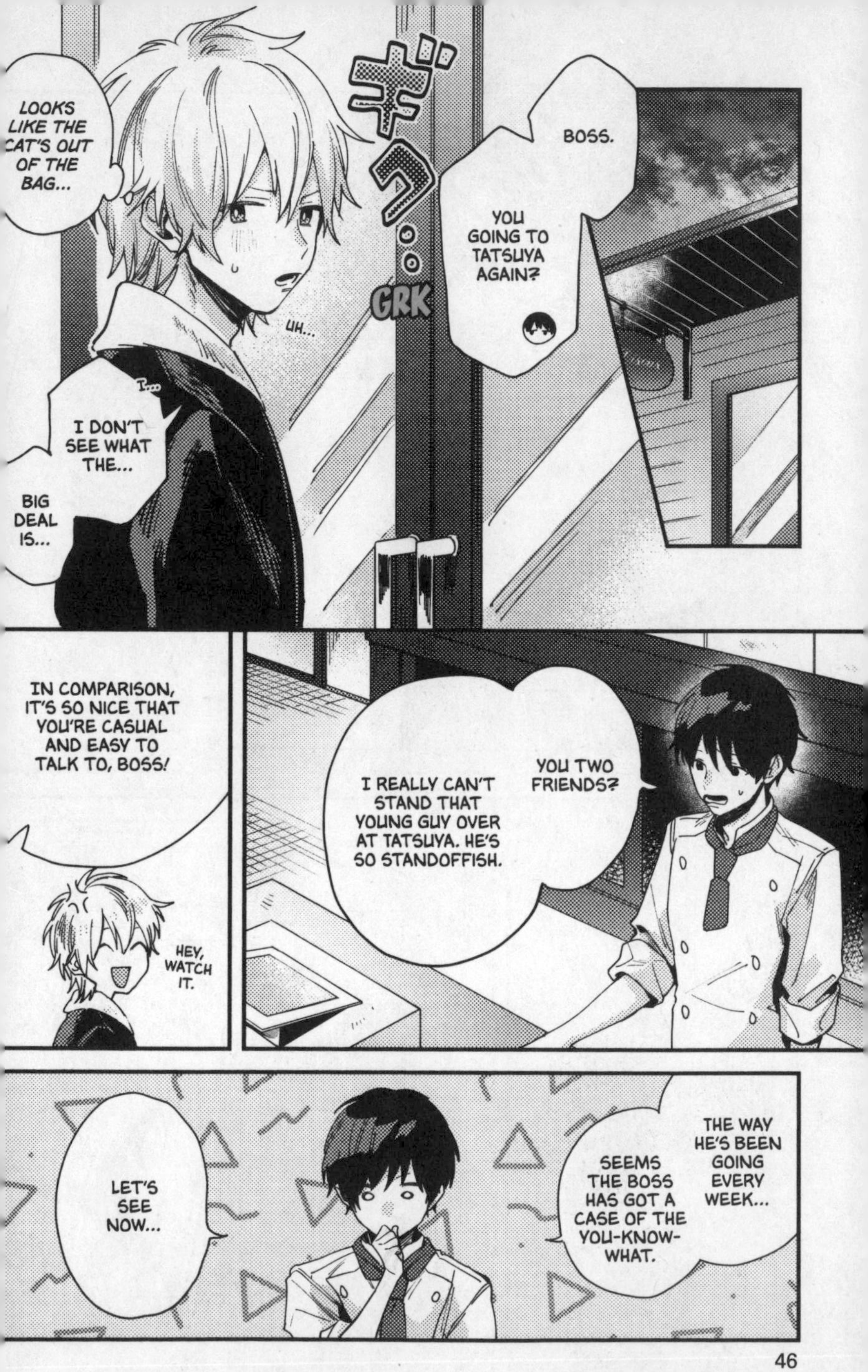
BOSS.
YOU GOING TO TATSUYA AGAIN?
GRK
LOOKS LIKE THE CAT'S OUT OF THE BAG...
UH...
I...
I DON'T SEE WHAT THE...
BIG DEAL IS...
YOU TWO FRIENDS?
I REALLY CAN'T STAND THAT YOUNG GUY OVER AT TATSUYA. HE'S SO STANDOFFISH.
IN COMPARISON, IT'S SO NICE THAT YOU'RE CASUAL AND EASY TO TALK TO, BOSS!
HEY, WATCH IT.
THE WAY HE'S BEEN GOING EVERY WEEK...
SEEMS THE BOSS HAS GOT A CASE OF THE YOU-KNOW-WHAT.
LET'S SEE NOW...

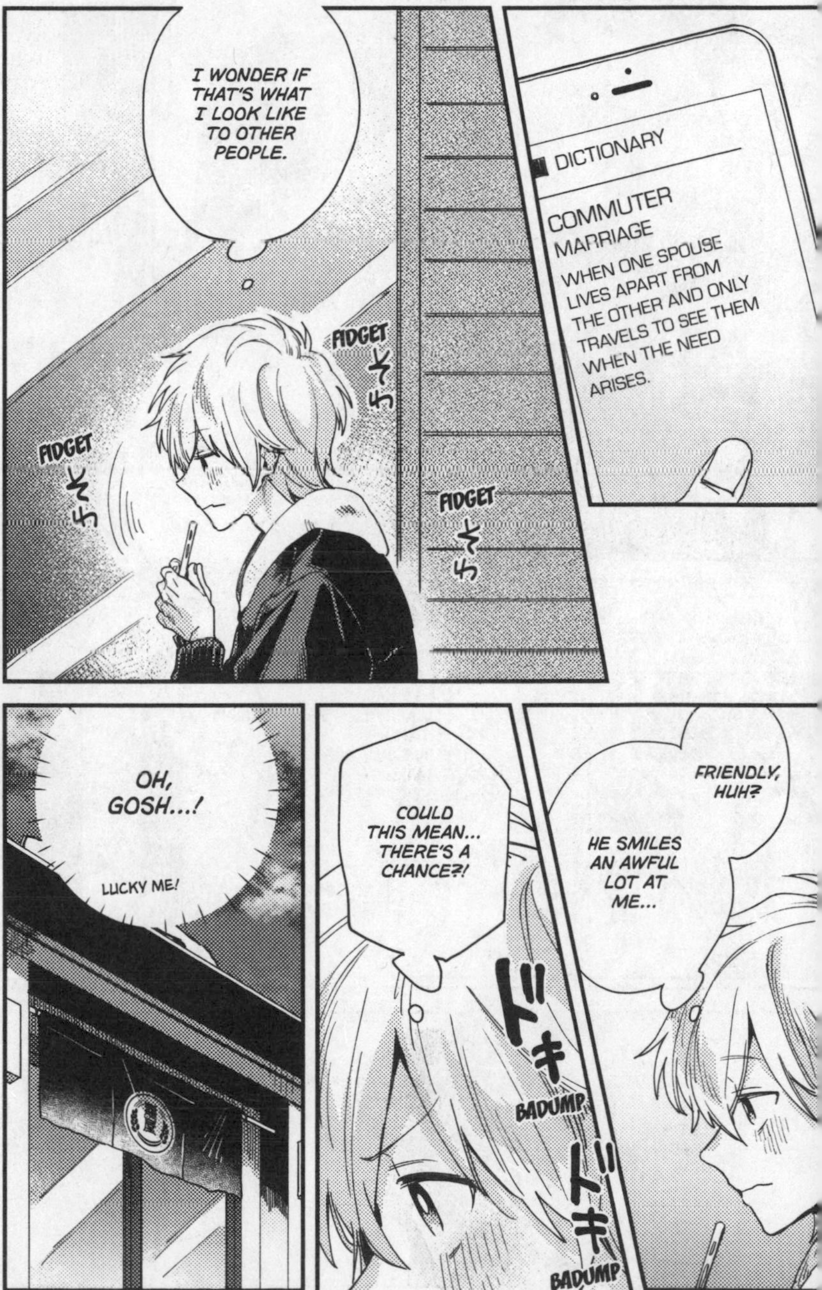
DICTIONARY
COMMUTER MARRIAGE
WHEN ONE SPOUSE LIVES APART FROM THE OTHER AND ONLY TRAVELS TO SEE THEM WHEN THE NEED ARISES.
I WONDER IF THAT'S WHAT I LOOK LIKE TO OTHER PEOPLE.
FIDGET
FIDGET
FIDGET
FRIENDLY, HUH?
HE SMILES AN AWFUL LOT AT ME...
COULD THIS MEAN... THERE'S A CHANCE?!
BADUMP
BADUMP
OH, GOSH...!
LUCKY ME!

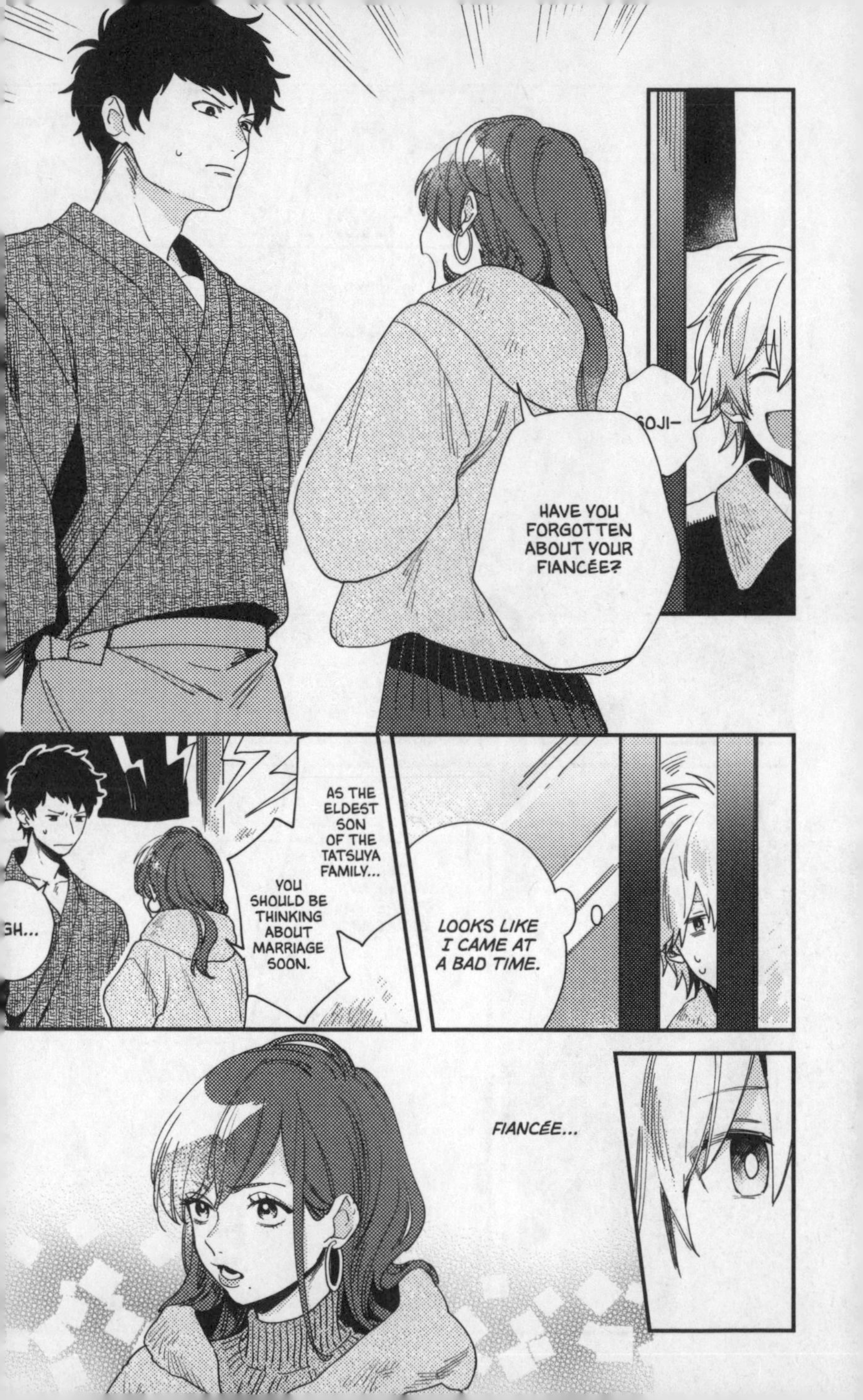
SOJI—
HAVE YOU FORGOTTEN ABOUT YOUR FIANCÉE?
LOOKS LIKE I CAME AT A BAD TIME.
AS THE ELDEST SON OF THE TATSUYA FAMILY...
YOU SHOULD BE THINKING ABOUT MARRIAGE SOON.
GH...
FIANCÉE...

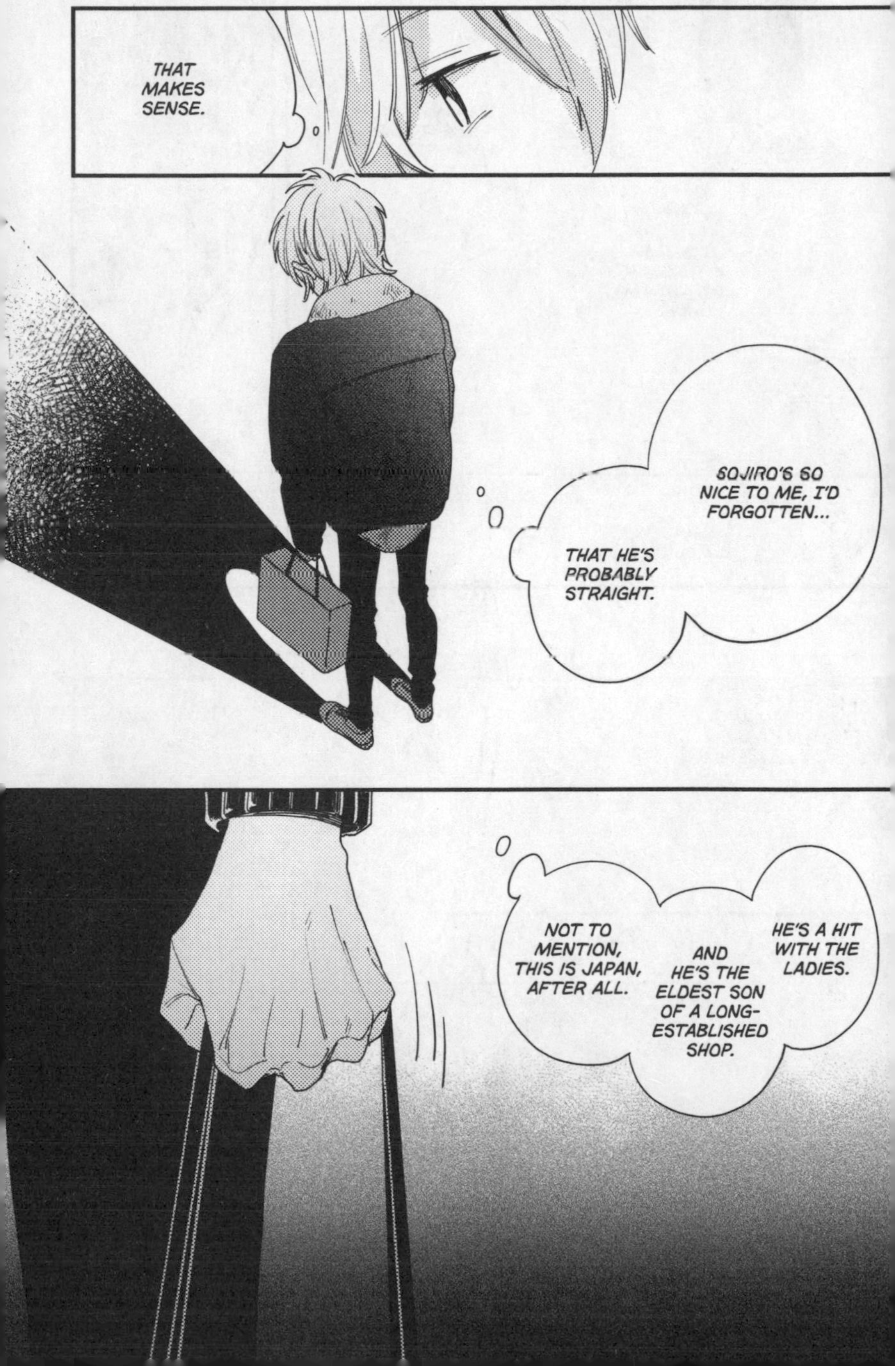
THAT MAKES SENSE.
SOJIRO'S SO NICE TO ME, I'D FORGOTTEN...
THAT HE'S PROBABLY STRAIGHT.
HE'S A HIT WITH THE LADIES.
AND HE'S THE ELDEST SON OF A LONG-ESTABLISHED SHOP.
NOT TO MENTION, THIS IS JAPAN, AFTER ALL.

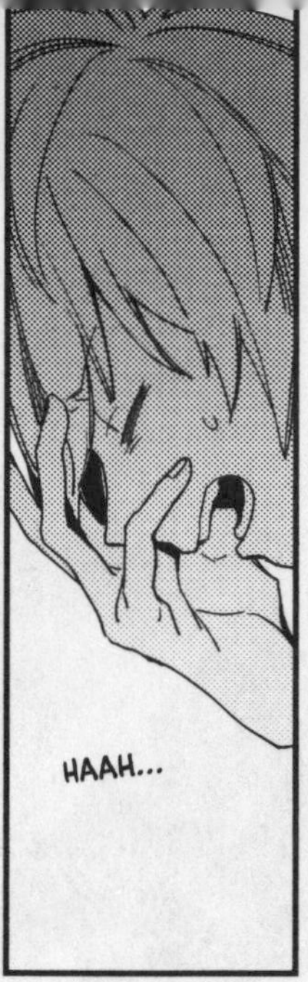
HAAH...
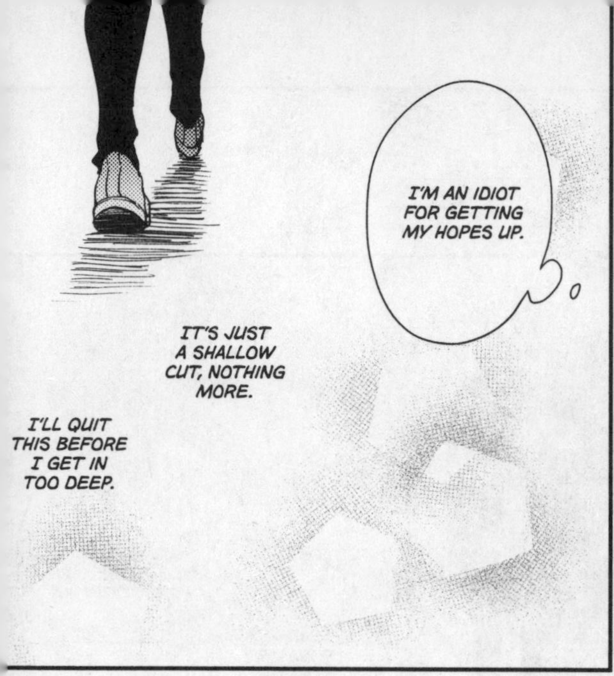
I'M AN IDIOT FOR GETTING MY HOPES UP.
IT'S JUST A SHALLOW CUT, NOTHING MORE.
I'LL QUIT THIS BEFORE I GET IN TOO DEEP.
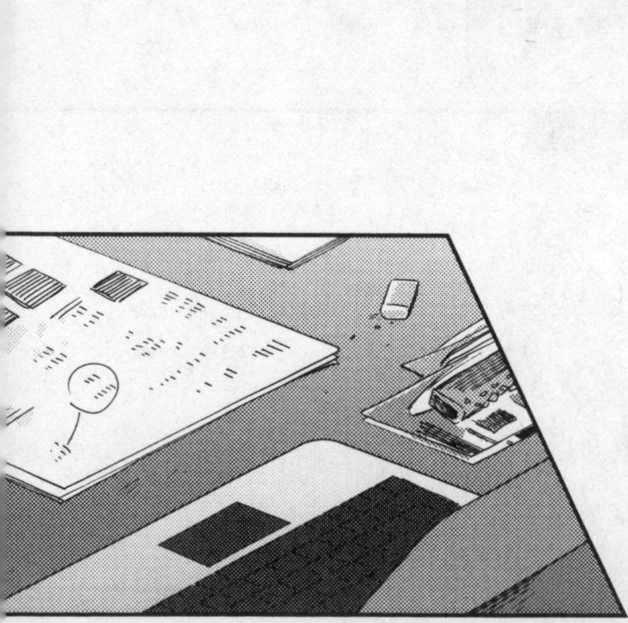

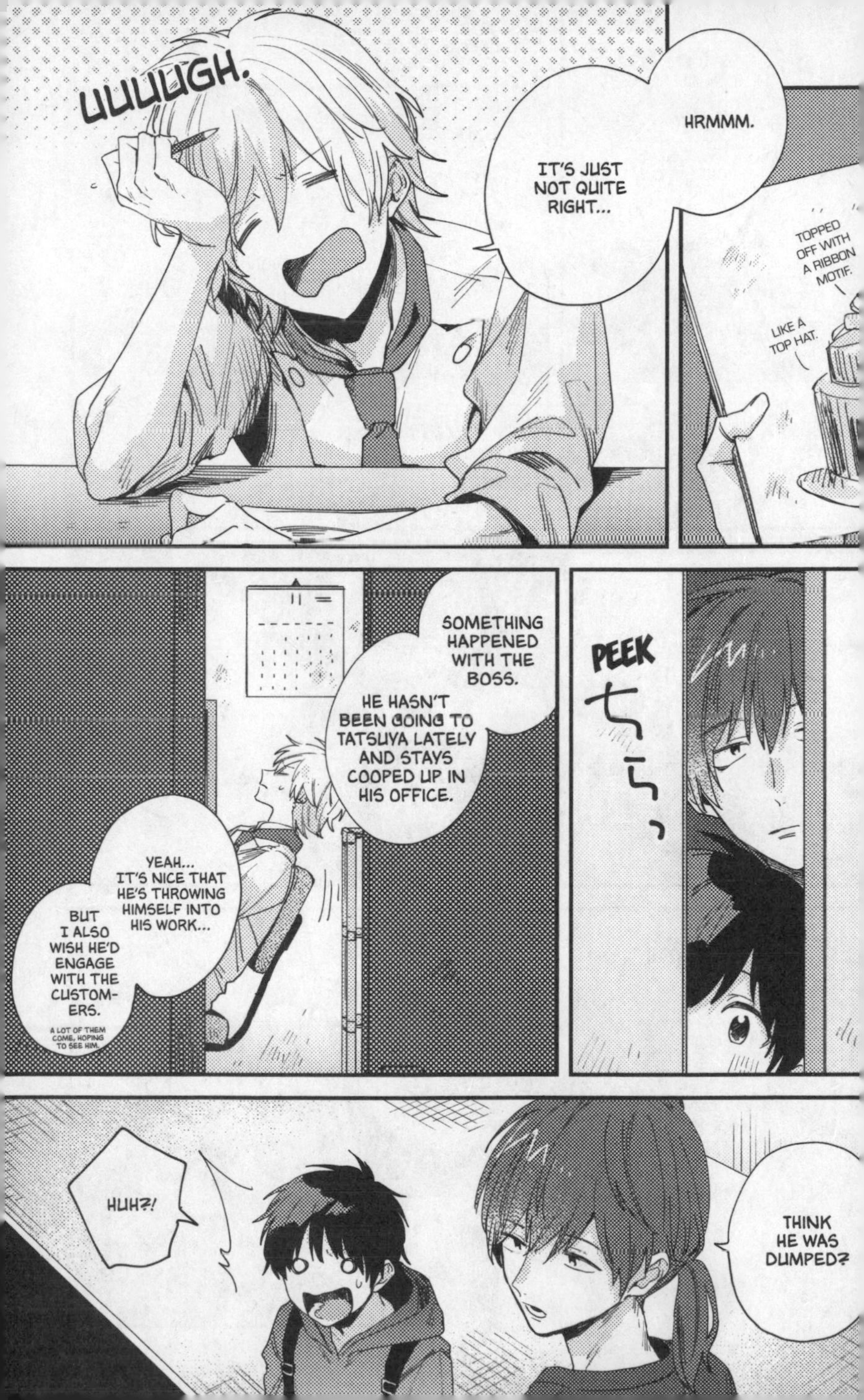
HRMMM.
IT'S JUST NOT QUITE RIGHT...
TOPPED OFF WITH A RIBBON MOTIF.
LIKE A TOP HAT.
UUUUGH.
PEEK
SOMETHING HAPPENED WITH THE BOSS.
HE HASN'T BEEN GOING TO TATSUYA LATELY AND STAYS COOPED UP IN HIS OFFICE.
YEAH... IT'S NICE THAT HE'S THROWING HIMSELF INTO HIS WORK...
BUT I ALSO WISH HE'D ENGAGE WITH THE CUSTOMERS.
A LOT OF THEM COME, HOPING TO SEE HIM.
THINK HE WAS DUMPED?
HUH?!

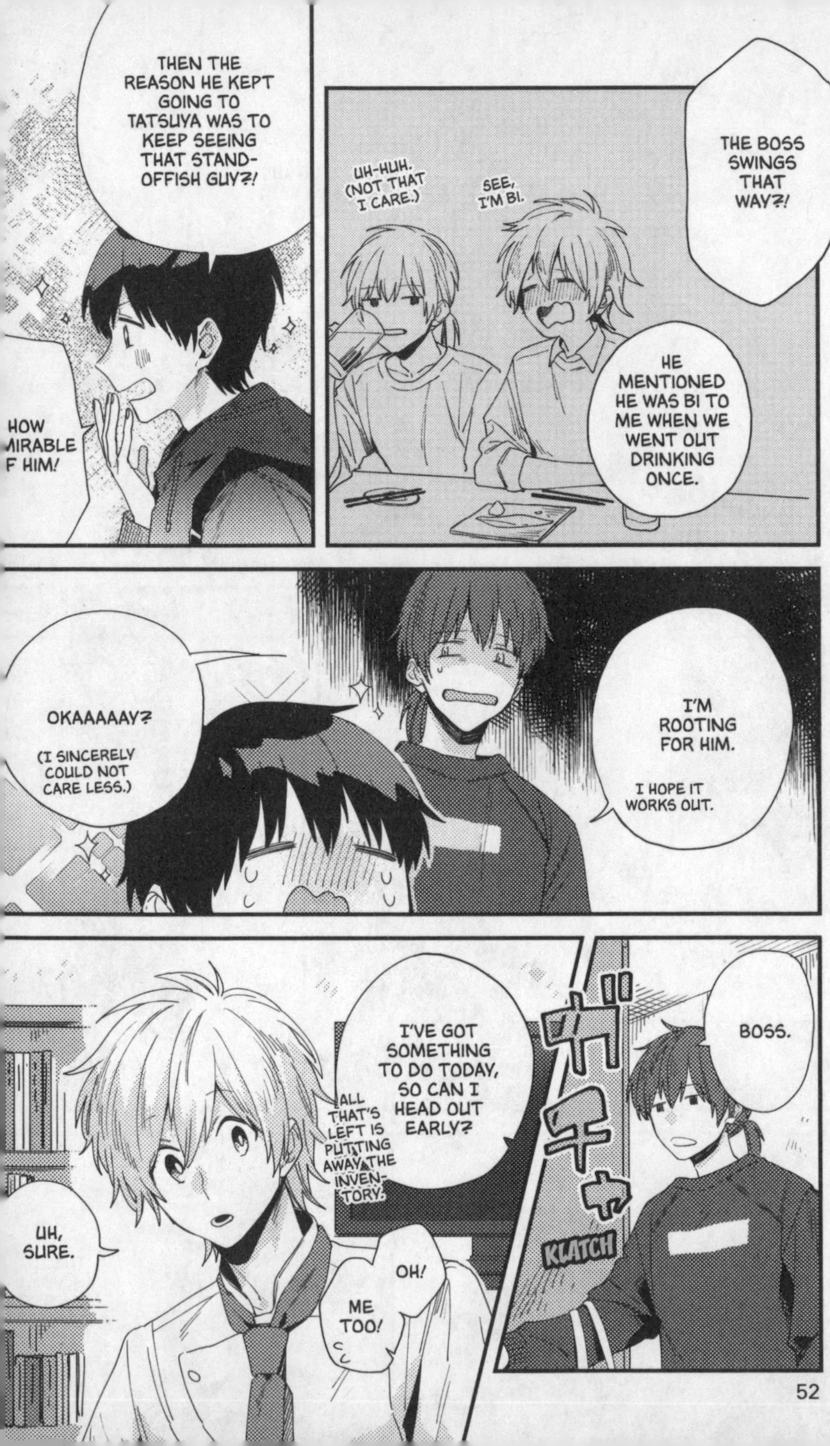
THE BOSS SWINGS THAT WAY?!
SEE, I'M BI.
UH-HUH. (NOT THAT I CARE.)
HE MENTIONED HE WAS BI TO ME WHEN WE WENT OUT DRINKING ONCE.
THEN THE REASON HE KEPT GOING TO TATSUYA WAS TO KEEP SEEING THAT STAND-OFFISH GUY?!
HOW MIRABLE F HIM!
I'M ROOTING FOR HIM.
I HOPE IT WORKS OUT.
OKAAAAAY?
(I SINCERELY COULD NOT CARE LESS.)
BOSS.
ガチャ
KLATCH
I'VE GOT SOMETHING TO DO TODAY, SO CAN I HEAD OUT EARLY?
ALL THAT'S LEFT IS PUTTING AWAY THE INVENTORY.
UH, SURE.
OH!
ME TOO!

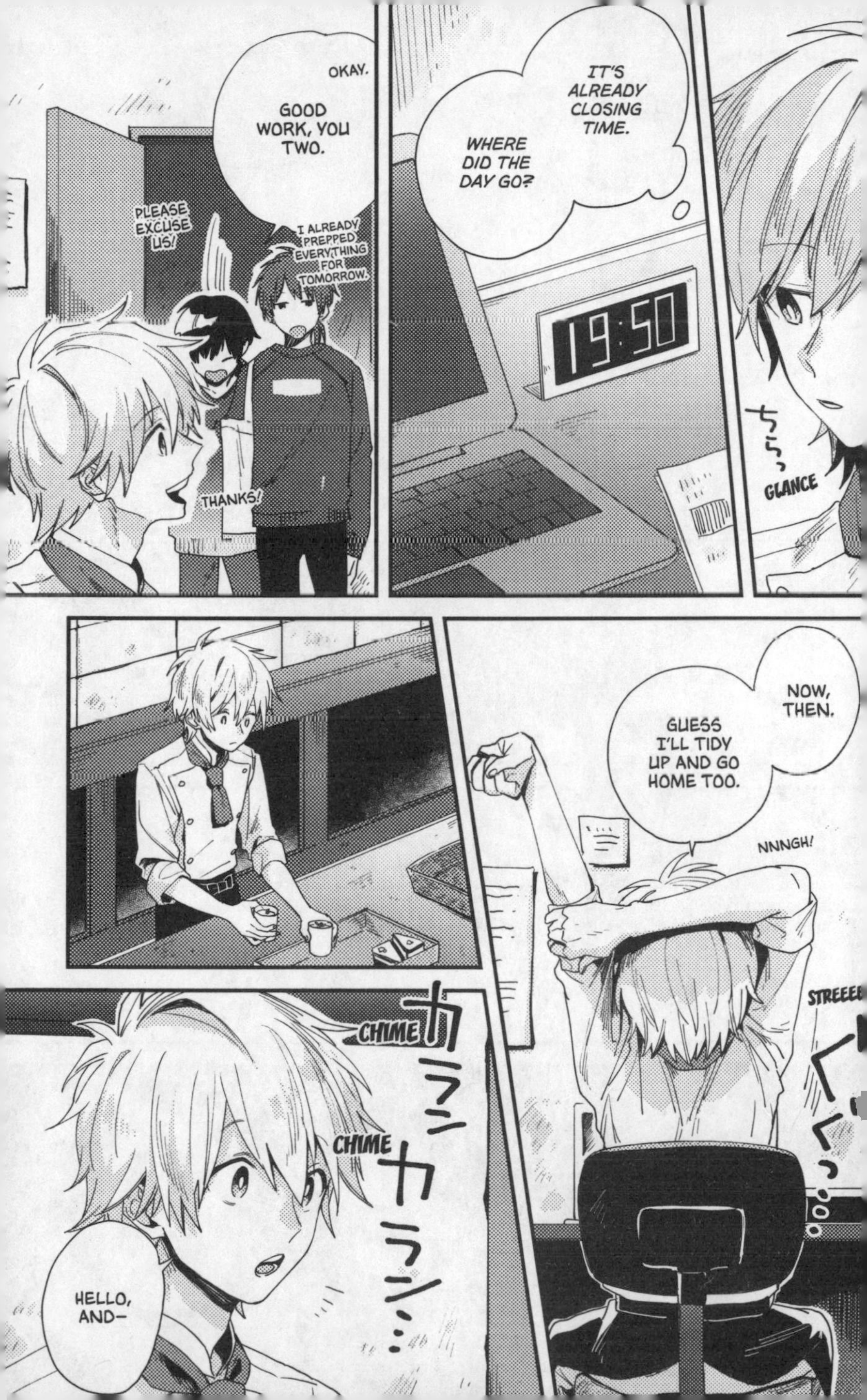
ちらっ
GLANCE
IT'S ALREADY CLOSING TIME.
WHERE DID THE DAY GO?
19:50
OKAY.
GOOD WORK, YOU TWO.
I ALREADY PREPPED EVERYTHING FOR TOMORROW.
PLEASE EXCUSE US!
THANKS!
NOW, THEN.
GUESS I'LL TIDY UP AND GO HOME TOO.
NNNGH!
STREEEE
ぐぐっ
CHIME
カラン
CHIME
カラン
HELLO, AND—

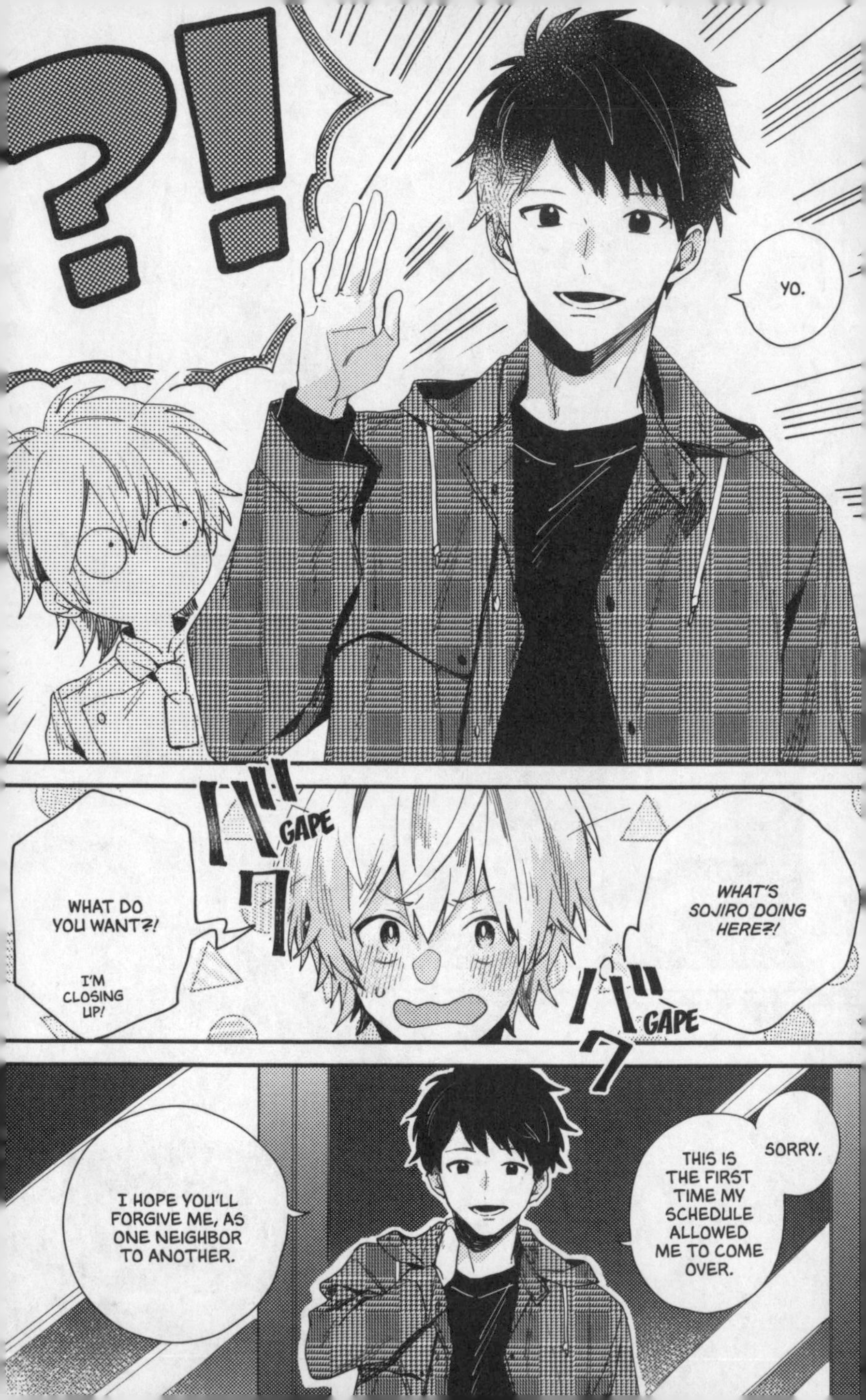
YO.
?!
WHAT'S SOJIRO DOING HERE?!
GAPE
GAPE
WHAT DO YOU WANT?!
I'M CLOSING UP!
SORRY.
THIS IS THE FIRST TIME MY SCHEDULE ALLOWED ME TO COME OVER.
I HOPE YOU'LL FORGIVE ME, AS ONE NEIGHBOR TO ANOTHER.

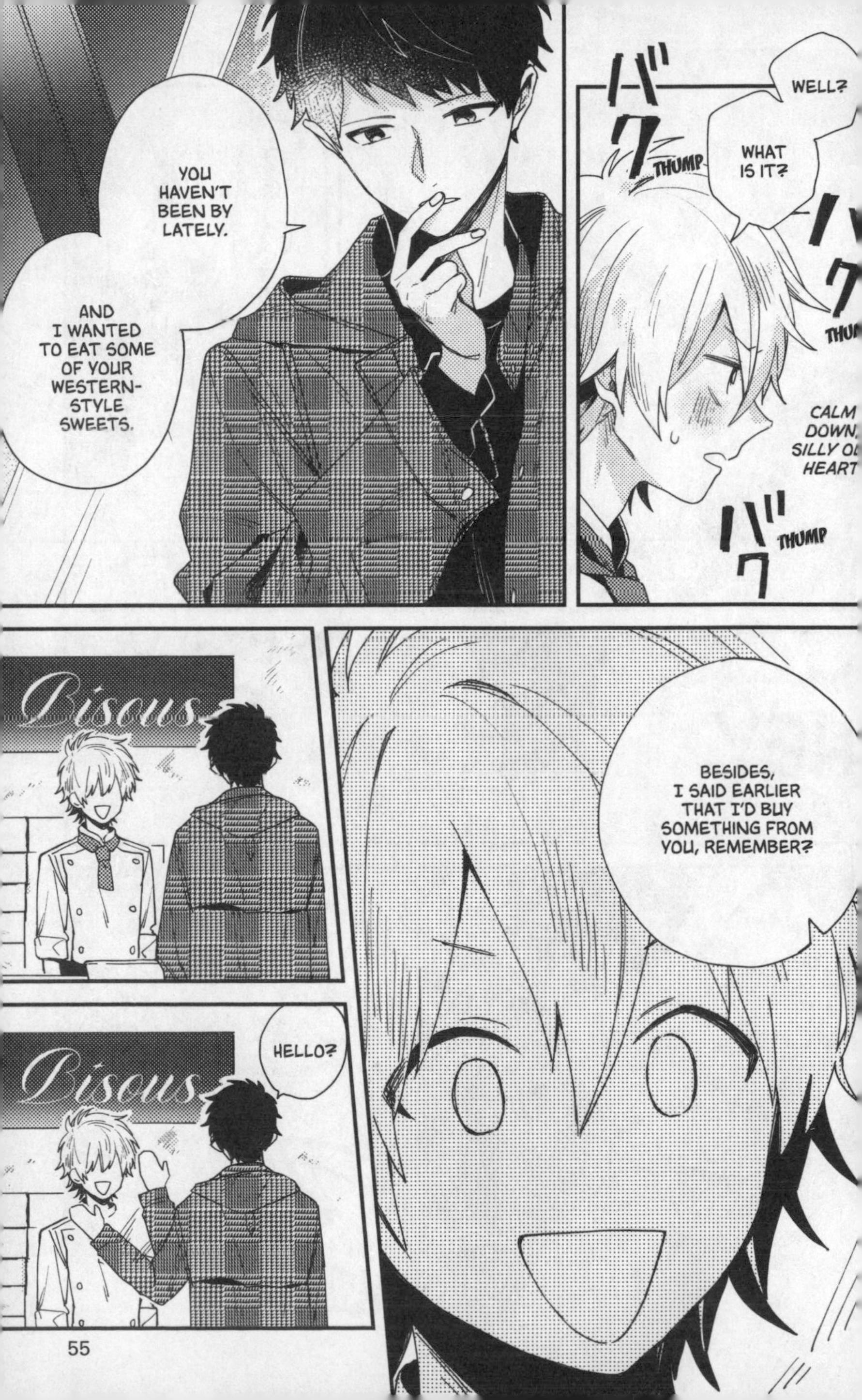
WELL?
WHAT IS IT?
バク THUMP
バク THU
CALM DOWN, SILLY OL HEART
バク THUMP
YOU HAVEN'T BEEN BY LATELY.
AND I WANTED TO EAT SOME OF YOUR WESTERN-STYLE SWEETS.
BESIDES, I SAID EARLIER THAT I'D BUY SOMETHING FROM YOU, REMEMBER?
Bisous
Bisous
HELLO?

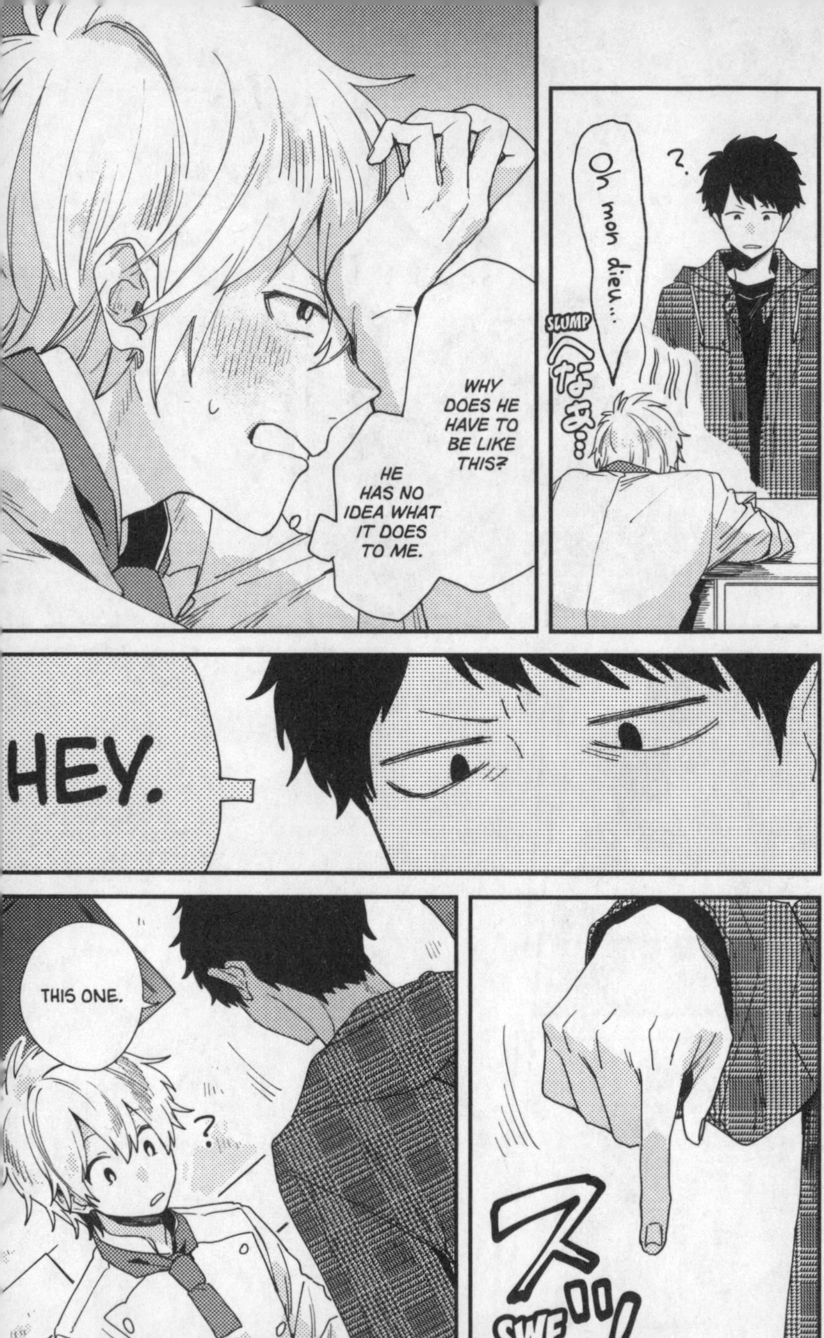
Oh mon dieu...
SLUMP
へなぁ…
WHY DOES HE HAVE TO BE LIKE THIS?
HE HAS NO IDEA WHAT IT DOES TO ME.
HEY.
ス
SWF
THIS ONE.

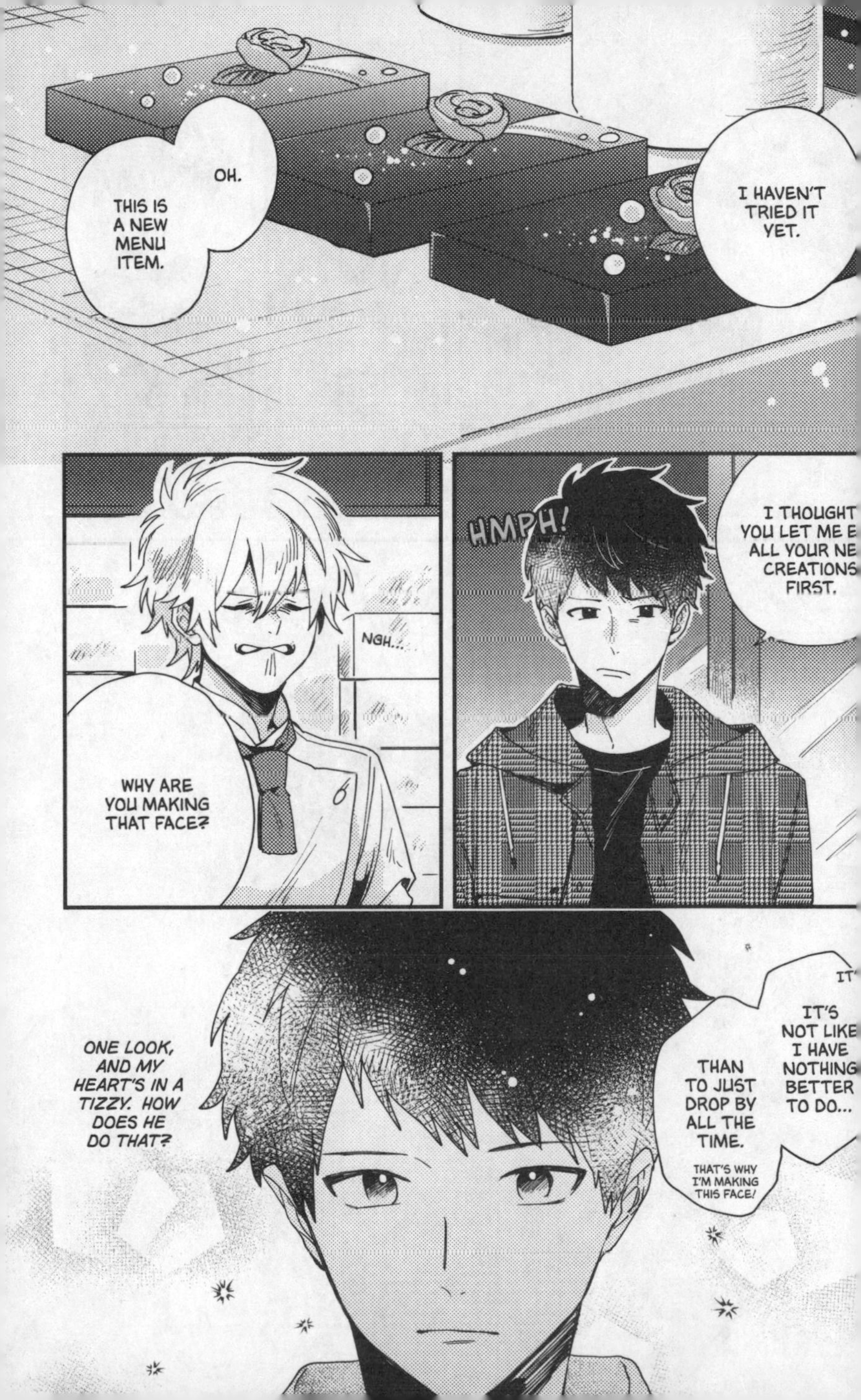
OH.
THIS IS A NEW MENU ITEM.
I HAVEN'T TRIED IT YET.
HMPH!
I THOUGHT YOU LET ME E ALL YOUR NE CREATIONS FIRST.
NGH...
WHY ARE YOU MAKING THAT FACE?
IT'
IT'S NOT LIKE I HAVE NOTHING BETTER TO DO...
THAN TO JUST DROP BY ALL THE TIME.
THAT'S WHY I'M MAKING THIS FACE!
ONE LOOK, AND MY HEART'S IN A TIZZY. HOW DOES HE DO THAT?

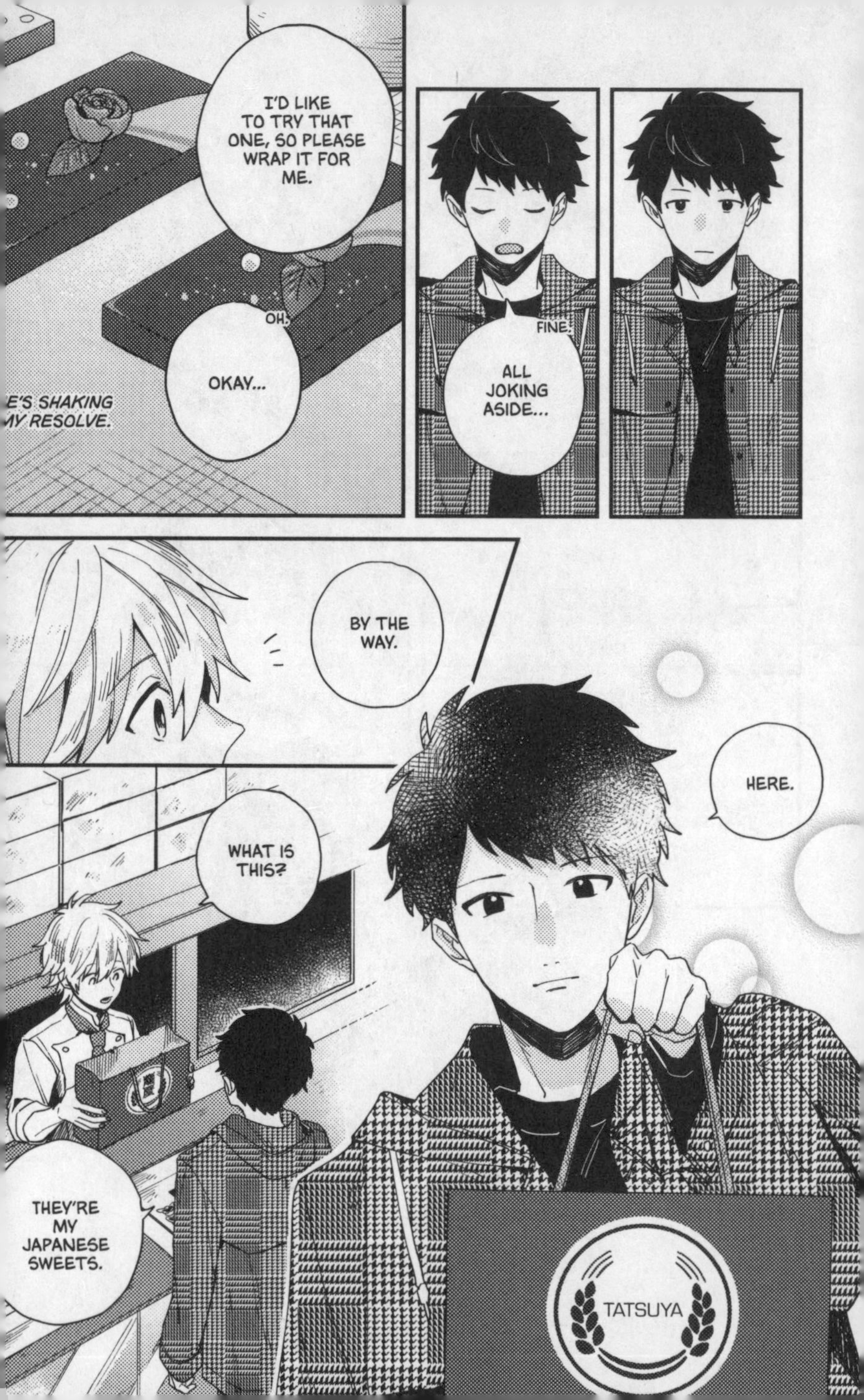
ALL JOKING ASIDE...
FINE.
I'D LIKE TO TRY THAT ONE, SO PLEASE WRAP IT FOR ME.
OH.
OKAY...
E'S SHAKING MY RESOLVE.
BY THE WAY.
HERE.
WHAT IS THIS?
THEY'RE MY JAPANESE SWEETS.
TATSUYA

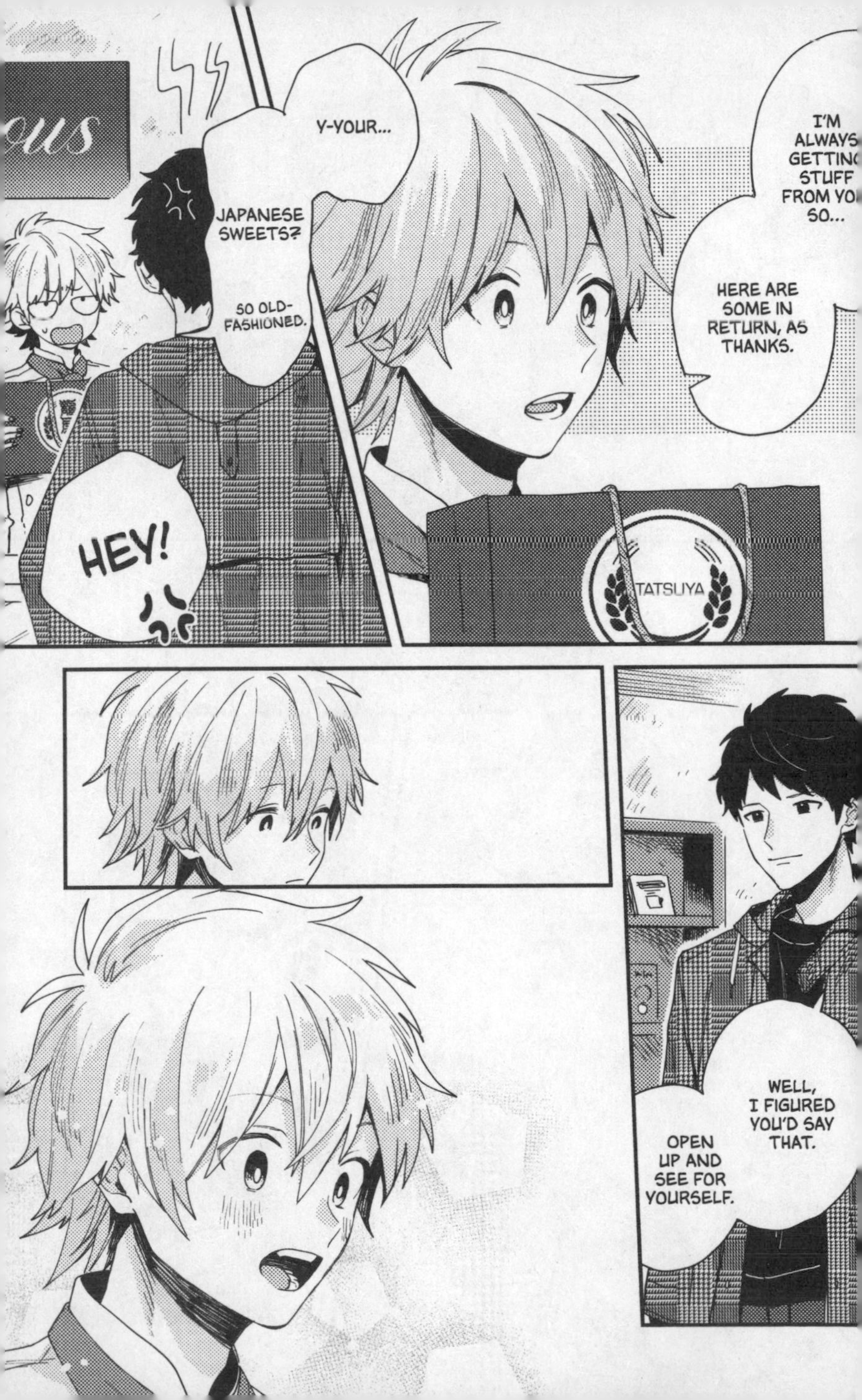
I'M ALWAYS GETTIN STUFF FROM YO SO...
HERE ARE SOME IN RETURN, AS THANKS.
TATSUYA
Y-YOUR...
JAPANESE SWEETS?
SO OLD-FASHIONED.
HEY!
WELL, I FIGURED YOU'D SAY THAT.
OPEN UP AND SEE FOR YOURSELF.

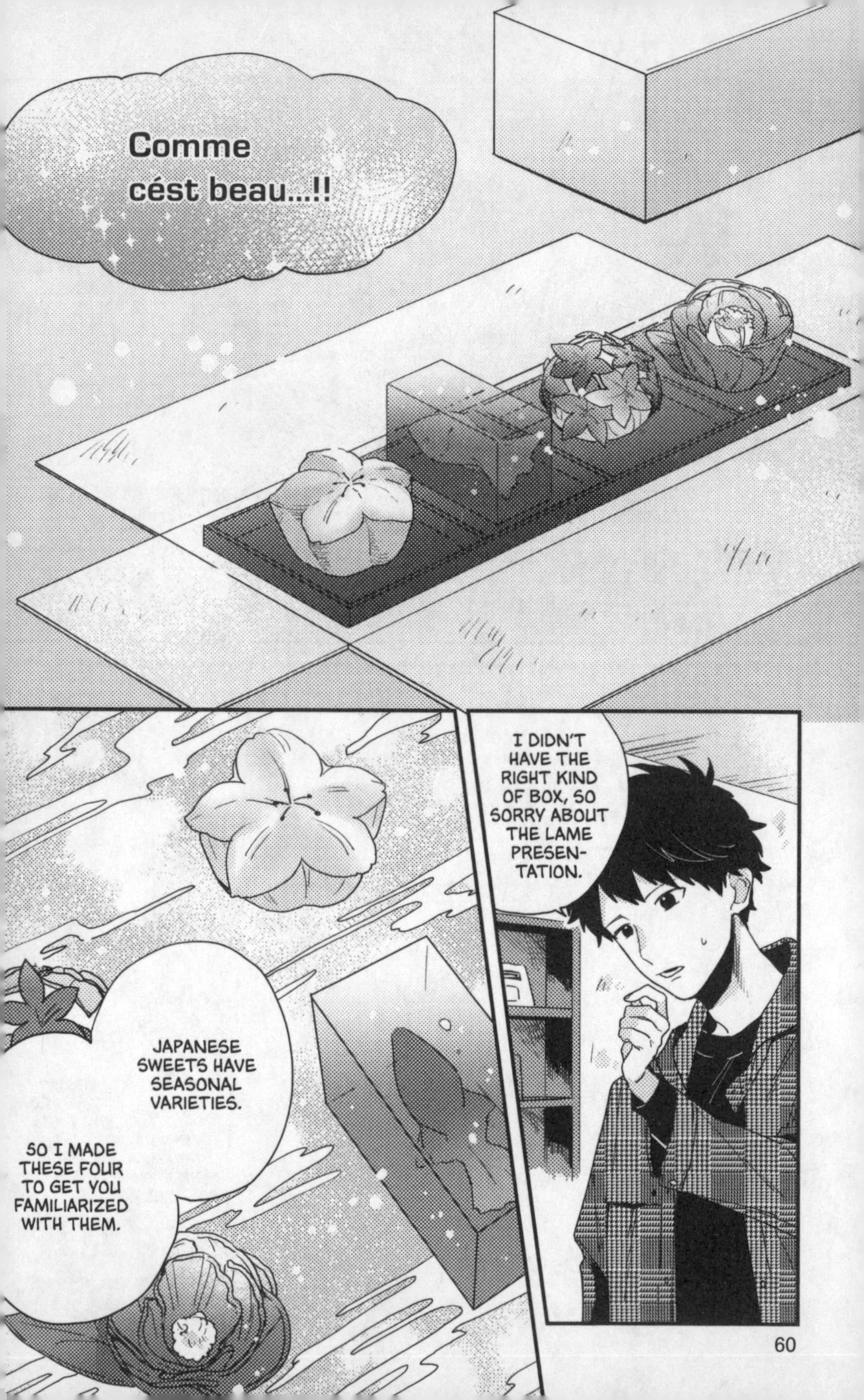
Comme cést beau...!!
I DIDN'T HAVE THE RIGHT KIND OF BOX, SO SORRY ABOUT THE LAME PRESEN-TATION.
JAPANESE SWEETS HAVE SEASONAL VARIETIES.
SO I MADE THESE FOUR TO GET YOU FAMILIARIZED WITH THEM.

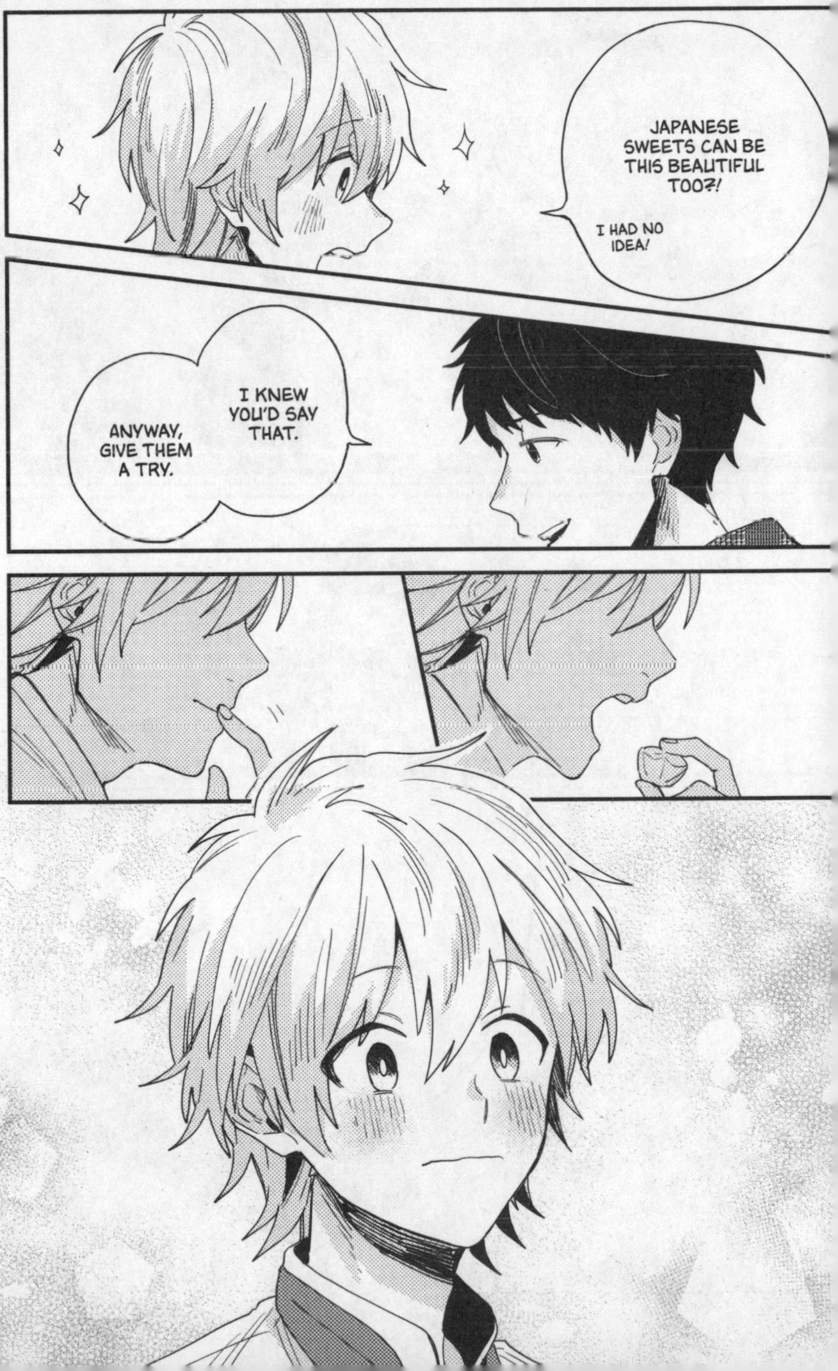

JAPANESE SWEETS CAN BE THIS BEAUTIFUL TOO?!
I HAD NO IDEA!
I KNEW YOU'D SAY THAT.
ANYWAY, GIVE THEM A TRY.

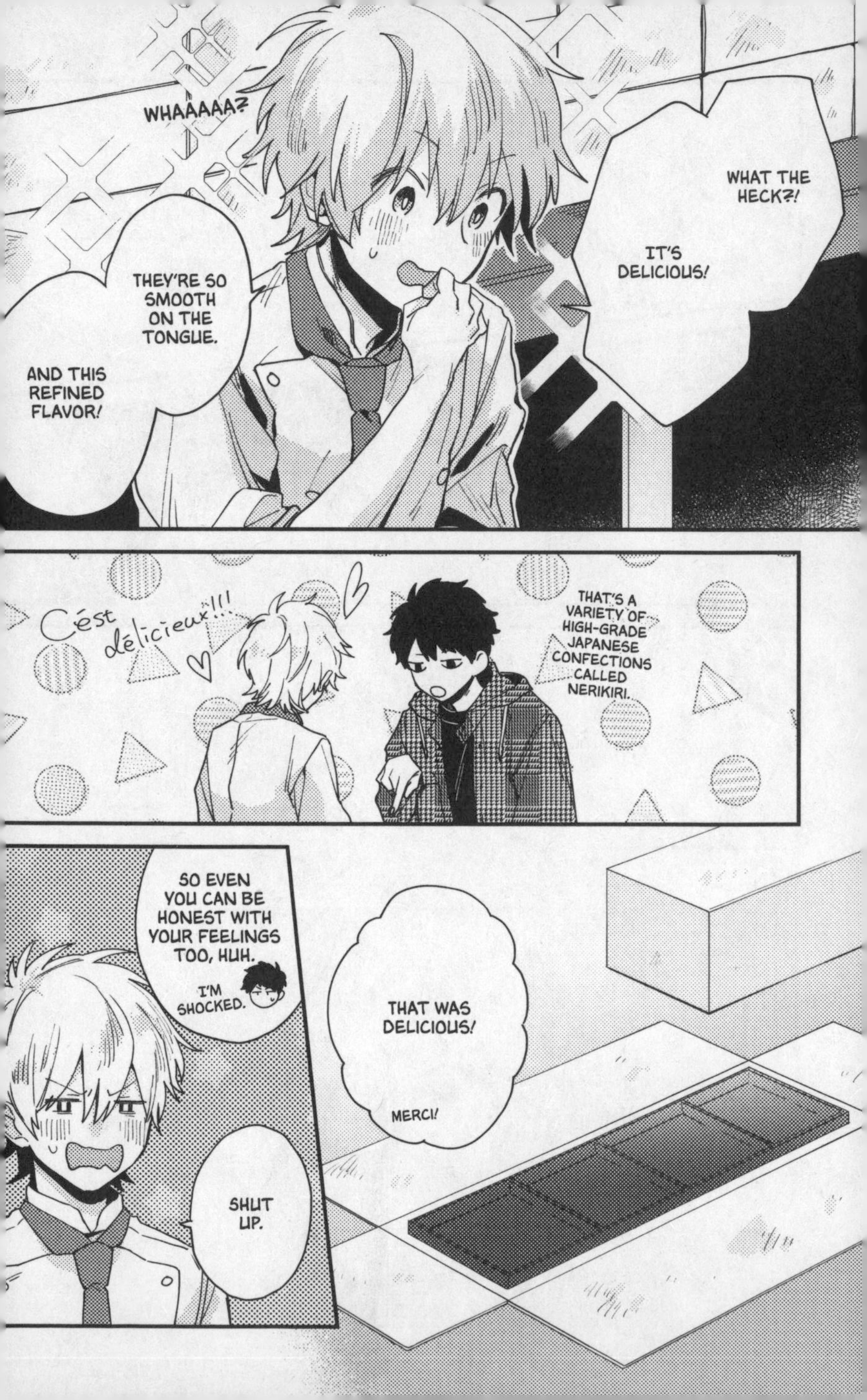
WHAT THE HECK?!
IT'S DELICIOUS!
WHAAAAA?
THEY'RE SO SMOOTH ON THE TONGUE.
AND THIS REFINED FLAVOR!
THAT'S A VARIETY OF HIGH-GRADE JAPANESE CONFECTIONS CALLED NERIKIRI.
Cést délicieux!!!
THAT WAS DELICIOUS!
MERCI!
SO EVEN YOU CAN BE HONEST WITH YOUR FEELINGS TOO, HUH.
I'M SHOCKED.
SHUT UP.

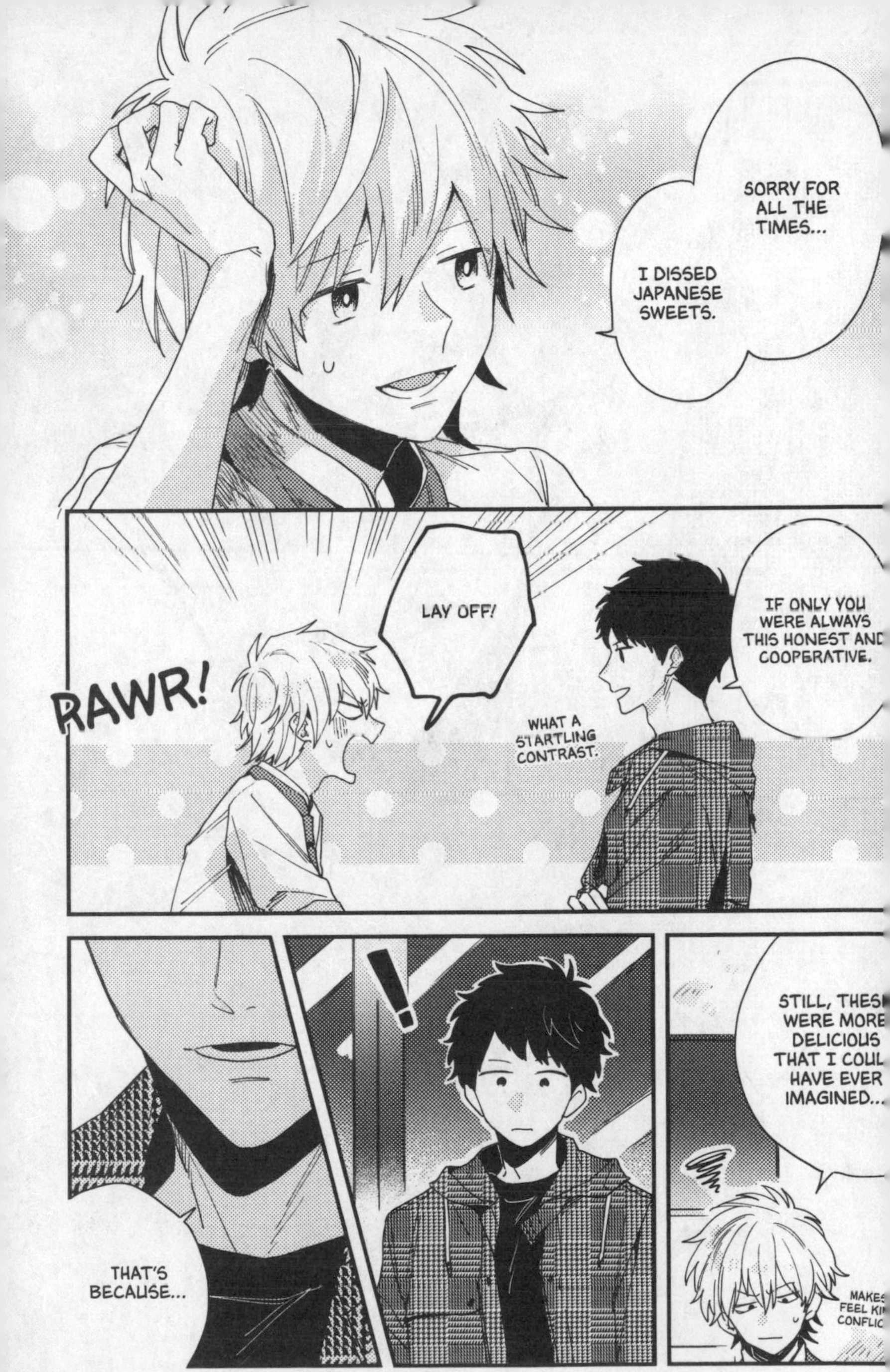
SORRY FOR ALL THE TIMES...
I DISSED JAPANESE SWEETS.
IF ONLY YOU WERE ALWAYS THIS HONEST AND COOPERATIVE.
LAY OFF!
WHAT A STARTLING CONTRAST.
RAWR!
STILL, THES WERE MORE DELICIOUS THAT I COUL HAVE EVER IMAGINED...
MAKES FEEL KI CONFLIC
!
THAT'S BECAUSE...

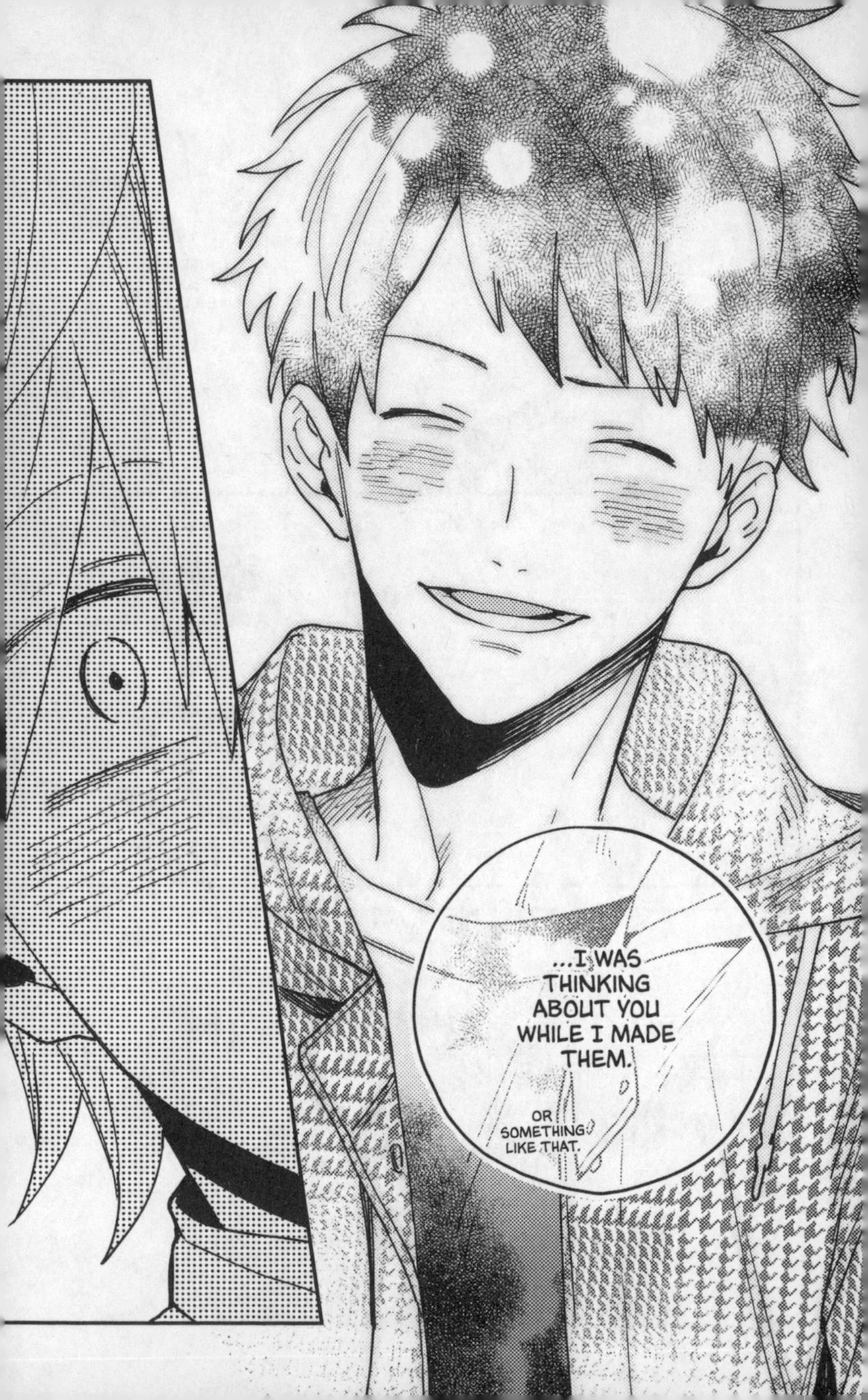
...I WAS THINKING ABOUT YOU WHILE I MADE THEM.
OR SOMETHING LIKE THAT.

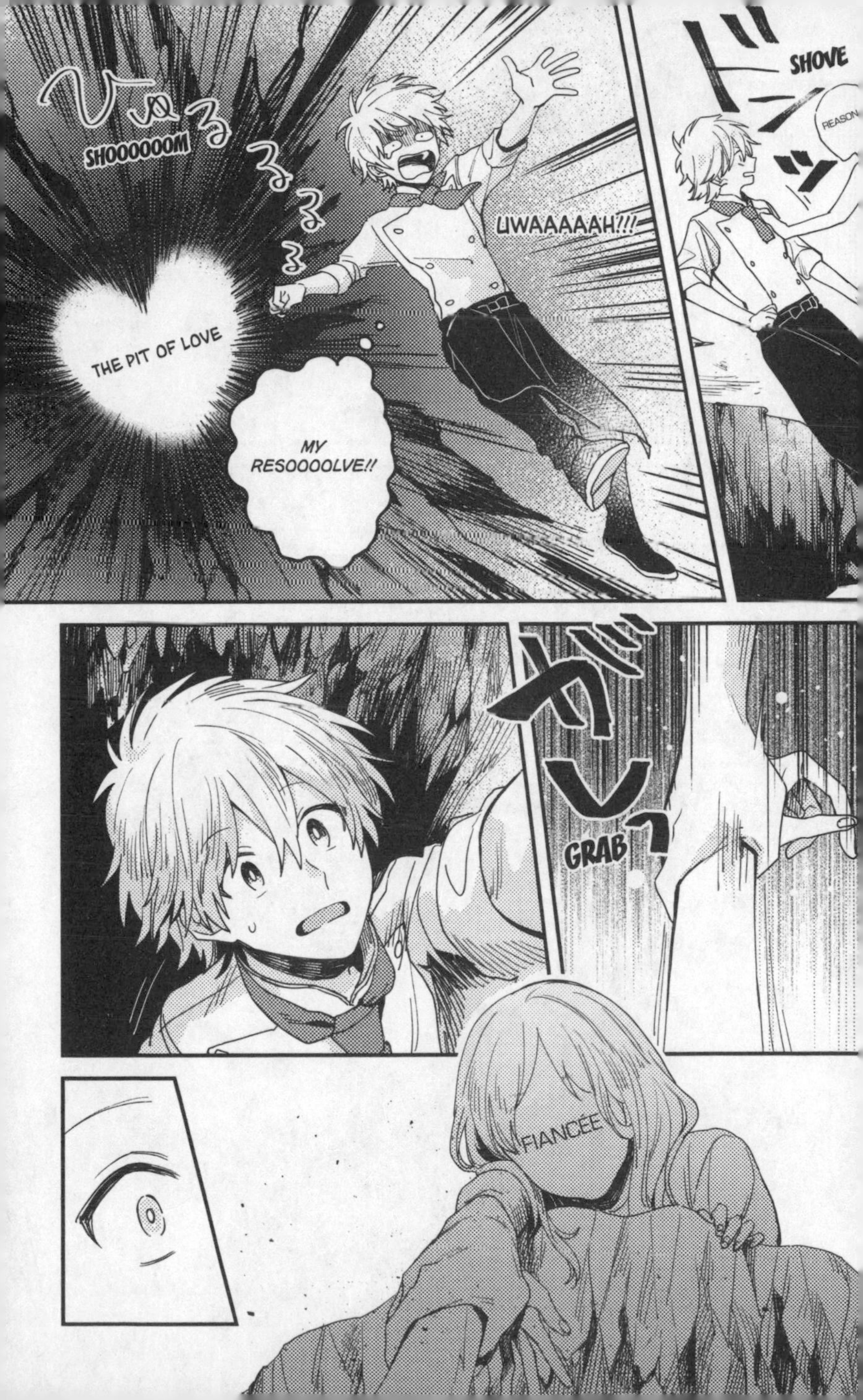
SHOVE
REASON
SHOOOOOOM
UWAAAAAH!!!
THE PIT OF LOVE
MY RESOOOOLVE!!
GRAB
FIANCÉE

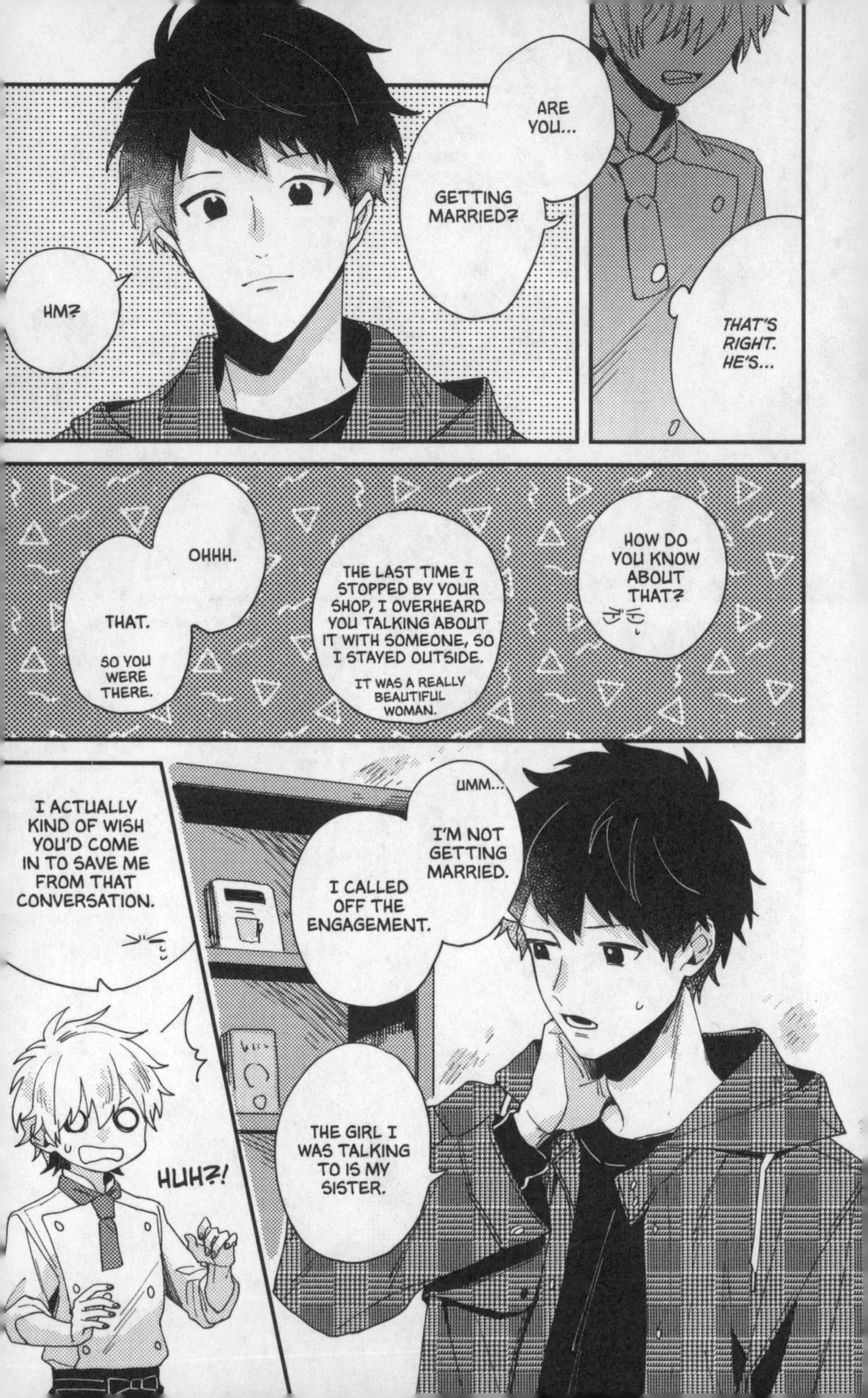
ARE YOU...
GETTING MARRIED?
THAT'S RIGHT. HE'S...
HM?
HOW DO YOU KNOW ABOUT THAT?
THE LAST TIME I STOPPED BY YOUR SHOP, I OVERHEARD YOU TALKING ABOUT IT WITH SOMEONE, SO I STAYED OUTSIDE.
IT WAS A REALLY BEAUTIFUL WOMAN.
OHHH.
THAT.
SO YOU WERE THERE.
UMM...
I'M NOT GETTING MARRIED.
I CALLED OFF THE ENGAGEMENT.
I ACTUALLY KIND OF WISH YOU'D COME IN TO SAVE ME FROM THAT CONVERSATION.
THE GIRL I WAS TALKING TO IS MY SISTER.
HUH?!

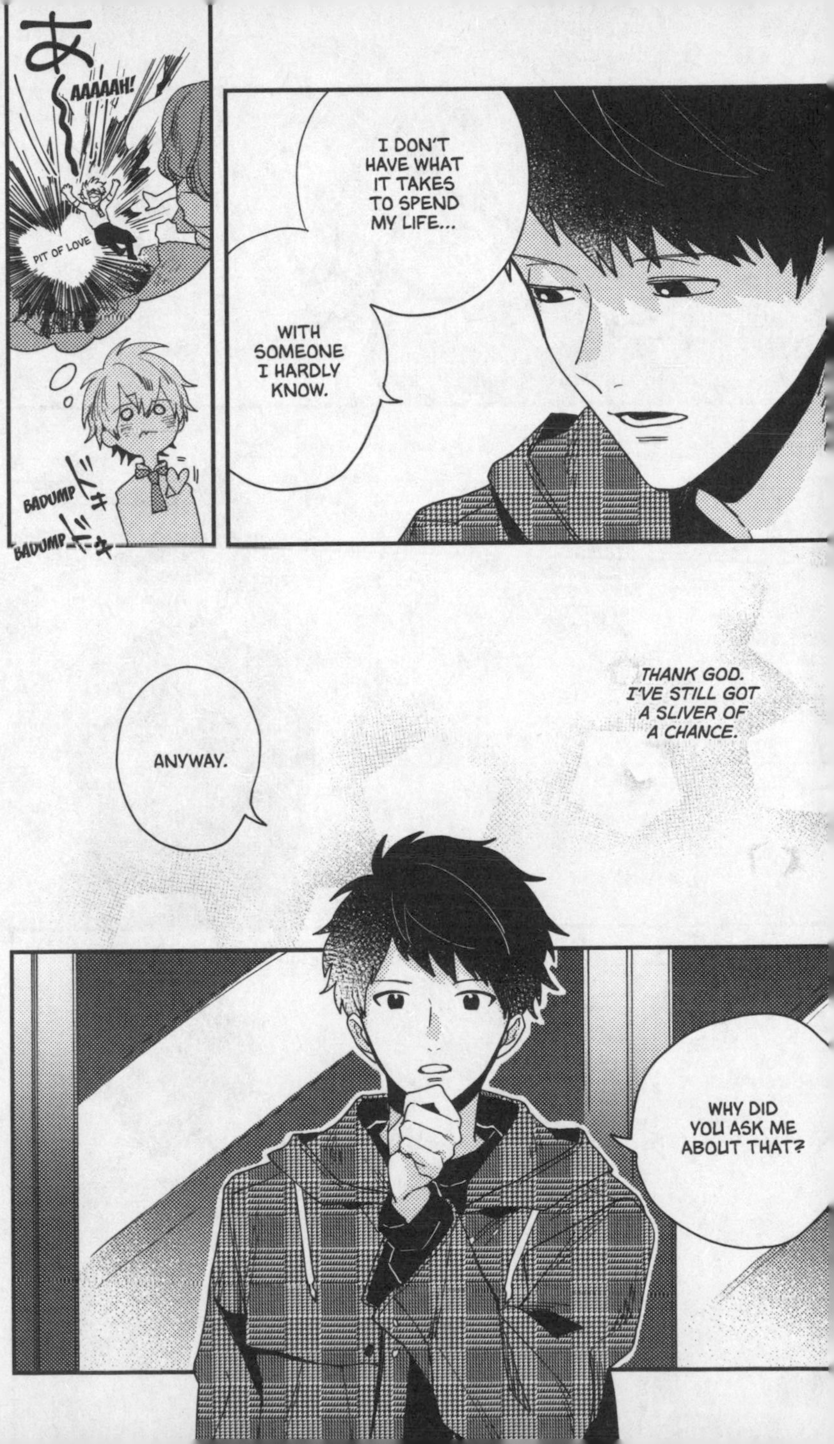
I DON'T HAVE WHAT IT TAKES TO SPEND MY LIFE...
WITH SOMEONE I HARDLY KNOW.
あ〜
AAAAAH!
PIT OF LOVE
BADUMP ドキ
BADUMP ドキ
THANK GOD. I'VE STILL GOT A SLIVER OF A CHANCE.
ANYWAY.
WHY DID YOU ASK ME ABOUT THAT?

!!!

?   ?

OH, CRAP!!

I JUST ASKED WHAT MY HEART WANTED ME TO!

THIS IS NONE OF MY BUSINESS, AND I DON'T WANT TO JUST BLURT OUT~!

AH!

I WAS JUST BEING NOSY. ANYONE WOULD BE CURIOUS IF THEY HEARD SOMETHING LIKE THAT, YOU KNOW?

HA HA!

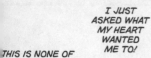
SPIN

SPIN

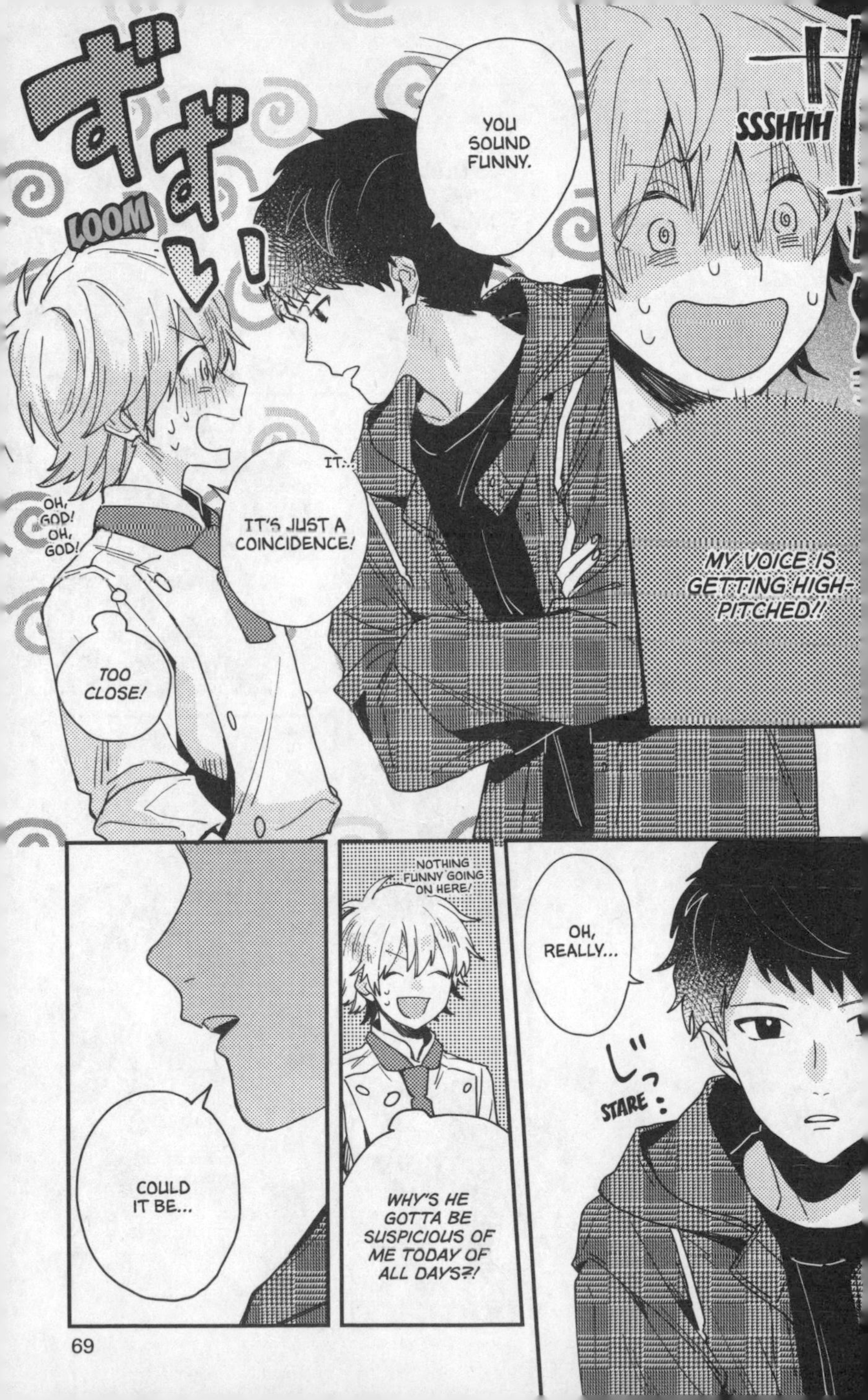
SSSHHH
MY VOICE IS GETTING HIGH-PITCHED!!
YOU SOUND FUNNY.
LOOM
IT...
IT'S JUST A COINCIDENCE!
OH, GOD! OH, GOD!
TOO CLOSE!
OH, REALLY...
じっ
STARE
NOTHING FUNNY GOING ON HERE!
WHY'S HE GOTTA BE SUSPICIOUS OF ME TODAY OF ALL DAYS?!
COULD IT BE...

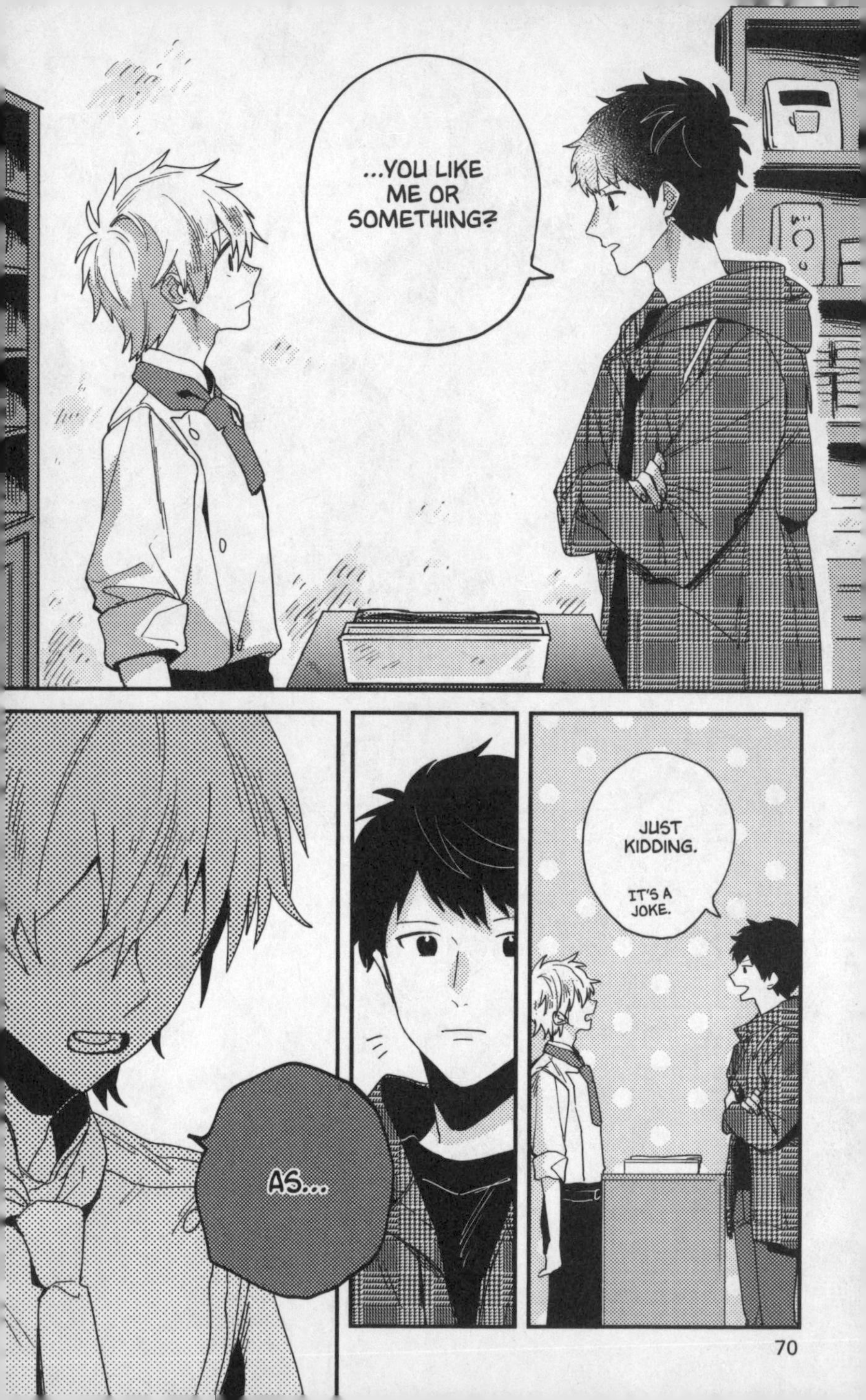
...YOU LIKE ME OR SOMETHING?
JUST KIDDING.
IT'S A JOKE.
AS...

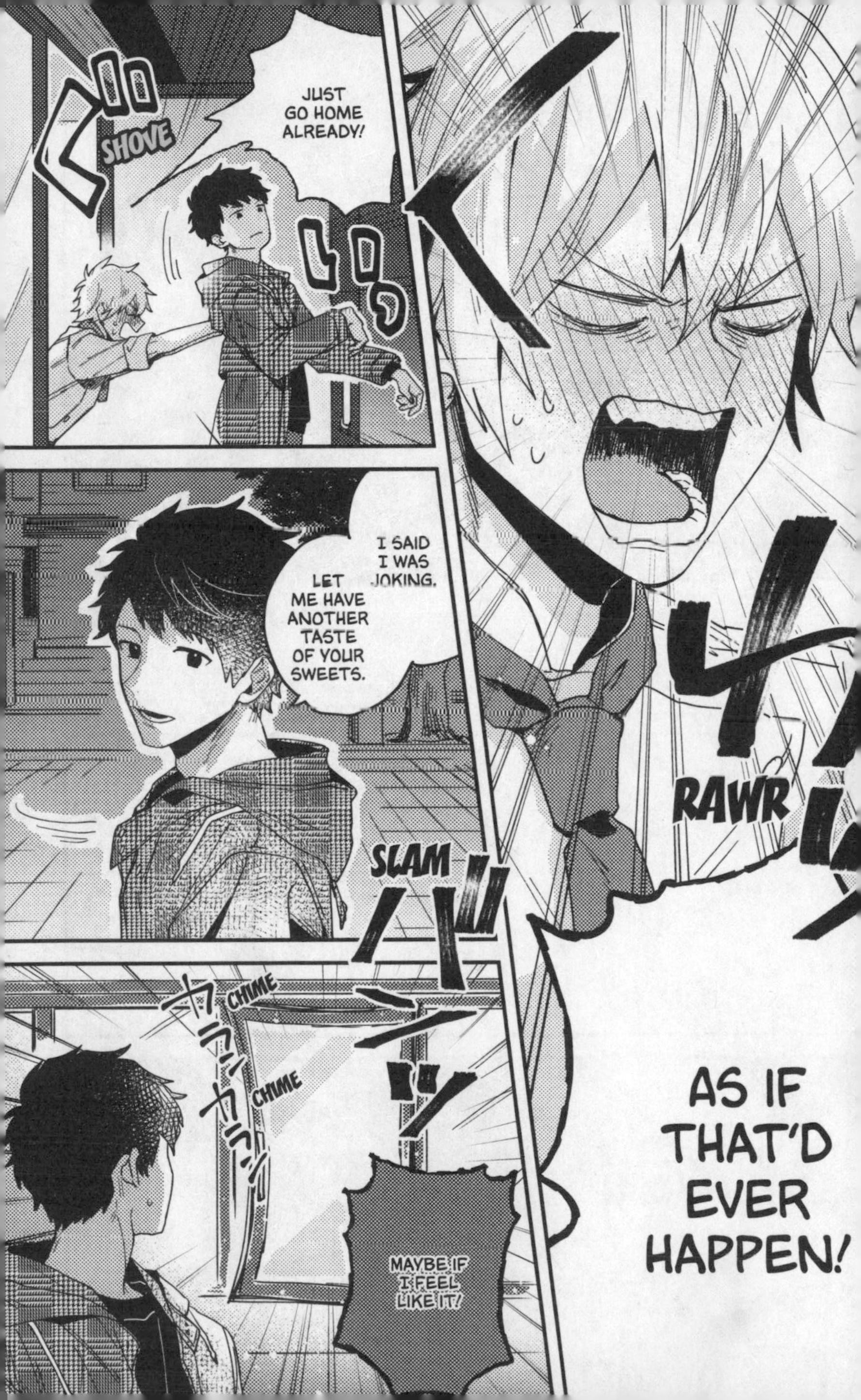
RAWR
AS IF THAT'D EVER HAPPEN!
SHOVE
JUST GO HOME ALREADY!
I SAID I WAS JOKING.
LET ME HAVE ANOTHER TASTE OF YOUR SWEETS.
SLAM
CHIME
CHIME
MAYBE IF I FEEL LIKE IT!

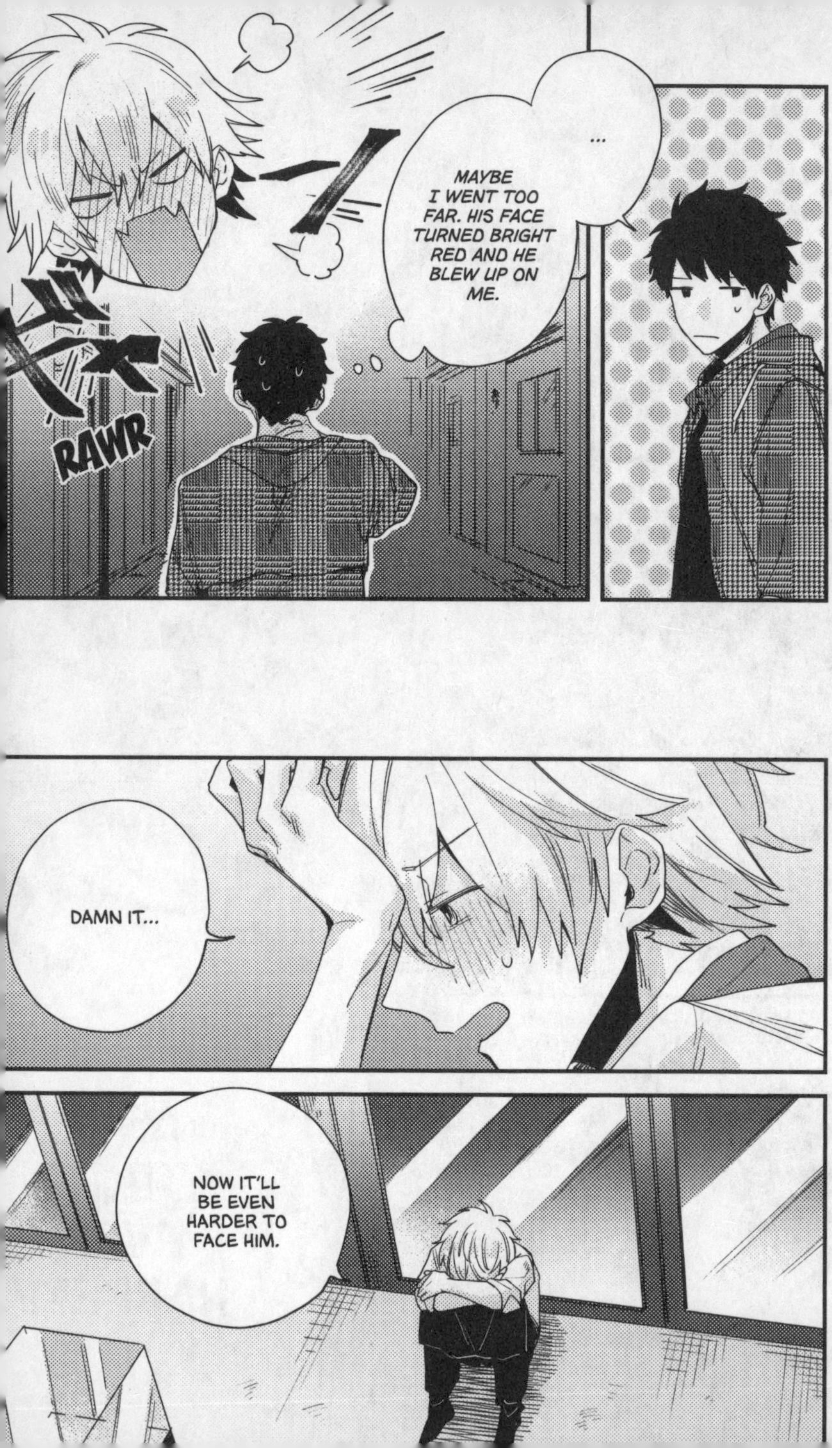
...
MAYBE I WENT TOO FAR. HIS FACE TURNED BRIGHT RED AND HE BLEW UP ON ME.
RAWR
DAMN IT...
NOW IT'LL BE EVEN HARDER TO FACE HIM.

Chéri, my destiny!

Chéri, my destiny!

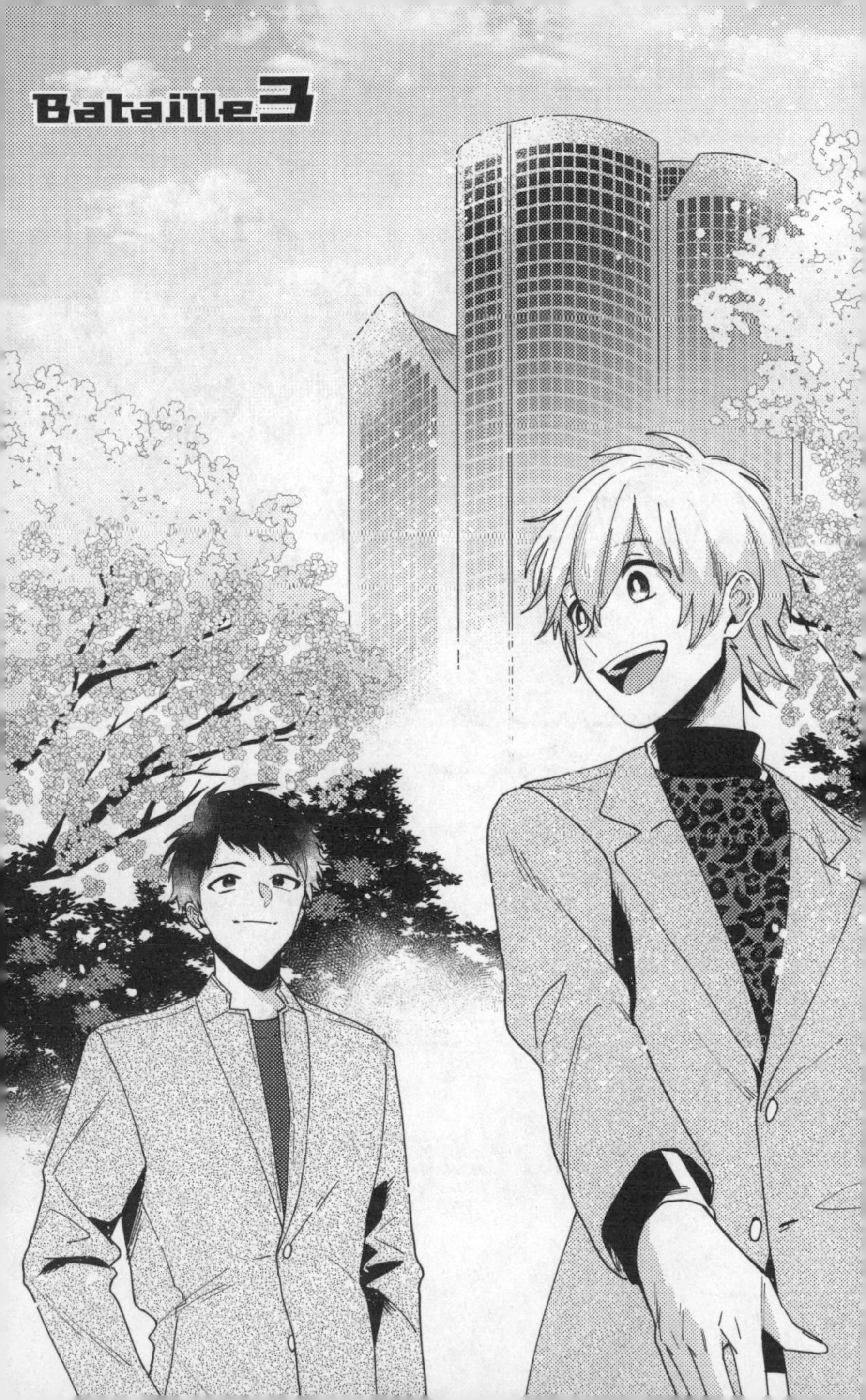
Bataille 3

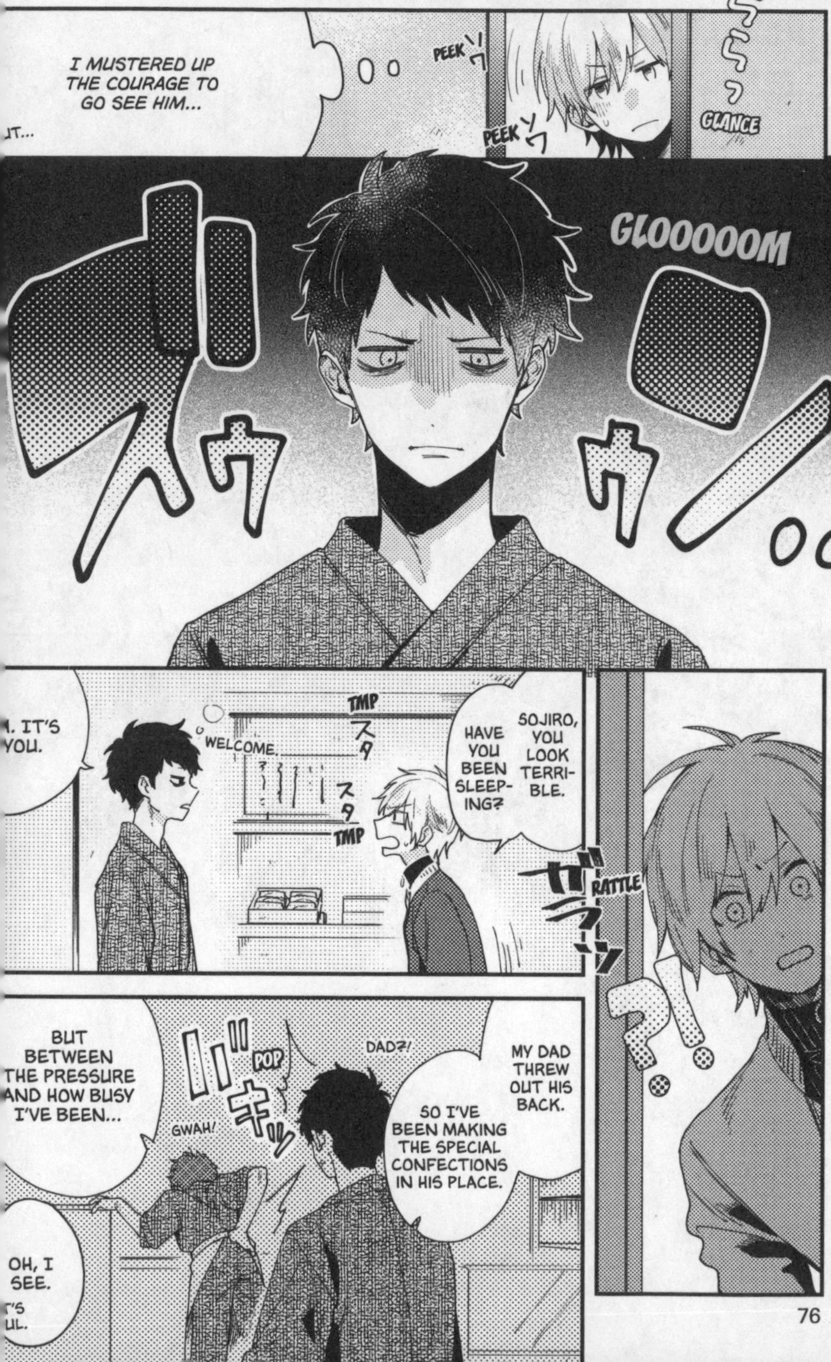
ちらっ
GLANCE
PEEK ソワ
PEEK ソワ
。。
I MUSTERED UP THE COURAGE TO GO SEE HIM...
UT...
GLOOOOOM
ズウウン。。
ガタッ
RATTLE
?!
SOJIRO, YOU LOOK TERRIBLE.
HAVE YOU BEEN SLEEPING?
TMP スタ
スタ TMP
WELCOME.
M. IT'S YOU.
MY DAD THREW OUT HIS BACK.
DAD?!
SO I'VE BEEN MAKING THE SPECIAL CONFECTIONS IN HIS PLACE.
POP ギッ
GWAH!
BUT BETWEEN THE PRESSURE AND HOW BUSY I'VE BEEN...
OH, I SEE.
T'S UL.

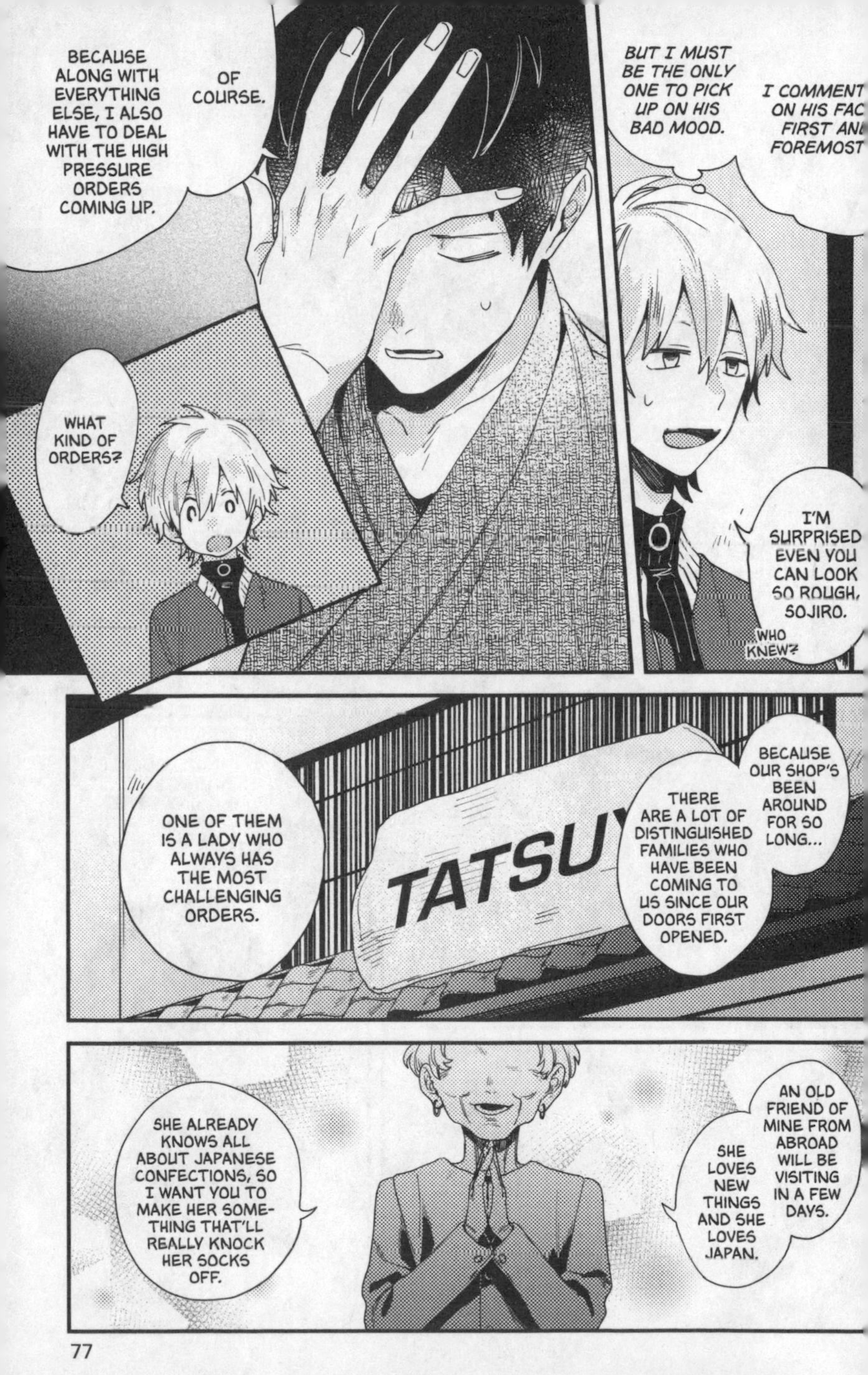
I COMMENT ON HIS FAC FIRST AN FOREMOST
BUT I MUST BE THE ONLY ONE TO PICK UP ON HIS BAD MOOD.
I'M SURPRISED EVEN YOU CAN LOOK SO ROUGH, SOJIRO.
WHO KNEW?
OF COURSE.
BECAUSE ALONG WITH EVERYTHING ELSE, I ALSO HAVE TO DEAL WITH THE HIGH PRESSURE ORDERS COMING UP.
WHAT KIND OF ORDERS?
BECAUSE OUR SHOP'S BEEN AROUND FOR SO LONG...
THERE ARE A LOT OF DISTINGUISHED FAMILIES WHO HAVE BEEN COMING TO US SINCE OUR DOORS FIRST OPENED.
TATSU
ONE OF THEM IS A LADY WHO ALWAYS HAS THE MOST CHALLENGING ORDERS.
AN OLD FRIEND OF MINE FROM ABROAD WILL BE VISITING IN A FEW DAYS.
SHE LOVES NEW THINGS AND SHE LOVES JAPAN.
SHE ALREADY KNOWS ALL ABOUT JAPANESE CONFECTIONS, SO I WANT YOU TO MAKE HER SOMETHING THAT'LL REALLY KNOCK HER SOCKS OFF.

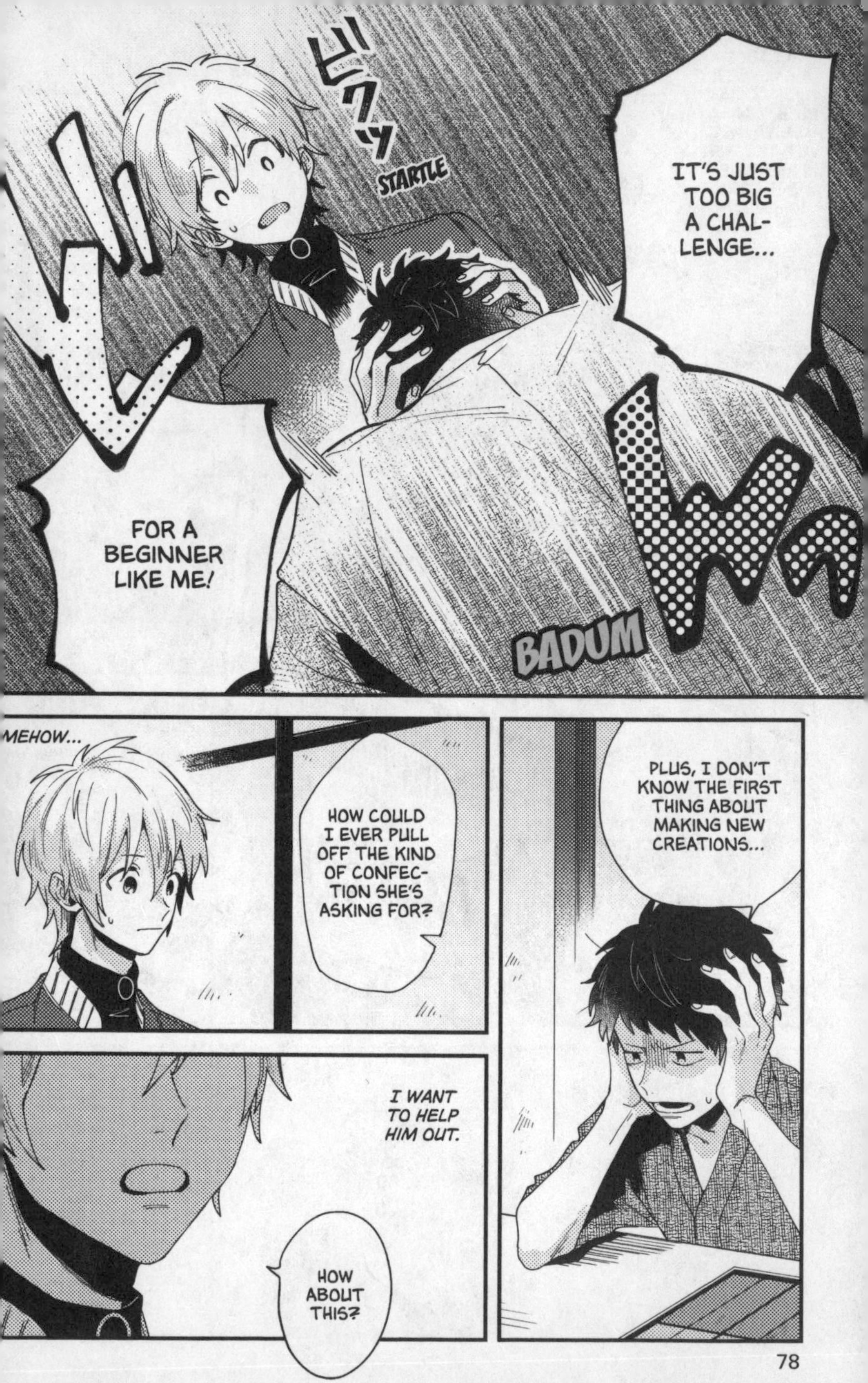
IT'S JUST TOO BIG A CHALLENGE...
STARTLE
FOR A BEGINNER LIKE ME!
BADUM
PLUS, I DON'T KNOW THE FIRST THING ABOUT MAKING NEW CREATIONS...
MEHOW...
HOW COULD I EVER PULL OFF THE KIND OF CONFECTION SHE'S ASKING FOR?
I WANT TO HELP HIM OUT.
HOW ABOUT THIS?

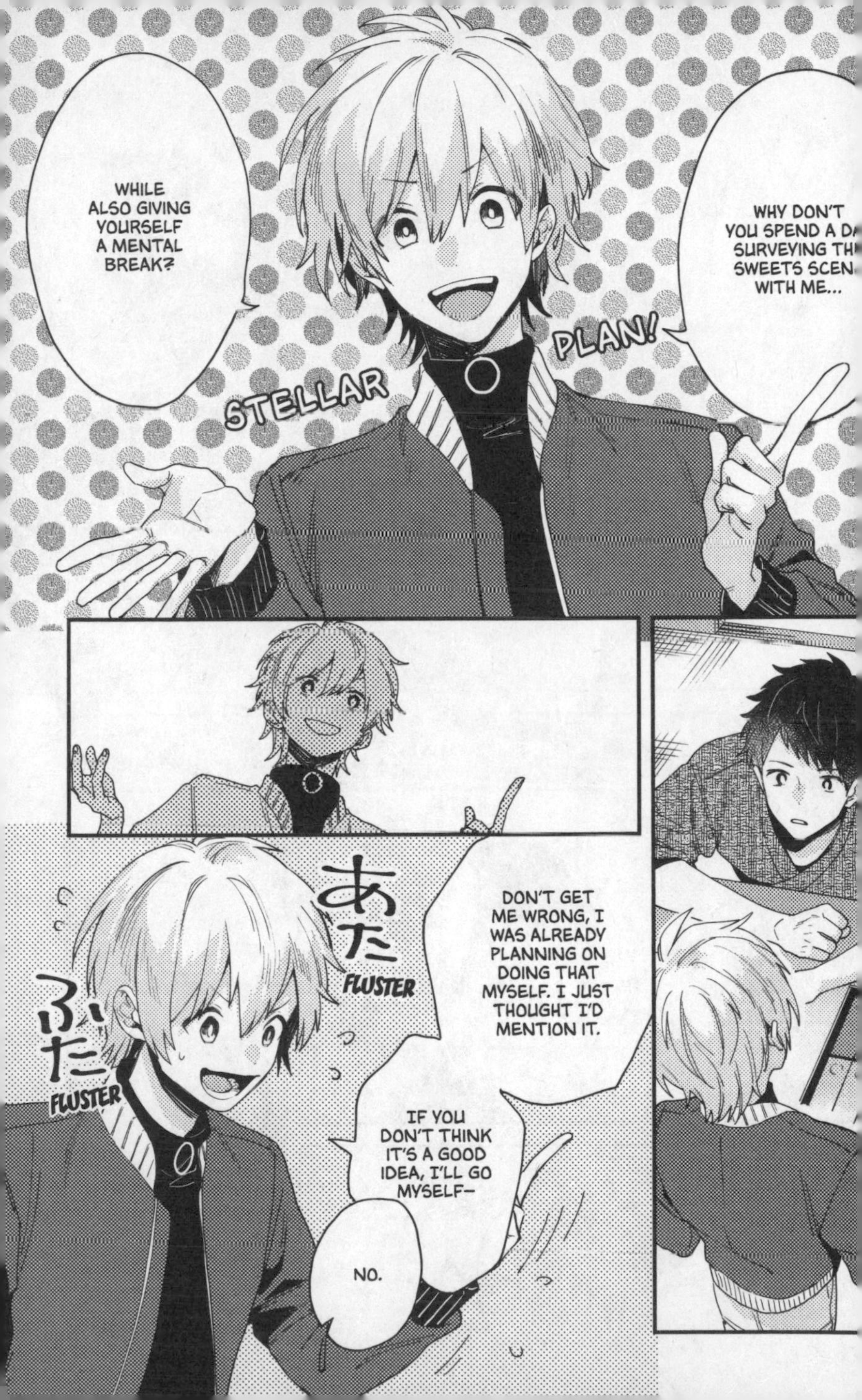
WHY DON'T YOU SPEND A DA SURVEYING TH SWEETS SCEN WITH ME...
STELLAR PLAN!
WHILE ALSO GIVING YOURSELF A MENTAL BREAK?
DON'T GET ME WRONG, I WAS ALREADY PLANNING ON DOING THAT MYSELF. I JUST THOUGHT I'D MENTION IT.
あた
FLUSTER
ふた
FLUSTER
IF YOU DON'T THINK IT'S A GOOD IDEA, I'LL GO MYSELF–
NO.

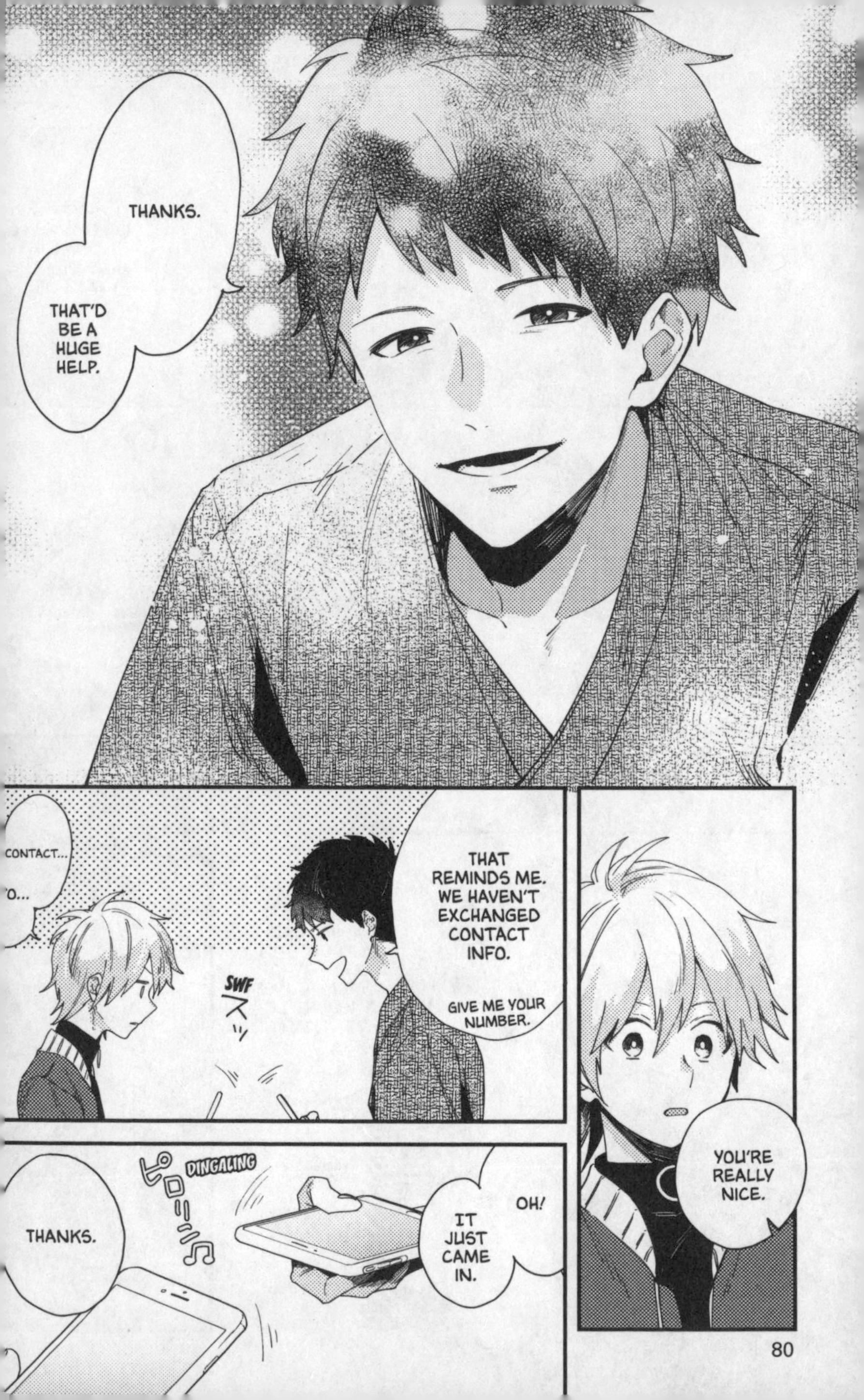
THANKS.
THAT'D BE A HUGE HELP.
YOU'RE REALLY NICE.
THAT REMINDS ME. WE HAVEN'T EXCHANGED CONTACT INFO.
GIVE ME YOUR NUMBER.
SWF
CONTACT...
OH!
IT JUST CAME IN.
DINGALING
THANKS.

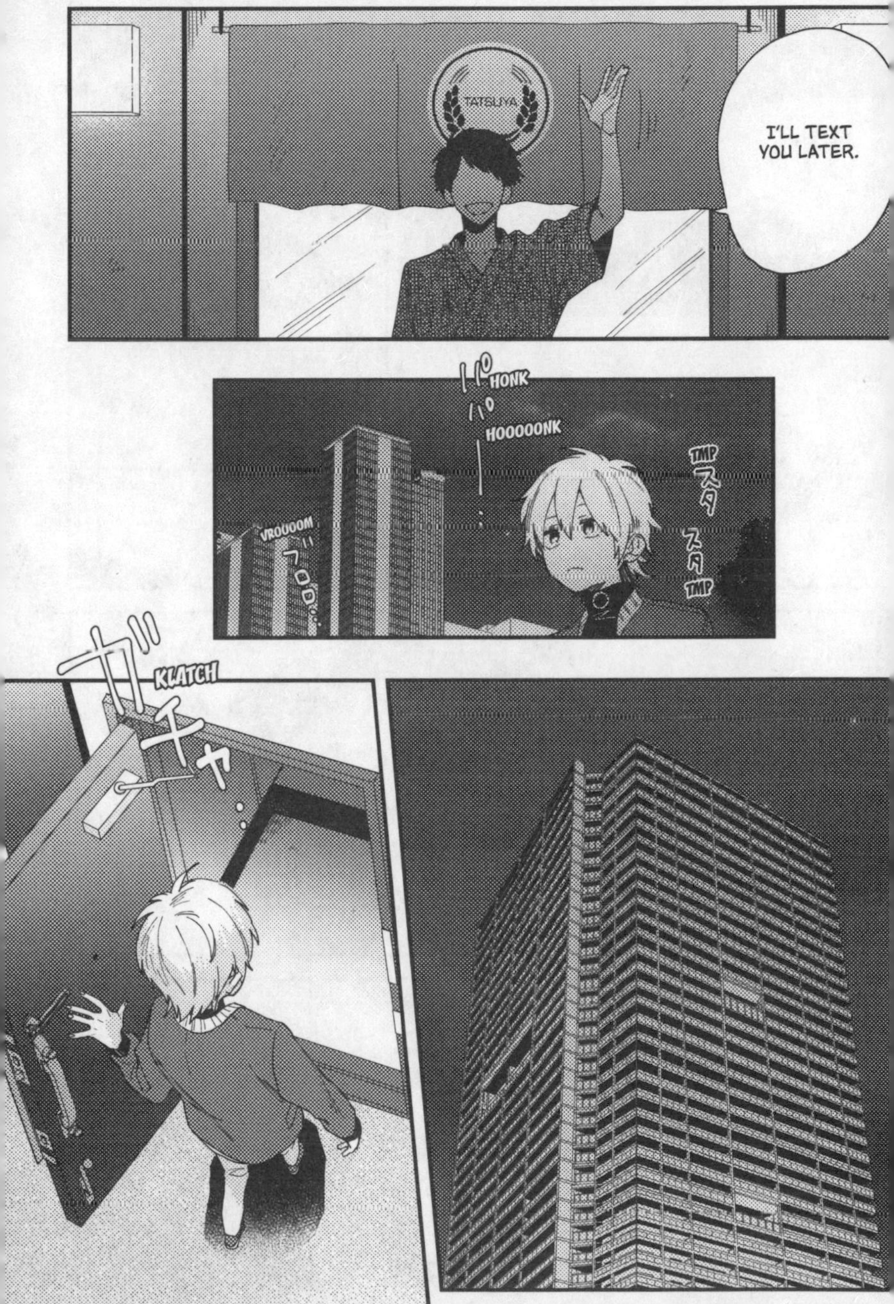
I'LL TEXT YOU LATER.
TATSUYA
TMP
TMP
HONK
HOOOOONK
VROUOOM
KLATCH

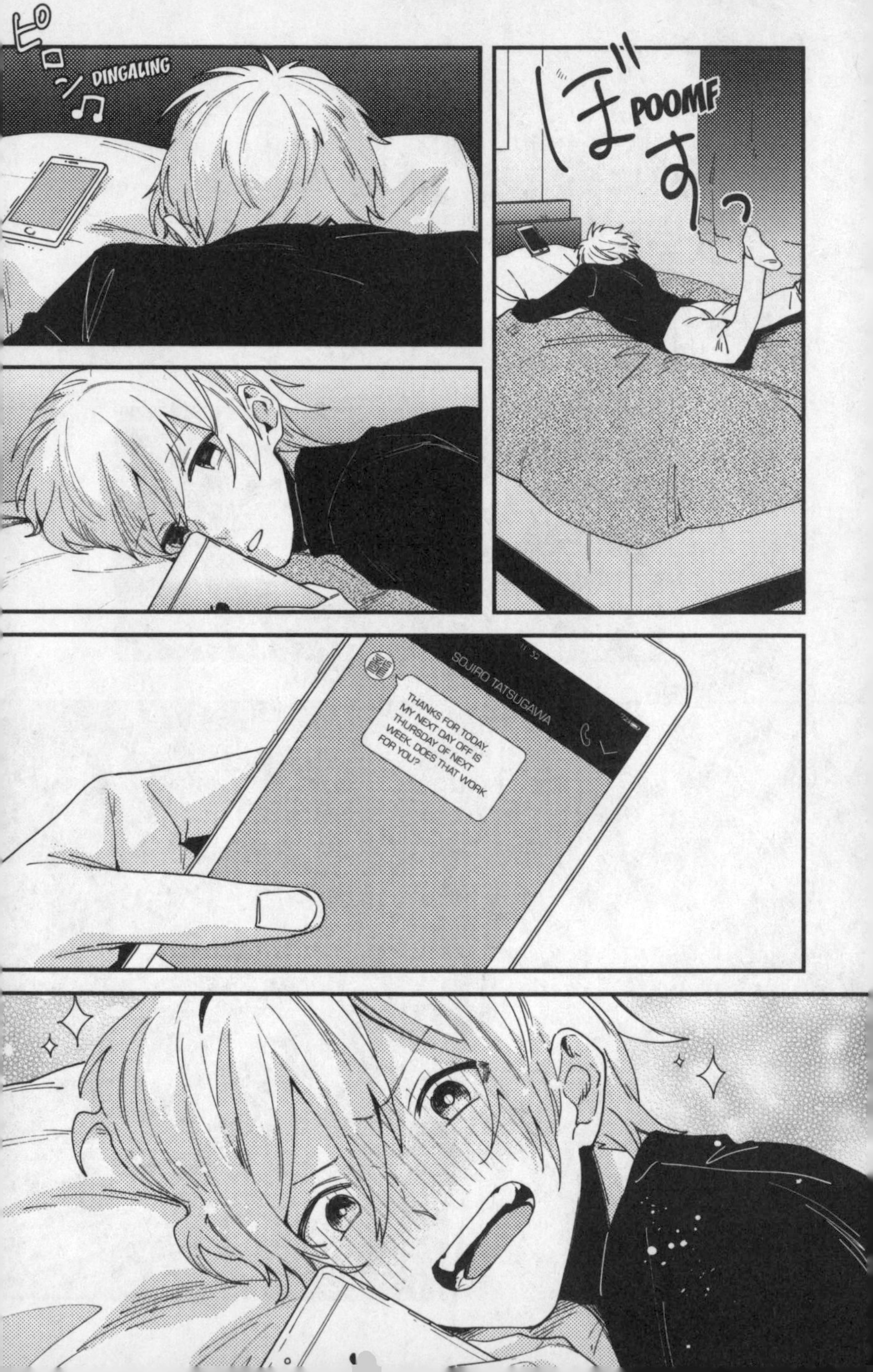
ぼすっ
POOMF
ピロン♪
DINGALING
SOJIRO TATSUGAWA
THANKS FOR TODAY. MY NEXT DAY OFF IS THURSDAY OF NEXT WEEK. DOES THAT WORK FOR YOU?

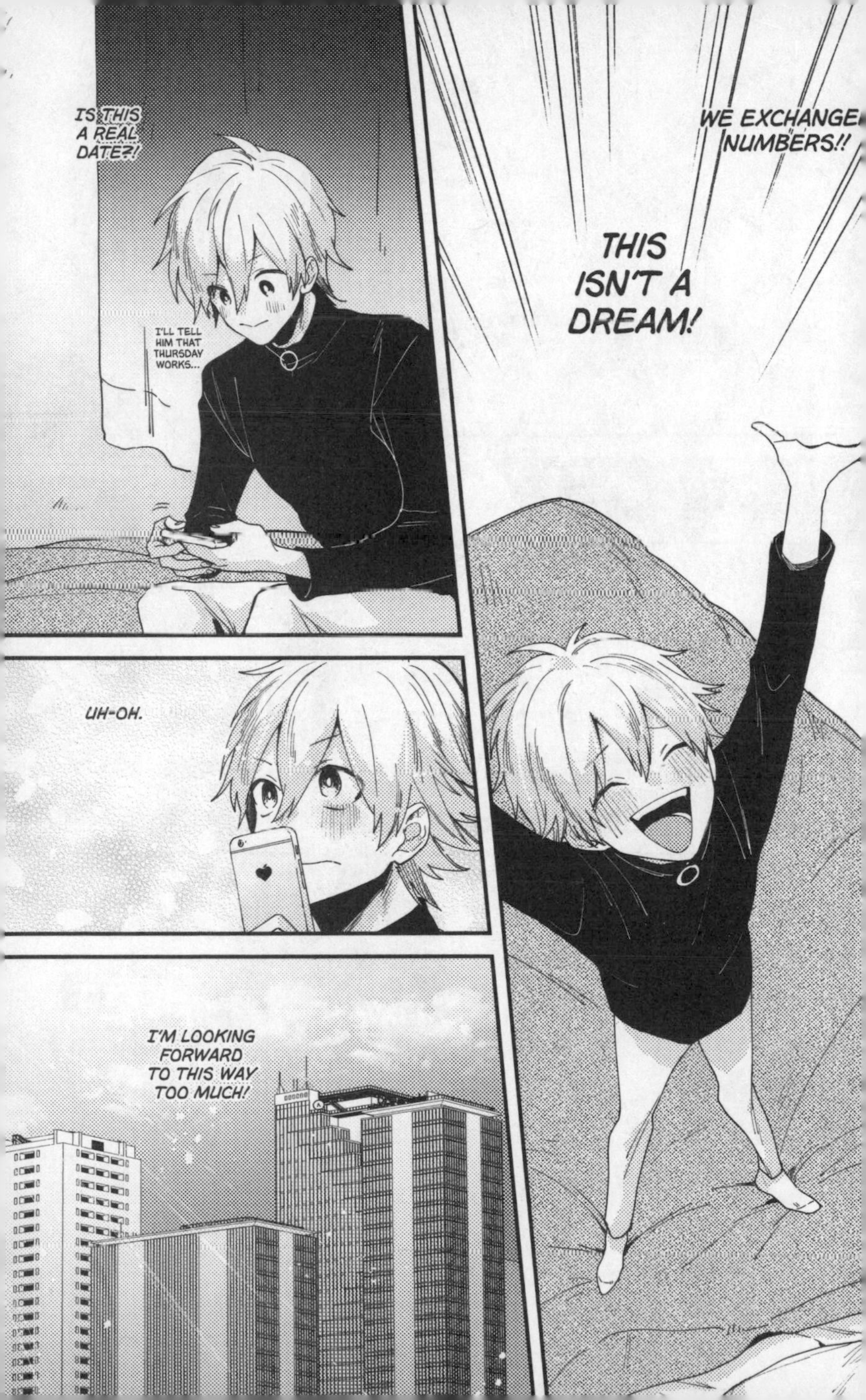
WE EXCHANGE NUMBERS!!
THIS ISN'T A DREAM!
IS THIS A REAL DATE?!
I'LL TELL HIM THAT THURSDAY WORKS...
UH-OH.
I'M LOOKING FORWARD TO THIS WAY TOO MUCH!

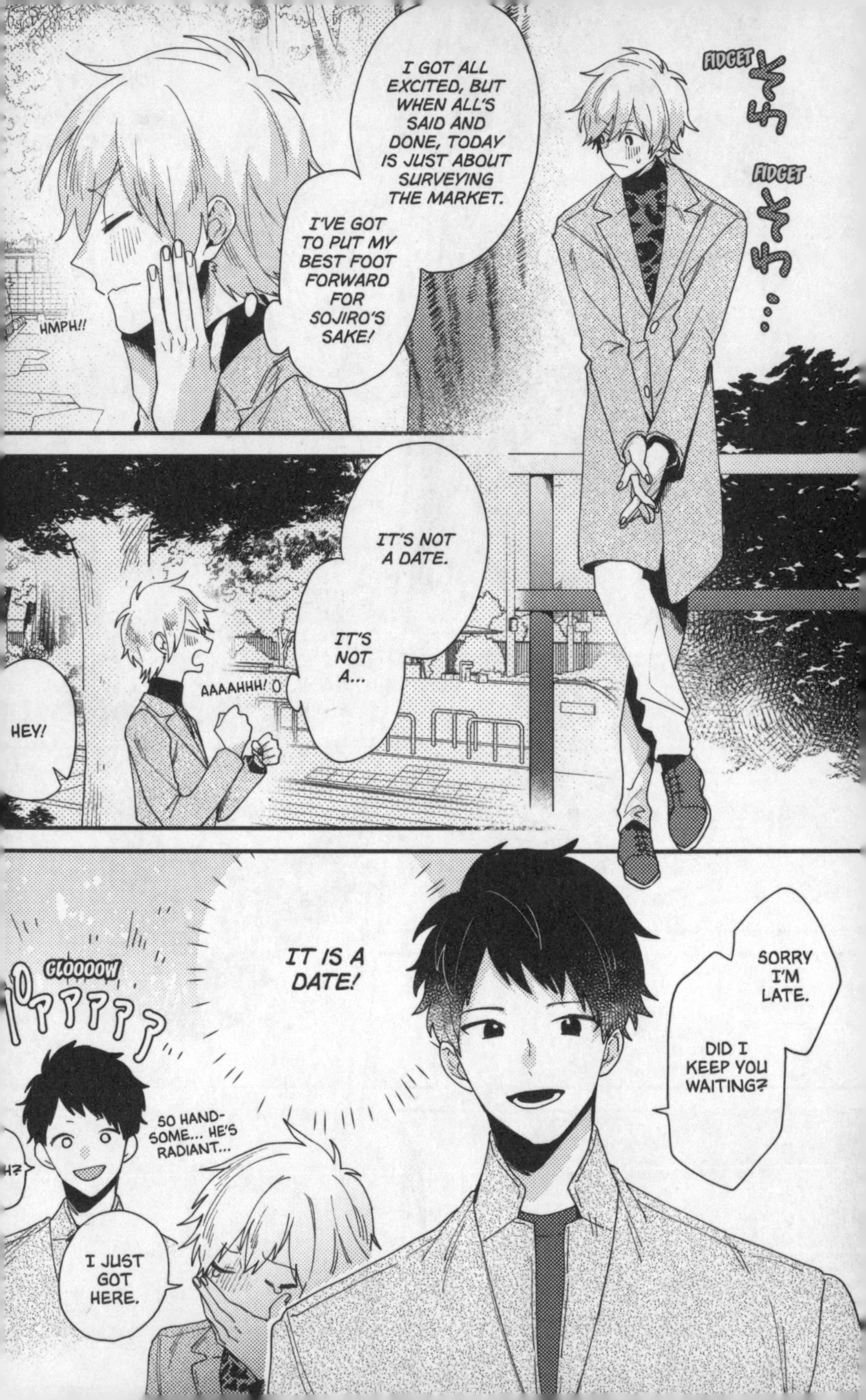
FIDGET
FIDGET
I GOT ALL EXCITED, BUT WHEN ALL'S SAID AND DONE, TODAY IS JUST ABOUT SURVEYING THE MARKET.
I'VE GOT TO PUT MY BEST FOOT FORWARD FOR SOJIRO'S SAKE!
HMPH!!
IT'S NOT A DATE.
IT'S NOT A...
AAAAHHH!
HEY!
SORRY I'M LATE.
DID I KEEP YOU WAITING?
IT IS A DATE!
GLOOOOW
SO HAND-SOME... HE'S RADIANT...
I JUST GOT HERE.

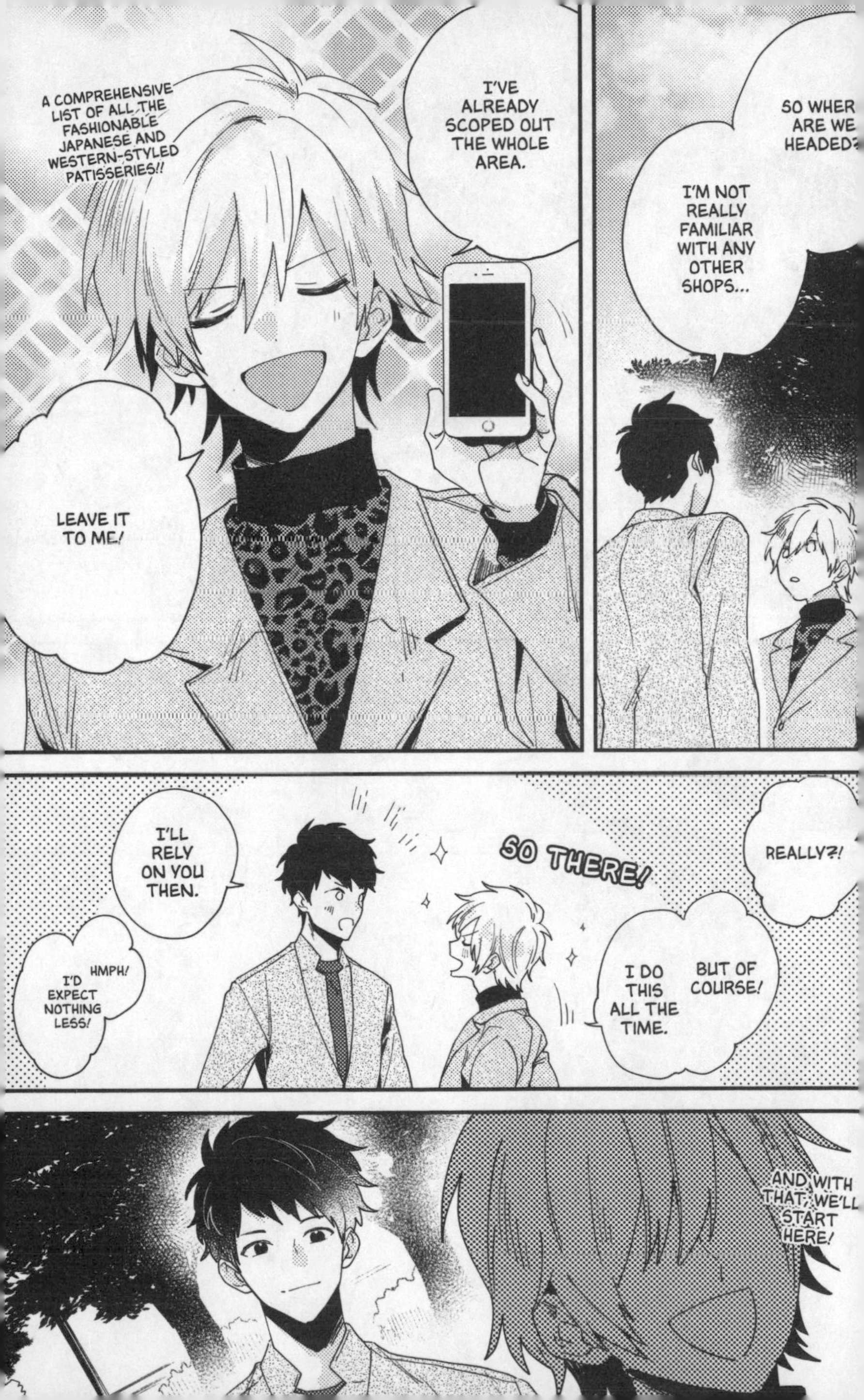
SO WHER ARE WE HEADED?
I'M NOT REALLY FAMILIAR WITH ANY OTHER SHOPS...
I'VE ALREADY SCOPED OUT THE WHOLE AREA.
A COMPREHENSIVE LIST OF ALL THE FASHIONABLE JAPANESE AND WESTERN-STYLED PATISSERIES!!
LEAVE IT TO ME!
REALLY?!
BUT OF COURSE!
I DO THIS ALL THE TIME.
SO THERE!
I'LL RELY ON YOU THEN.
HMPH!
I'D EXPECT NOTHING LESS!
AND WITH THAT, WE'LL START HERE!

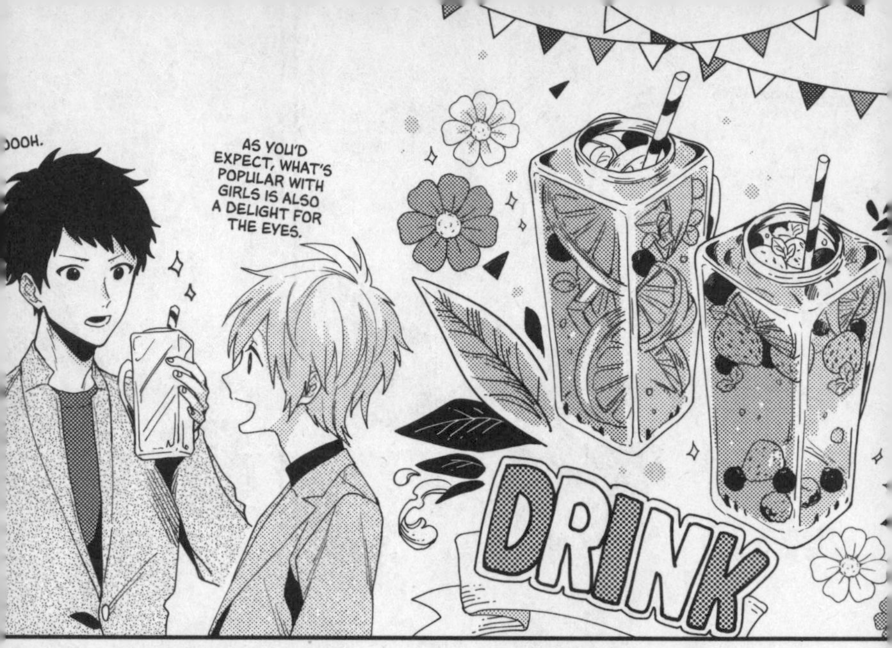
AS YOU'D EXPECT, WHAT'S POPULAR WITH GIRLS IS ALSO A DELIGHT FOR THE EYES.
OOOH.
DRINK

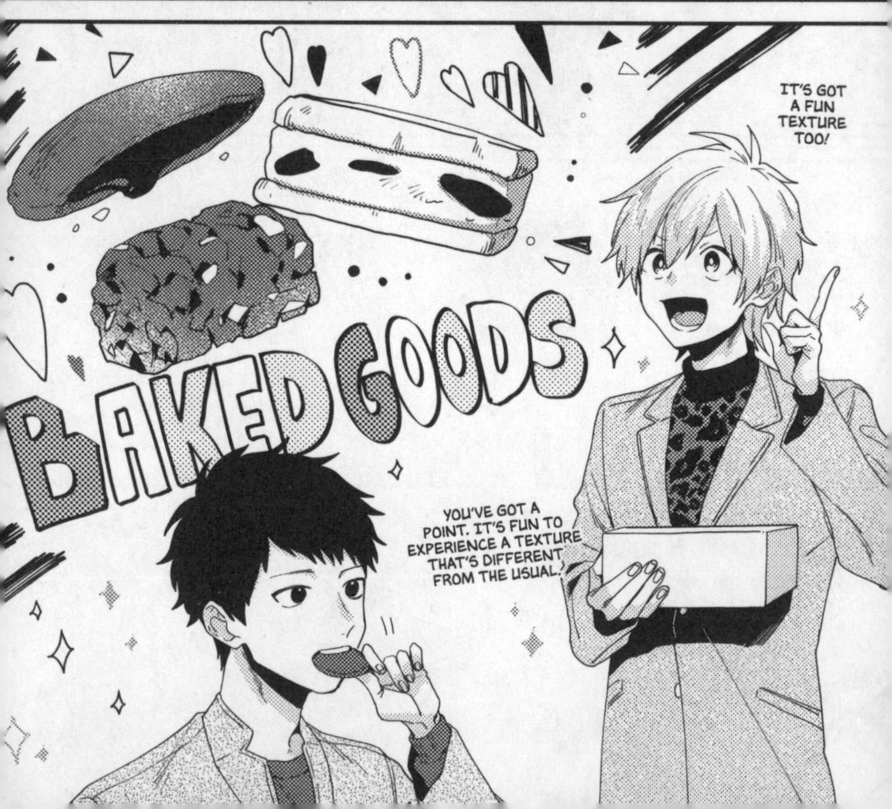
IT'S GOT A FUN TEXTURE TOO!
BAKED GOODS
YOU'VE GOT A POINT. IT'S FUN TO EXPERIENCE A TEXTURE THAT'S DIFFERENT FROM THE USUAL.

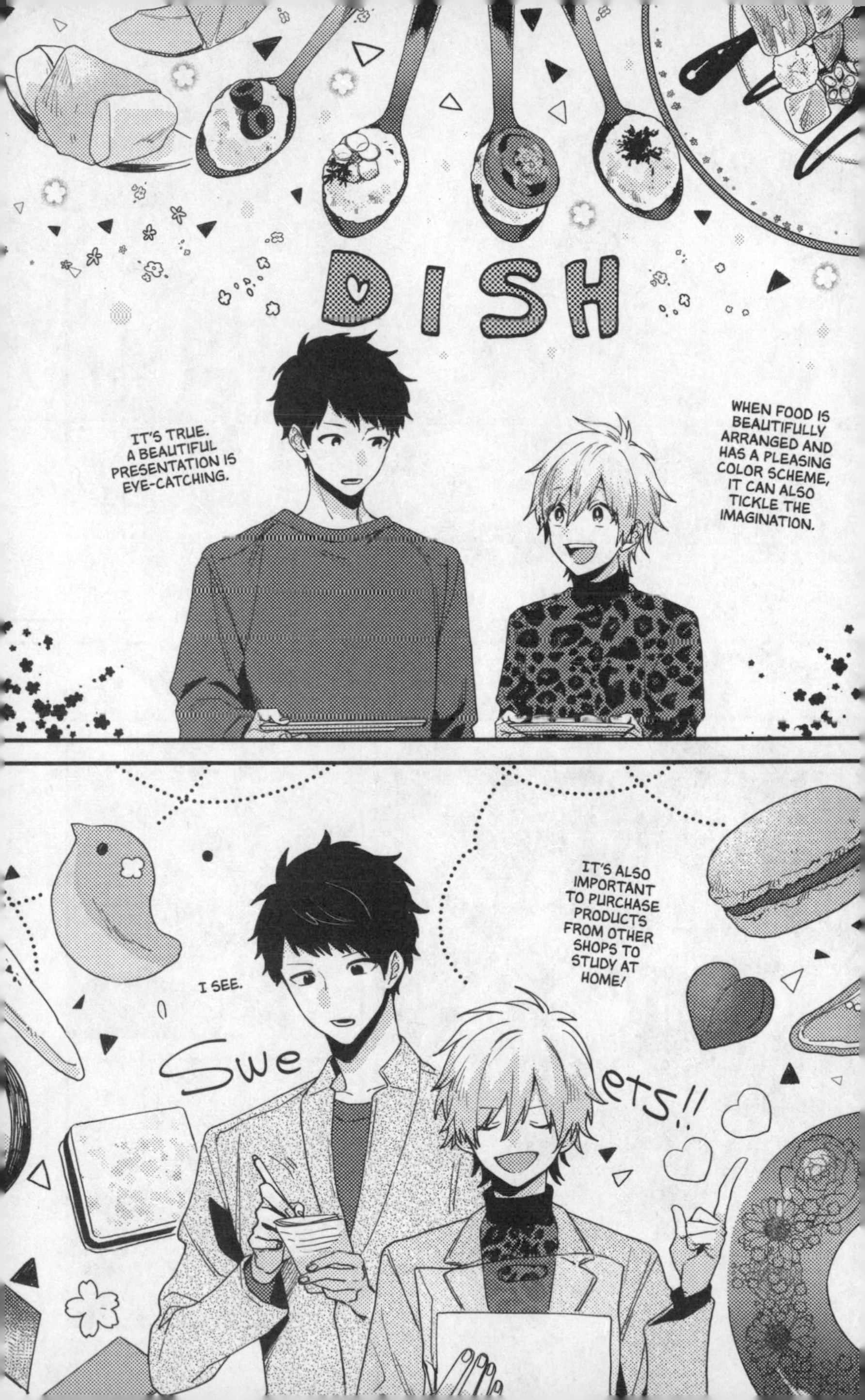
DISH
WHEN FOOD IS BEAUTIFULLY ARRANGED AND HAS A PLEASING COLOR SCHEME, IT CAN ALSO TICKLE THE IMAGINATION.
IT'S TRUE. A BEAUTIFUL PRESENTATION IS EYE-CATCHING.
IT'S ALSO IMPORTANT TO PURCHASE PRODUCTS FROM OTHER SHOPS TO STUDY AT HOME!
I SEE.
Swe ets!!

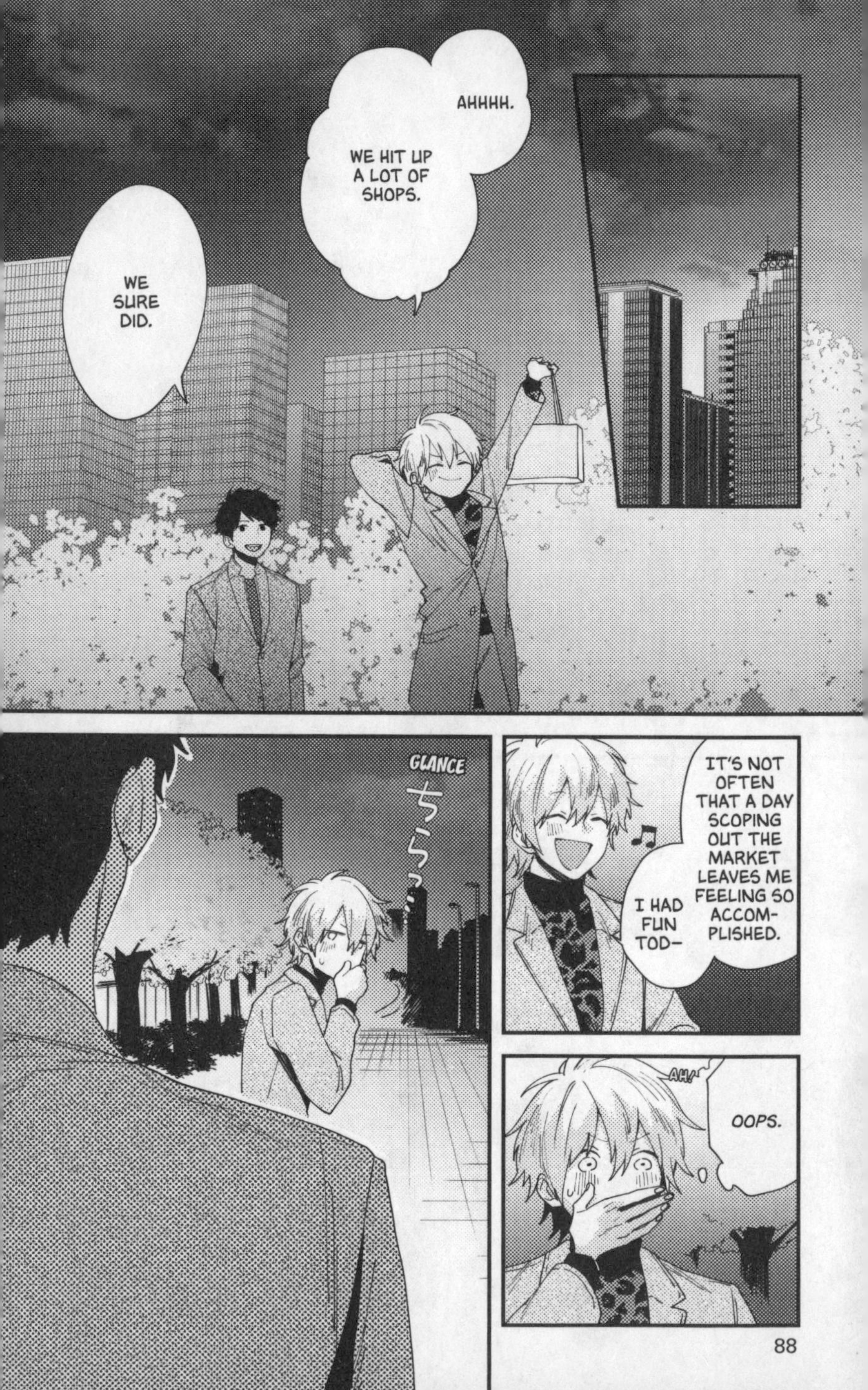
AHHHH.
WE HIT UP A LOT OF SHOPS.
WE SURE DID.
IT'S NOT OFTEN THAT A DAY SCOPING OUT THE MARKET LEAVES ME FEELING SO ACCOM-PLISHED.
I HAD FUN TOD—
AH!
OOPS.
GLANCE
ちらっ

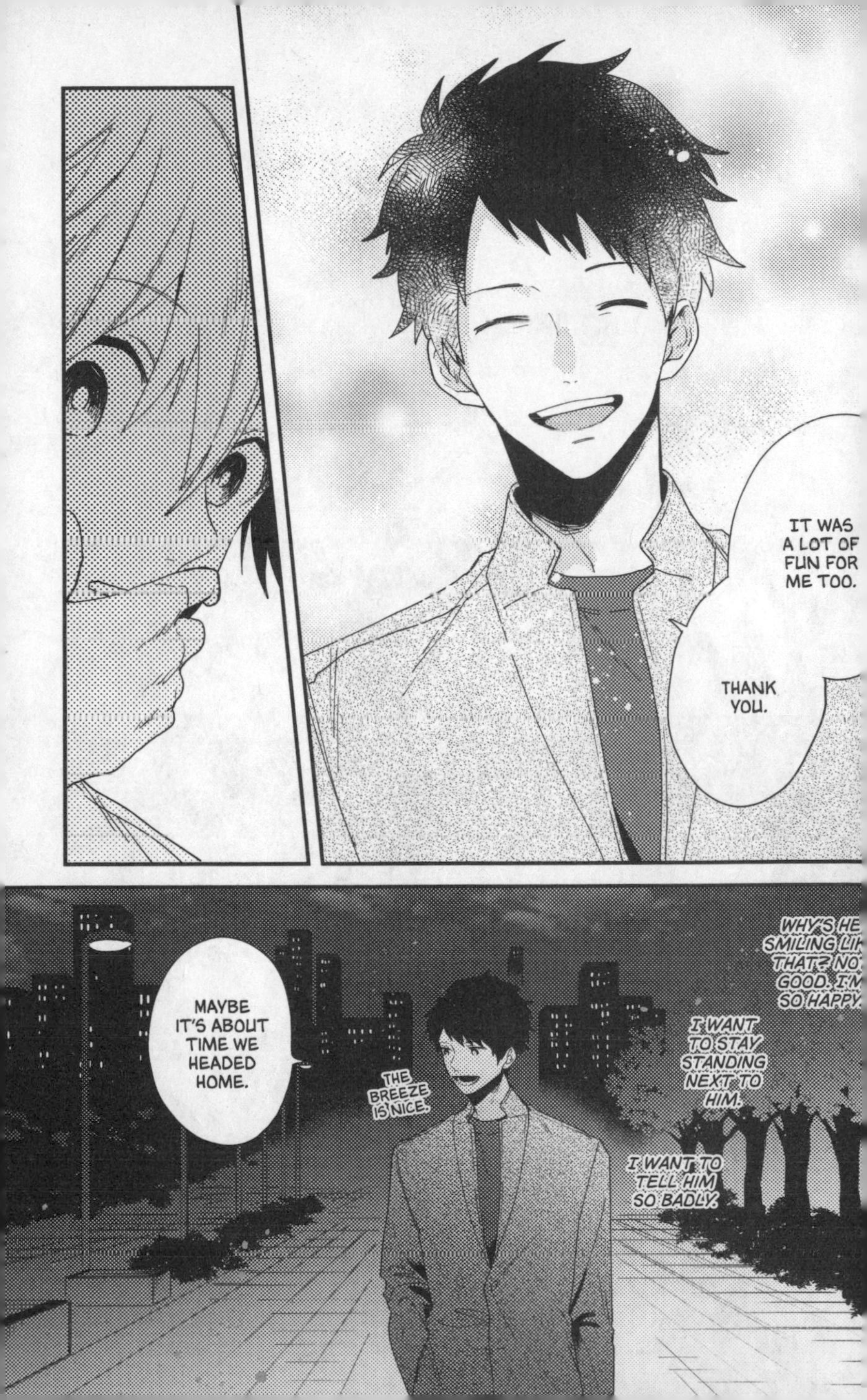
IT WAS A LOT OF FUN FOR ME TOO.
THANK YOU.
WHY'S HE SMILING LIK THAT? NO GOOD. I'M SO HAPPY.
I WANT TO STAY STANDING NEXT TO HIM.
I WANT TO TELL HIM SO BADLY.
THE BREEZE IS NICE.
MAYBE IT'S ABOUT TIME WE HEADED HOME.

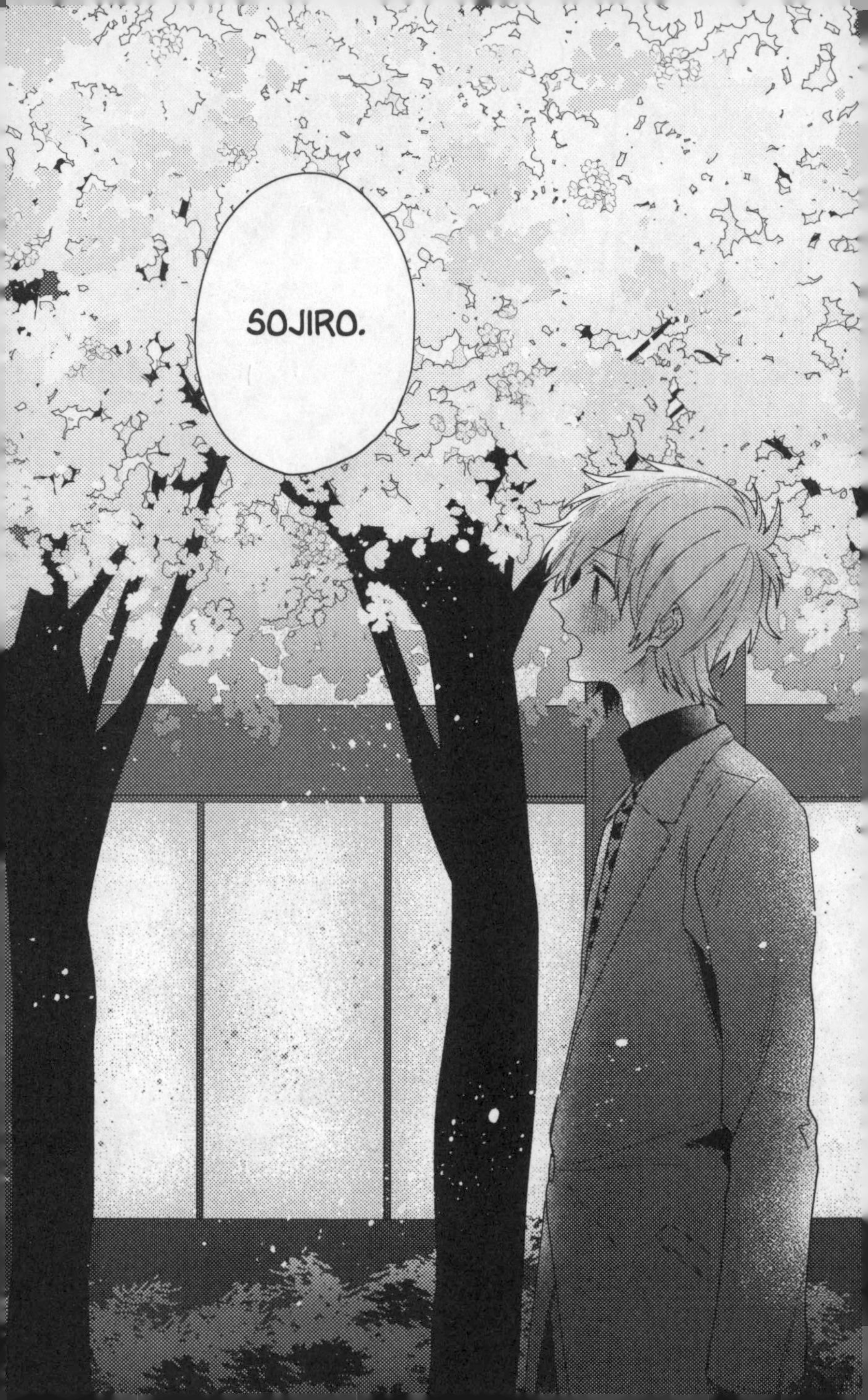
SOJIRO.

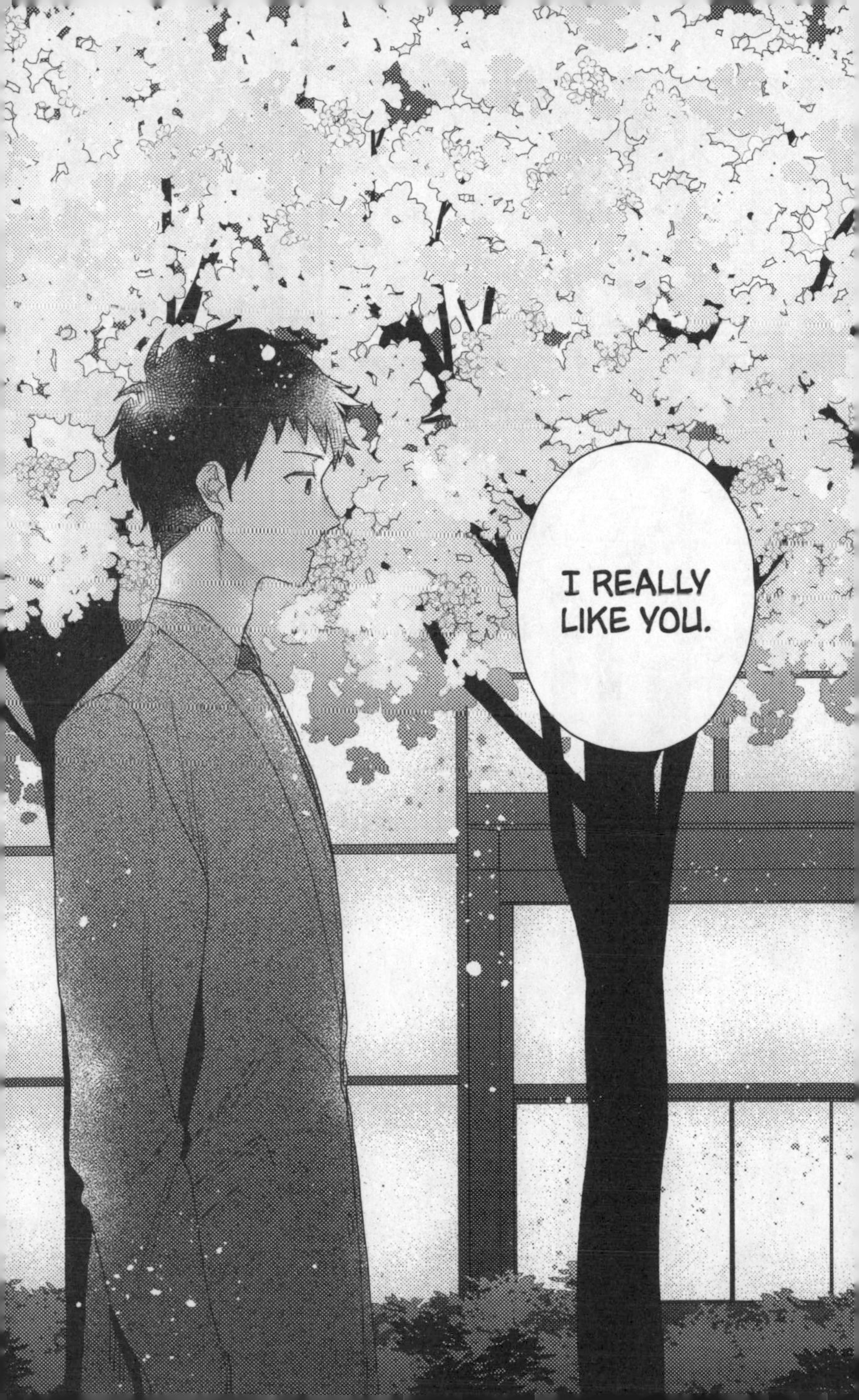
I REALLY LIKE YOU.

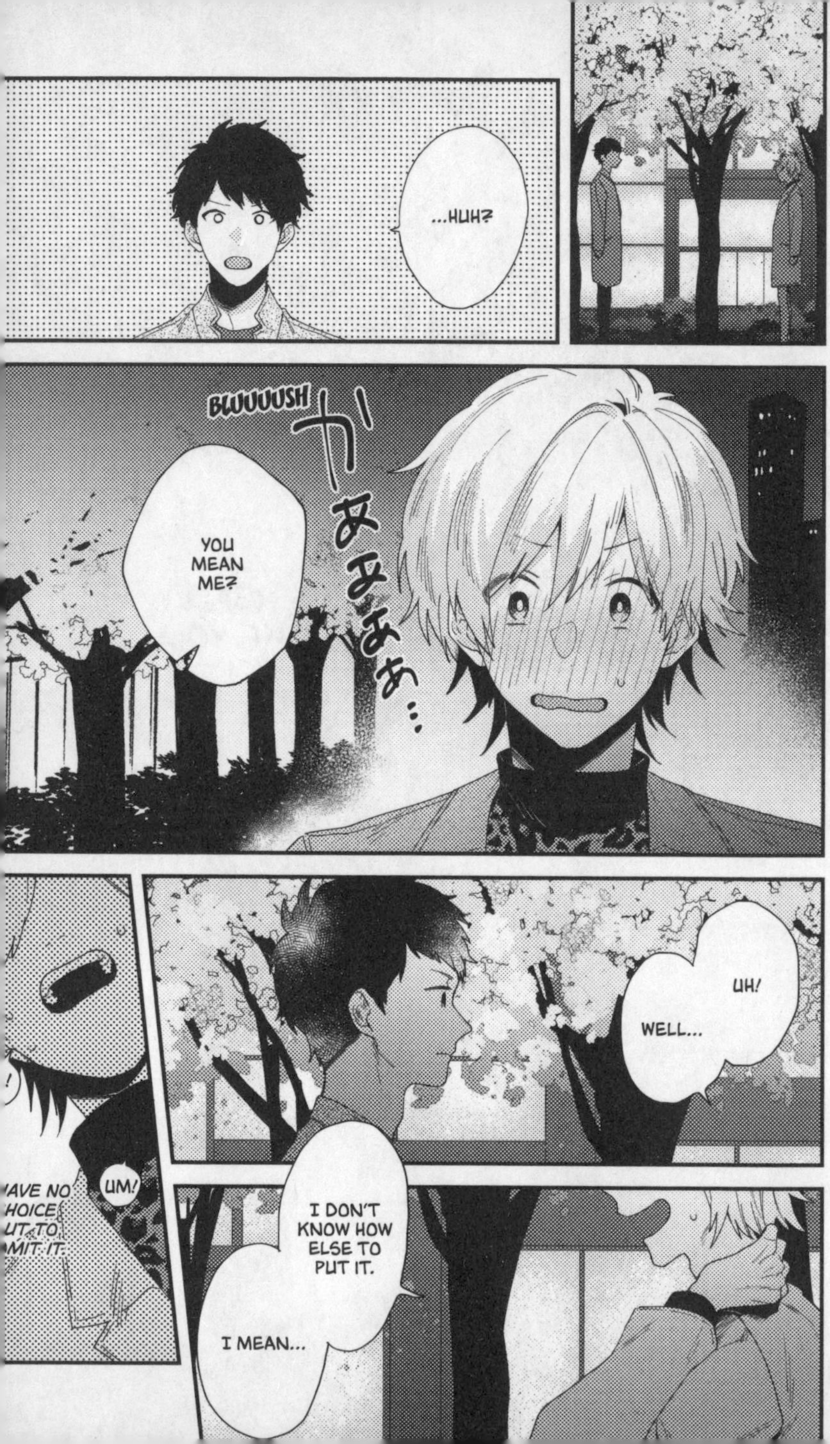
...HUH?
BLUUUUSH
やぁぁぁぁ…
YOU MEAN ME?
UH!
WELL...
I DON'T KNOW HOW ELSE TO PUT IT.
I MEAN...
UM!
AVE NO HOICE UT TO MIT IT.

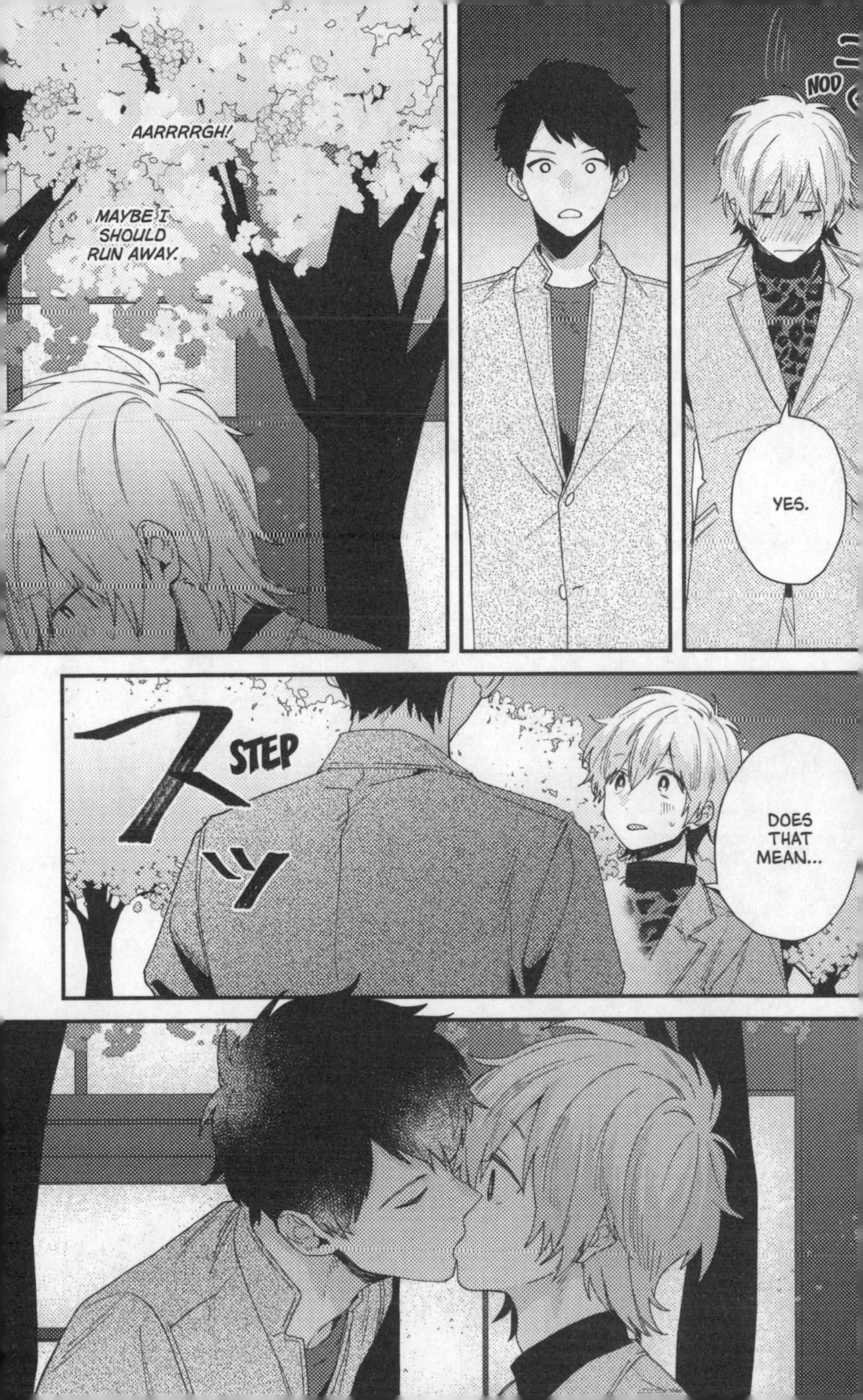
NOD
YES.
AARRRGH!
MAYBE I SHOULD RUN AWAY.
DOES THAT MEAN...
スッ
STEP

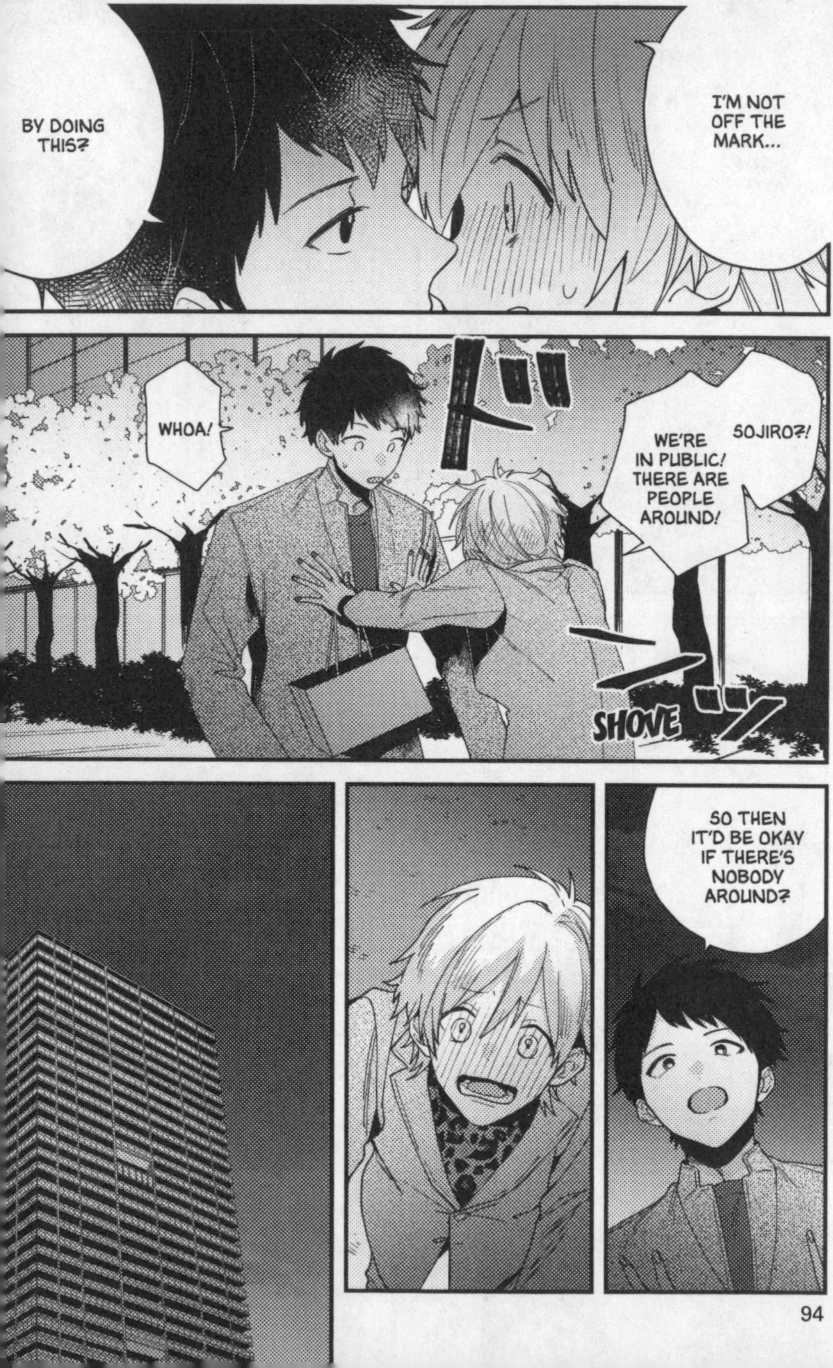
I'M NOT OFF THE MARK...
BY DOING THIS?
ドッ
SOJIRO?!
WE'RE IN PUBLIC! THERE ARE PEOPLE AROUND!
WHOA!
SHOVE
SO THEN IT'D BE OKAY IF THERE'S NOBODY AROUND?

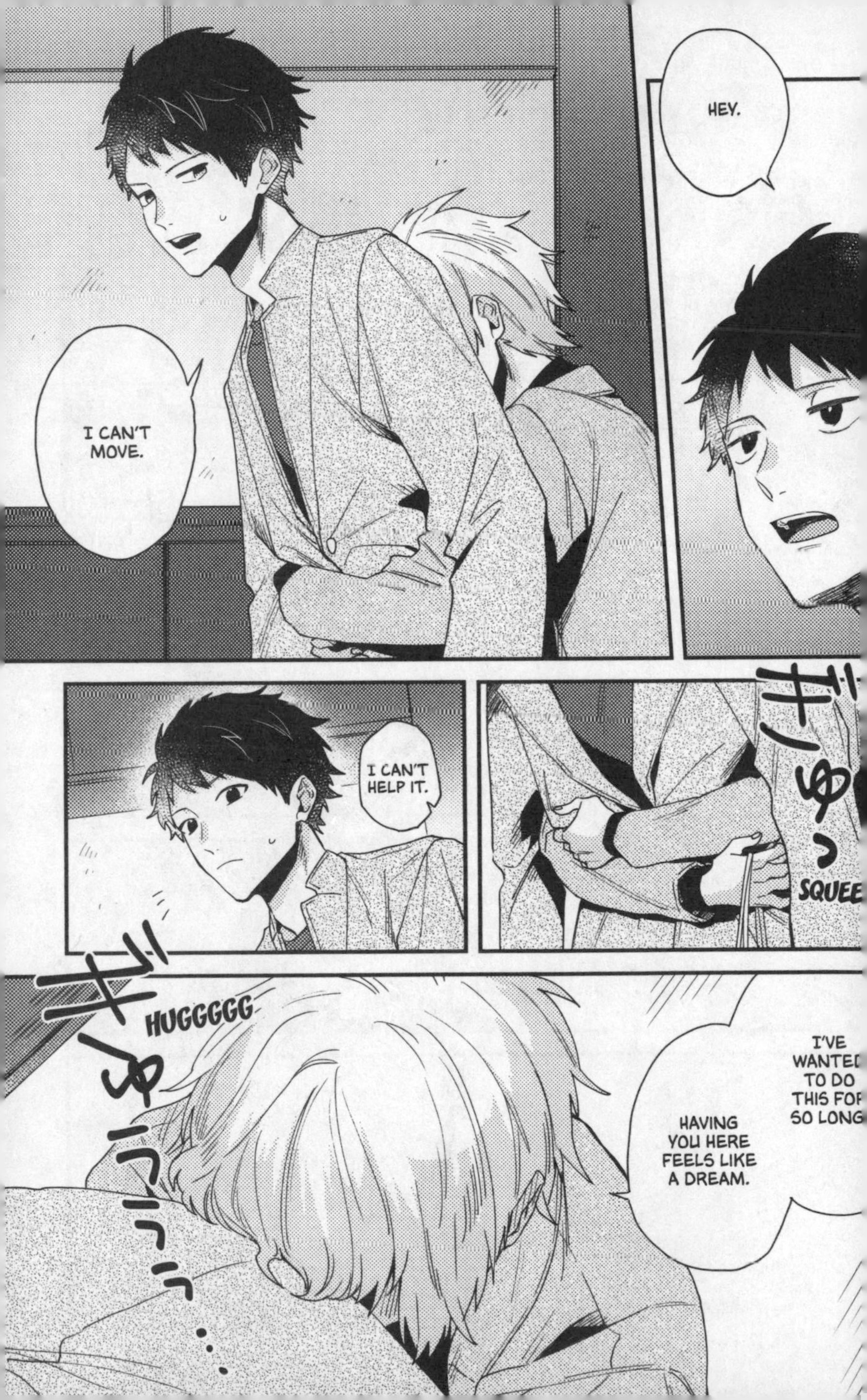
HEY.
I CAN'T MOVE.
ぎゅっ
SQUEE
I CAN'T HELP IT.
I'VE WANTED TO DO THIS FOR SO LONG
HAVING YOU HERE FEELS LIKE A DREAM.
ぎゅ
HUGGGGG

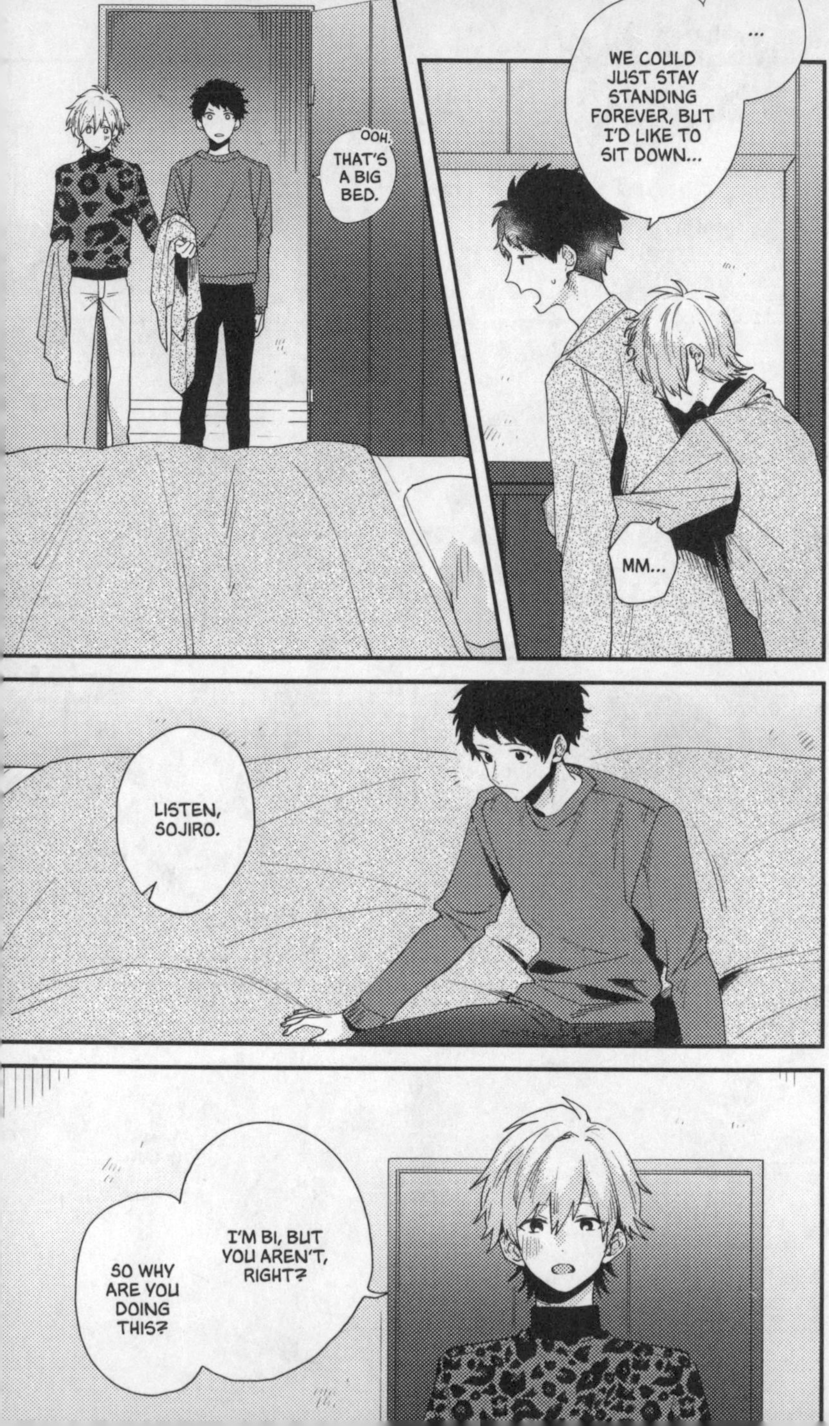
...
WE COULD JUST STAY STANDING FOREVER, BUT I'D LIKE TO SIT DOWN...
MM...
OOH. THAT'S A BIG BED.
LISTEN, SOJIRO.
I'M BI, BUT YOU AREN'T, RIGHT?
SO WHY ARE YOU DOING THIS?

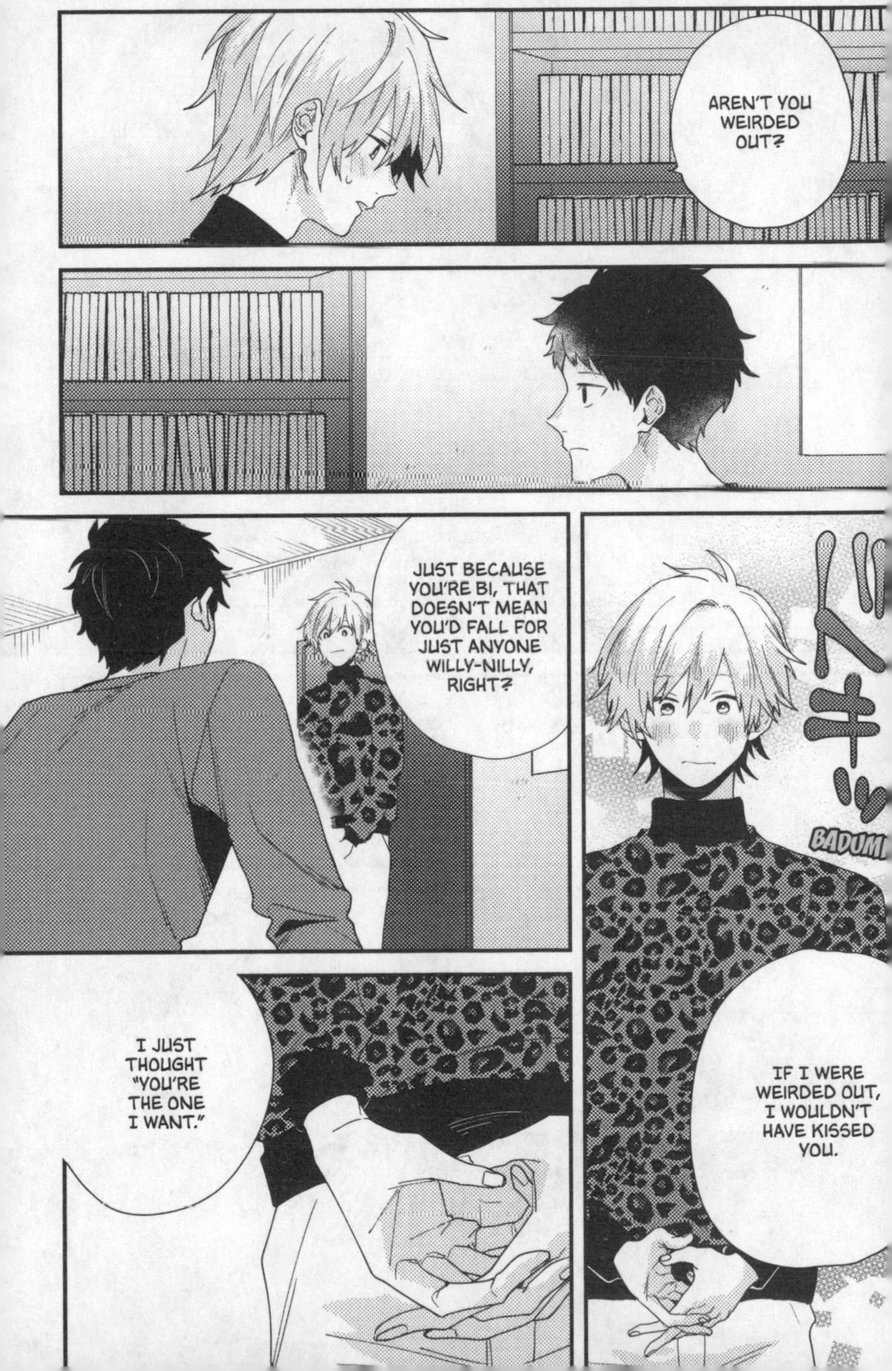
AREN'T YOU WEIRDED OUT?
ドキッ
BADUM
IF I WERE WEIRDED OUT, I WOULDN'T HAVE KISSED YOU.
JUST BECAUSE YOU'RE BI, THAT DOESN'T MEAN YOU'D FALL FOR JUST ANYONE WILLY-NILLY, RIGHT?
I JUST THOUGHT "YOU'RE THE ONE I WANT."

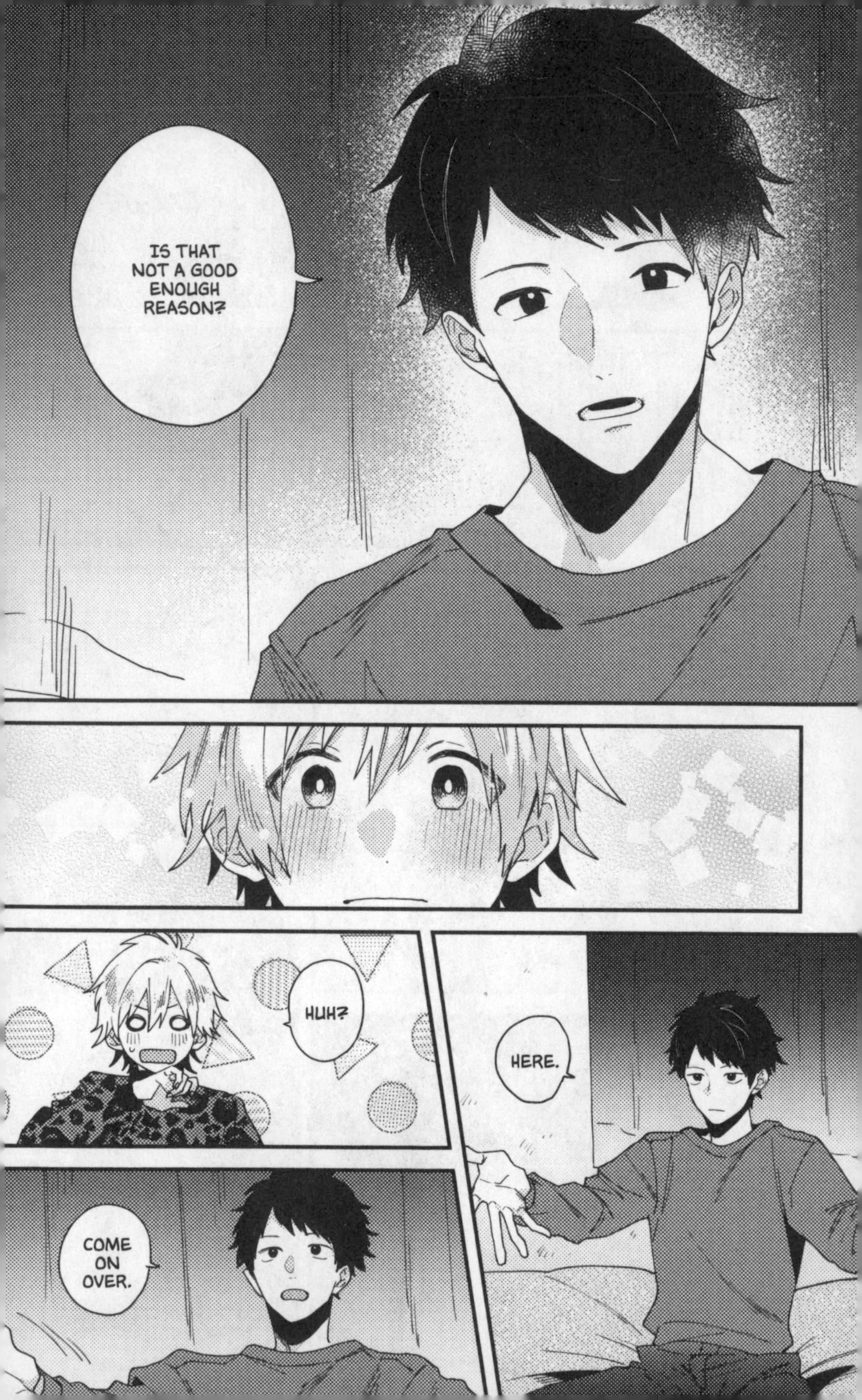
IS THAT NOT A GOOD ENOUGH REASON?
HERE.
HUH?
COME ON OVER.

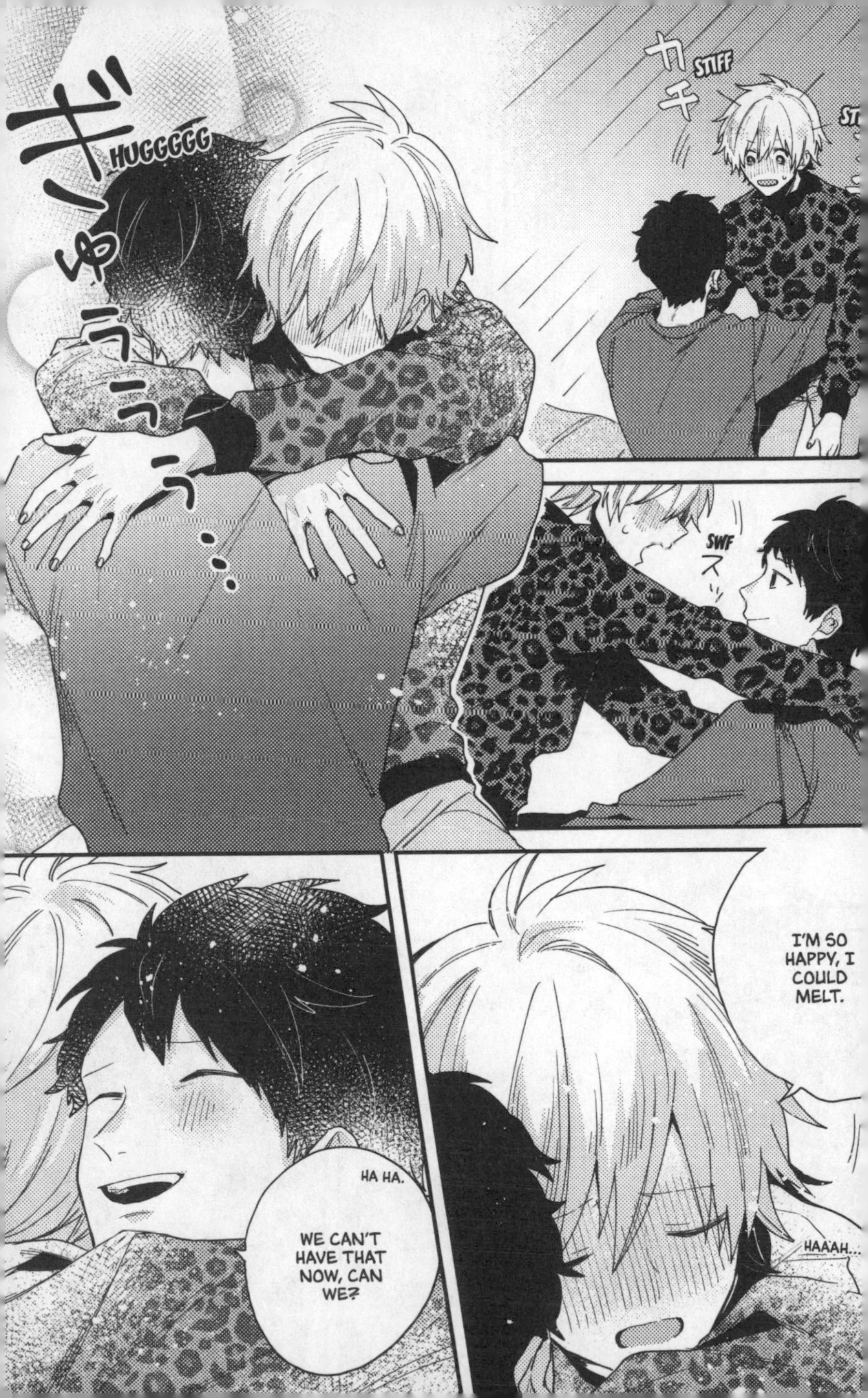
カチ
STIFF
SWF
スッ
ギゅぅぅぅぅ…
HUGGGGG
I'M SO HAPPY, I COULD MELT.
HAAAH...
HA HA.
WE CAN'T HAVE THAT NOW, CAN WE?

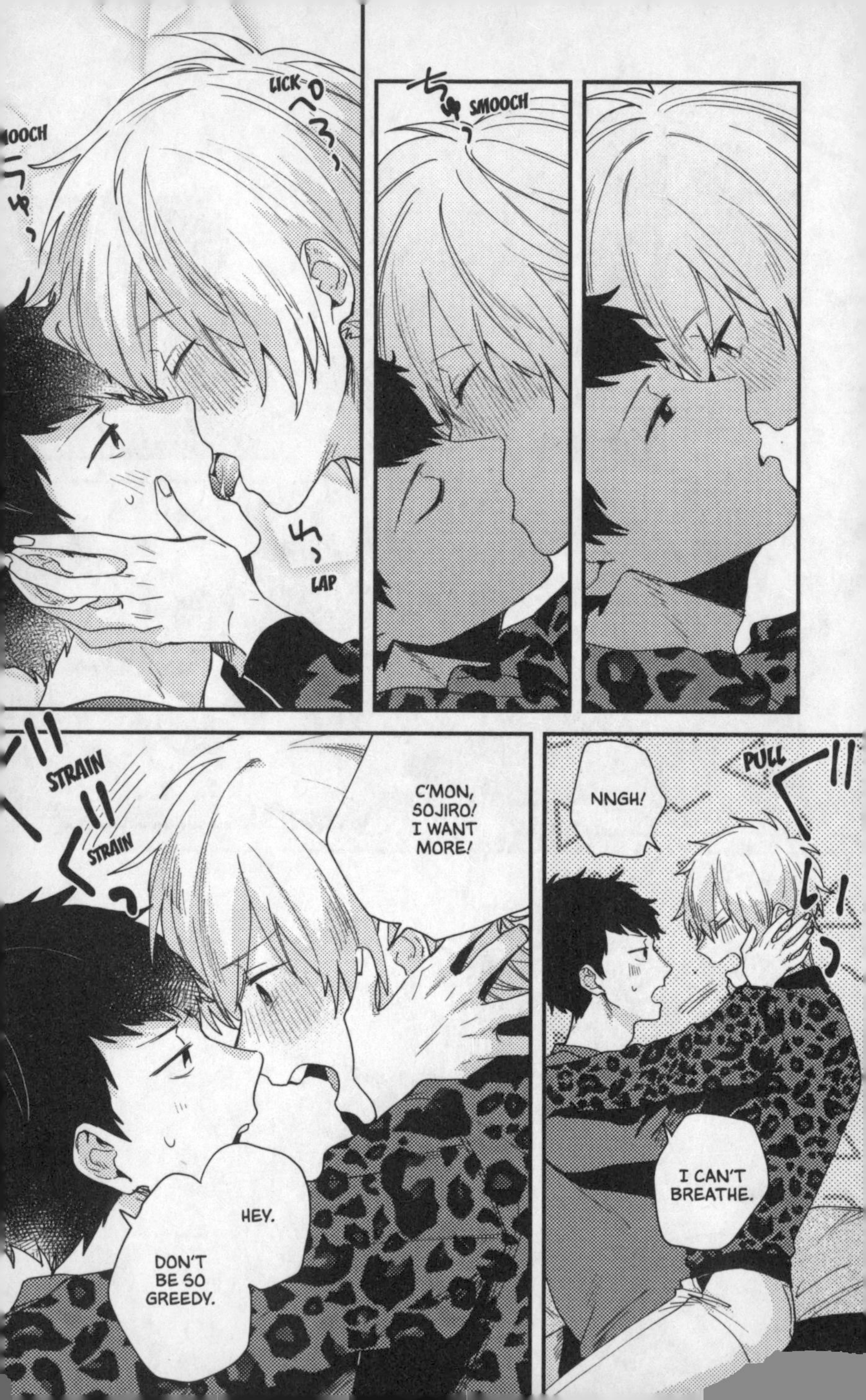
SMOOCH
LICK
SMOOCH
LAP
PULL
NNGH!
I CAN'T BREATHE.
STRAIN
STRAIN
C'MON, SOJIRO! I WANT MORE!
HEY.
DON'T BE SO GREEDY.

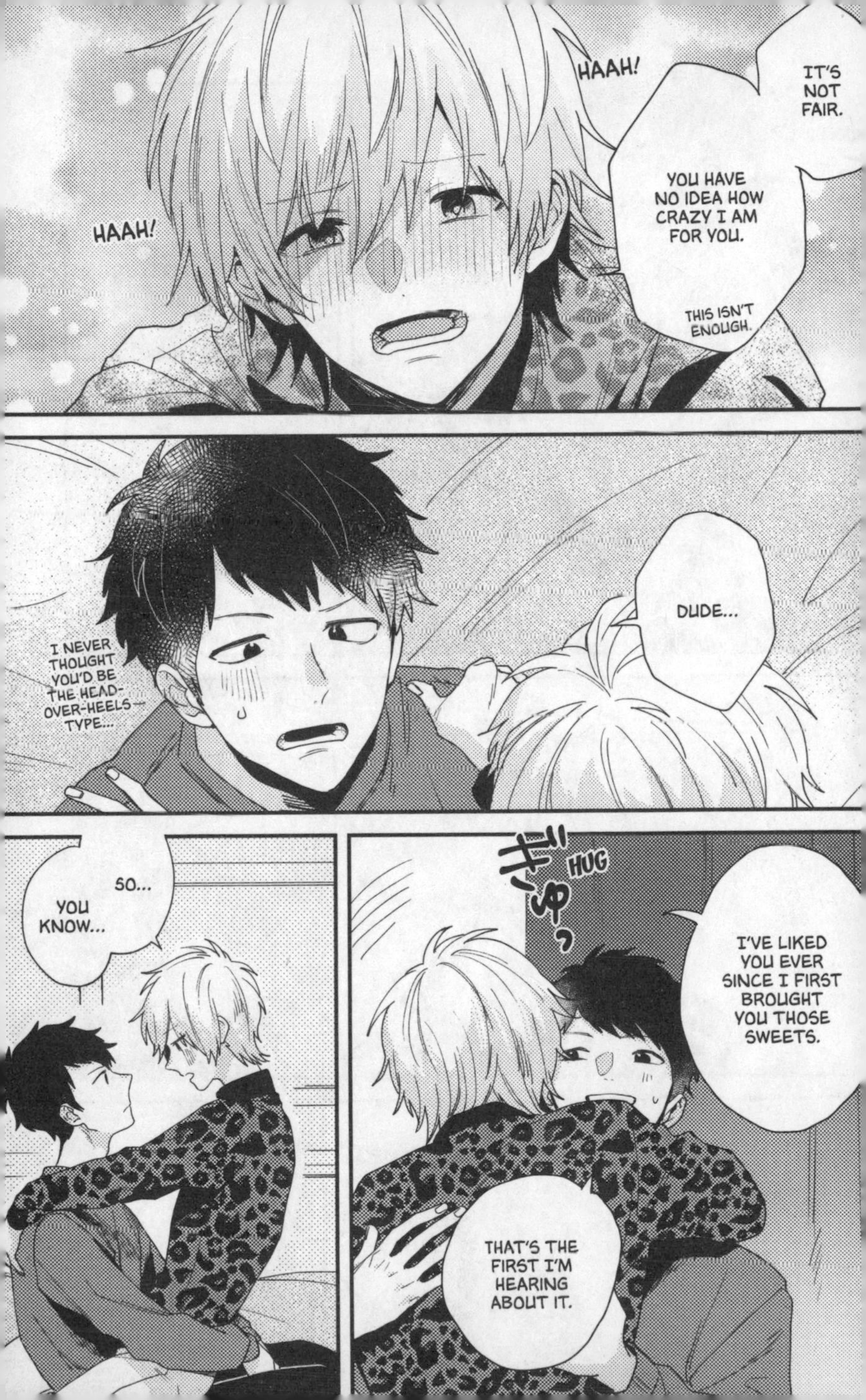

HAAH!
IT'S NOT FAIR.
YOU HAVE NO IDEA HOW CRAZY I AM FOR YOU.
THIS ISN'T ENOUGH.
HAAH!
DUDE...
I NEVER THOUGHT YOU'D BE THE HEAD-OVER-HEELS-TYPE...
ぎゅっ
HUG
I'VE LIKED YOU EVER SINCE I FIRST BROUGHT YOU THOSE SWEETS.
THAT'S THE FIRST I'M HEARING ABOUT IT.
SO...
YOU KNOW...

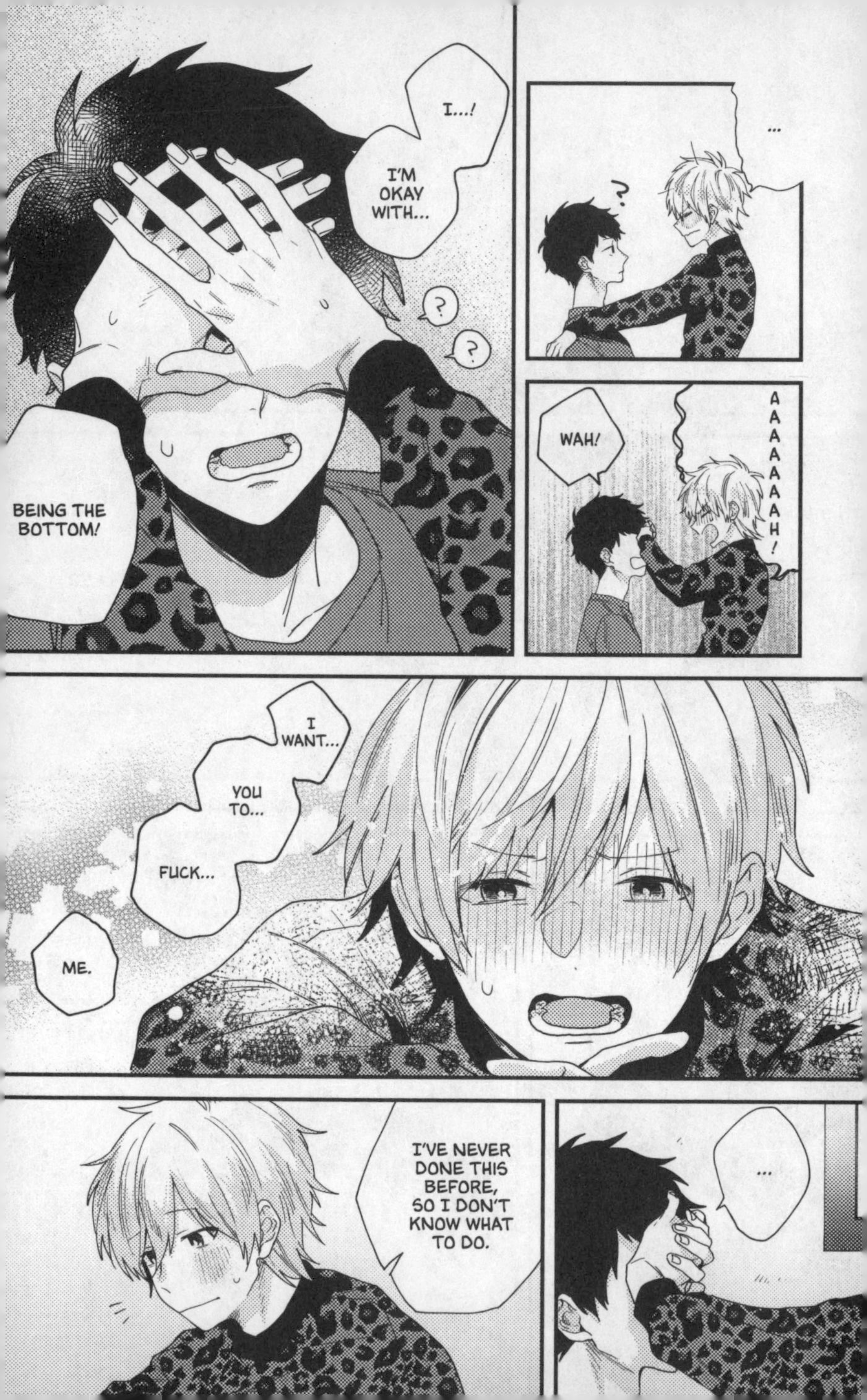
...
AAAAAAAAH!
WAH!
I...!
I'M OKAY WITH...
?
?
BEING THE BOTTOM!
I WANT...
YOU TO...
FUCK...
ME.
...
I'VE NEVER DONE THIS BEFORE, SO I DON'T KNOW WHAT TO DO.

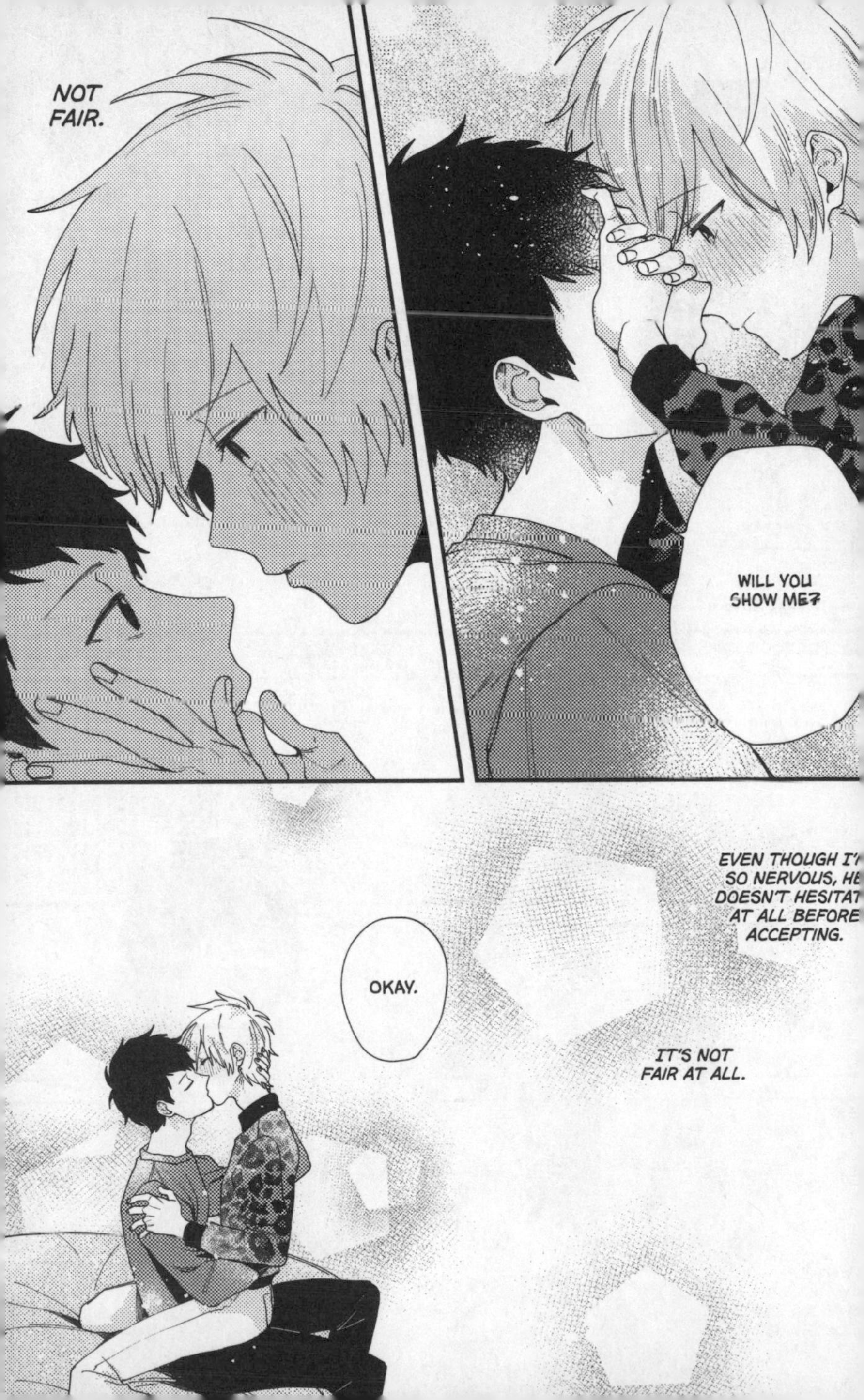
WILL YOU SHOW ME?
NOT FAIR.
EVEN THOUGH I' SO NERVOUS, HE DOESN'T HESITAT AT ALL BEFORE ACCEPTING.
OKAY.
IT'S NOT FAIR AT ALL.

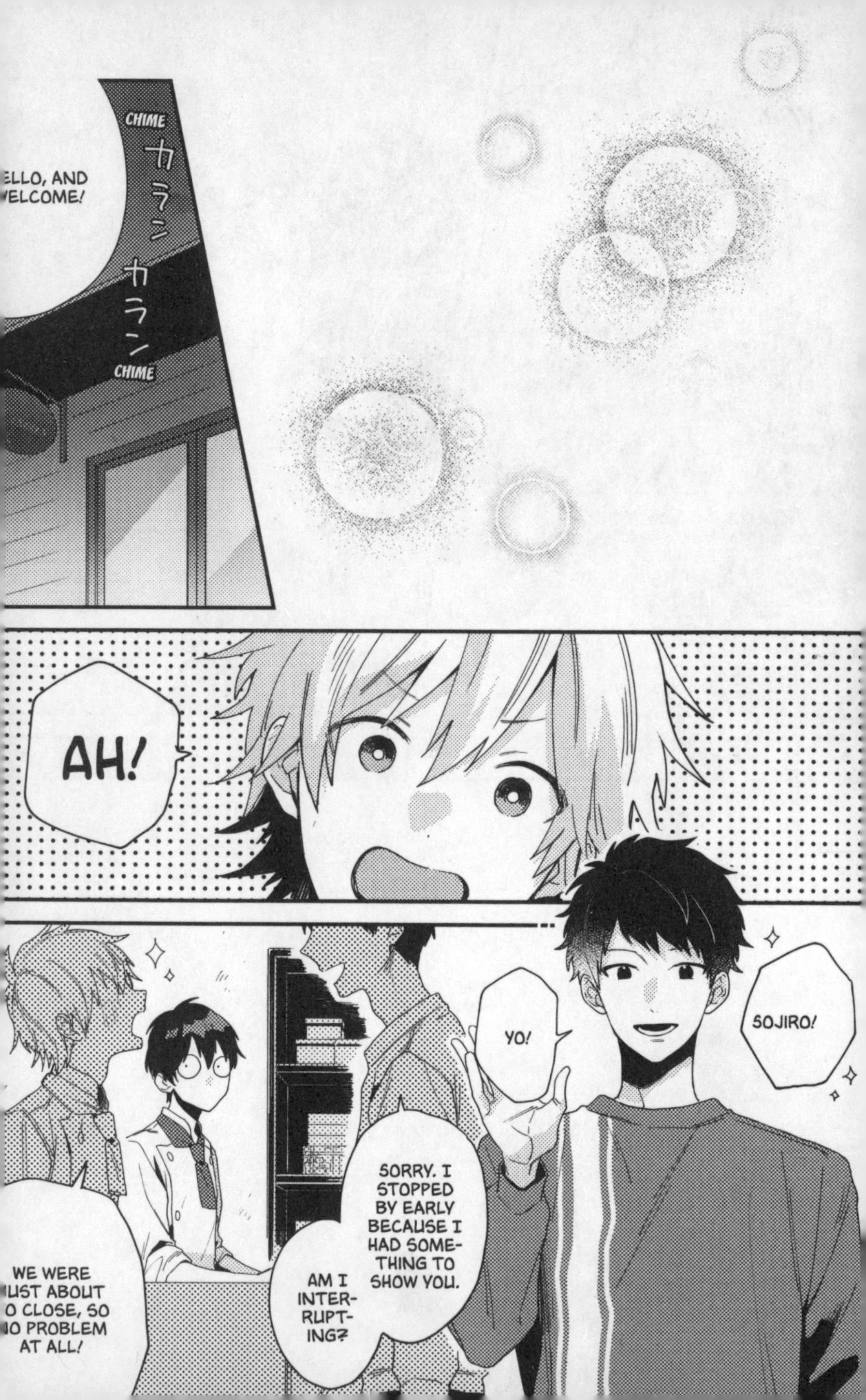
CHIME
カラン カラン
CHIME
ELLO, AND VELCOME!
AH!
SOJIRO!
YO!
SORRY. I STOPPED BY EARLY BECAUSE I HAD SOME-THING TO SHOW YOU.
AM I INTER-RUPT-ING?
WE WERE UST ABOUT O CLOSE, SO O PROBLEM AT ALL!

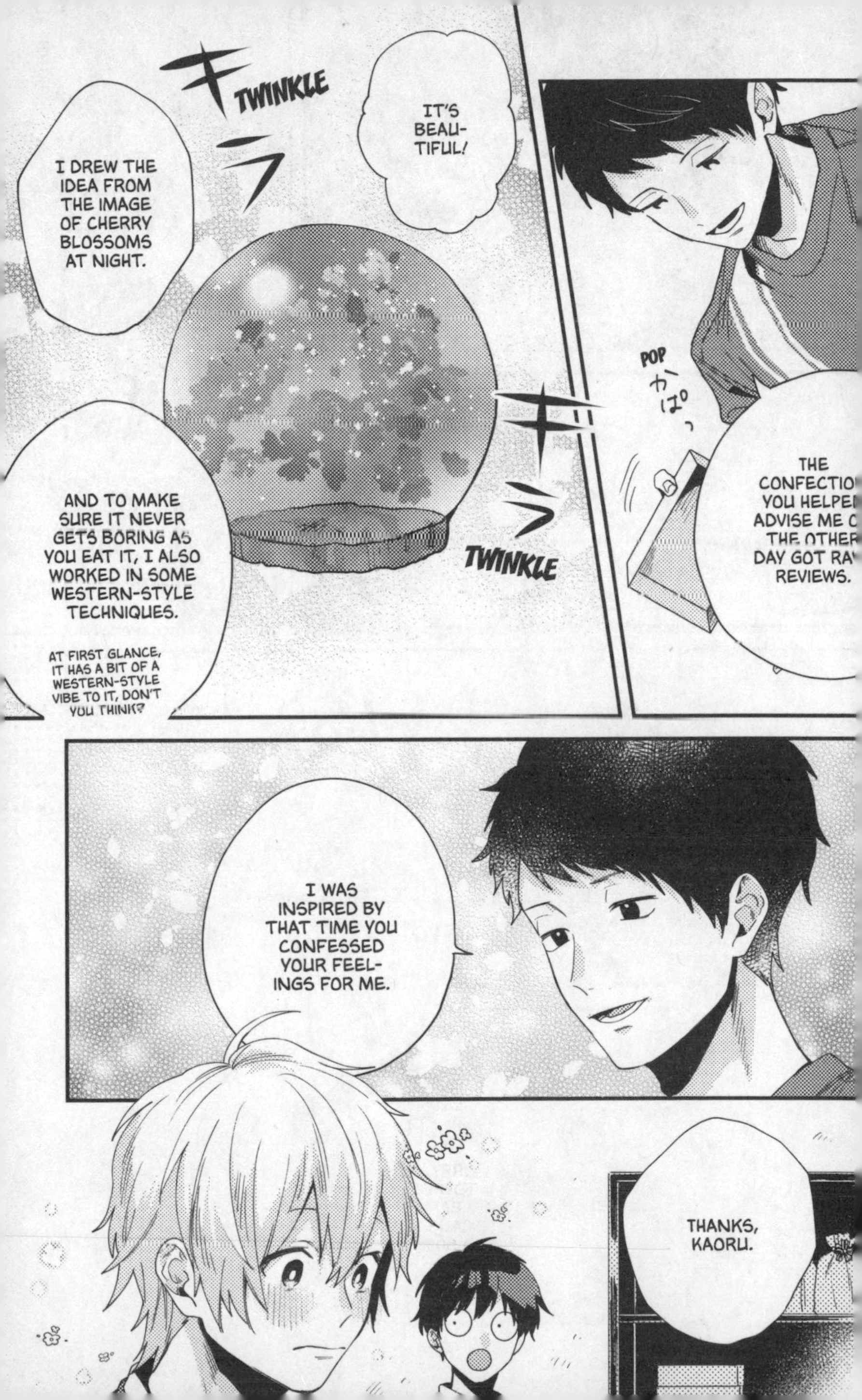
POP
かぽっ
THE CONFECTIO YOU HELPE ADVISE ME O THE OTHER DAY GOT RA REVIEWS.
TWINKLE
IT'S BEAU-TIFUL!
I DREW THE IDEA FROM THE IMAGE OF CHERRY BLOSSOMS AT NIGHT.
TWINKLE
AND TO MAKE SURE IT NEVER GETS BORING AS YOU EAT IT, I ALSO WORKED IN SOME WESTERN-STYLE TECHNIQUES.
AT FIRST GLANCE, IT HAS A BIT OF A WESTERN-STYLE VIBE TO IT, DON'T YOU THINK?
I WAS INSPIRED BY THAT TIME YOU CONFESSED YOUR FEEL-INGS FOR ME.
THANKS, KAORU.

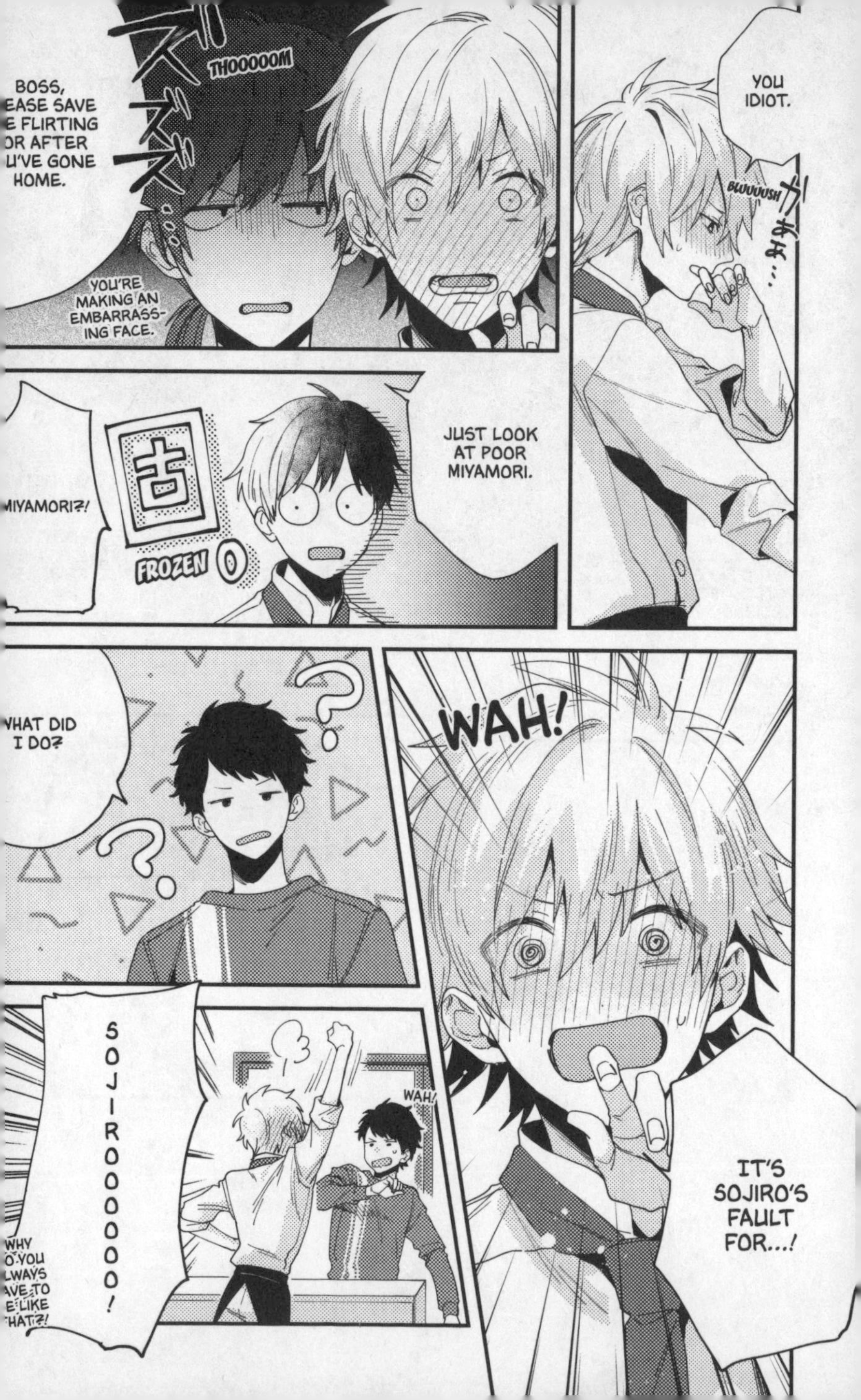
YOU IDIOT.
BLUUUUSH
THOOOOOM
BOSS, EASE SAVE E FLIRTING OR AFTER U'VE GONE HOME.
YOU'RE MAKING AN EMBARRASS-ING FACE.
JUST LOOK AT POOR MIYAMORI.
MIYAMORI?!
FROZEN
WAH!
IT'S SOJIRO'S FAULT FOR...!
WHAT DID I DO?
SOJIROOOOOOO!
WAH!
WHY O YOU LWAYS AVE TO E LIKE THAT?!

Chéri, my destiny!

Chéri, my destiny!

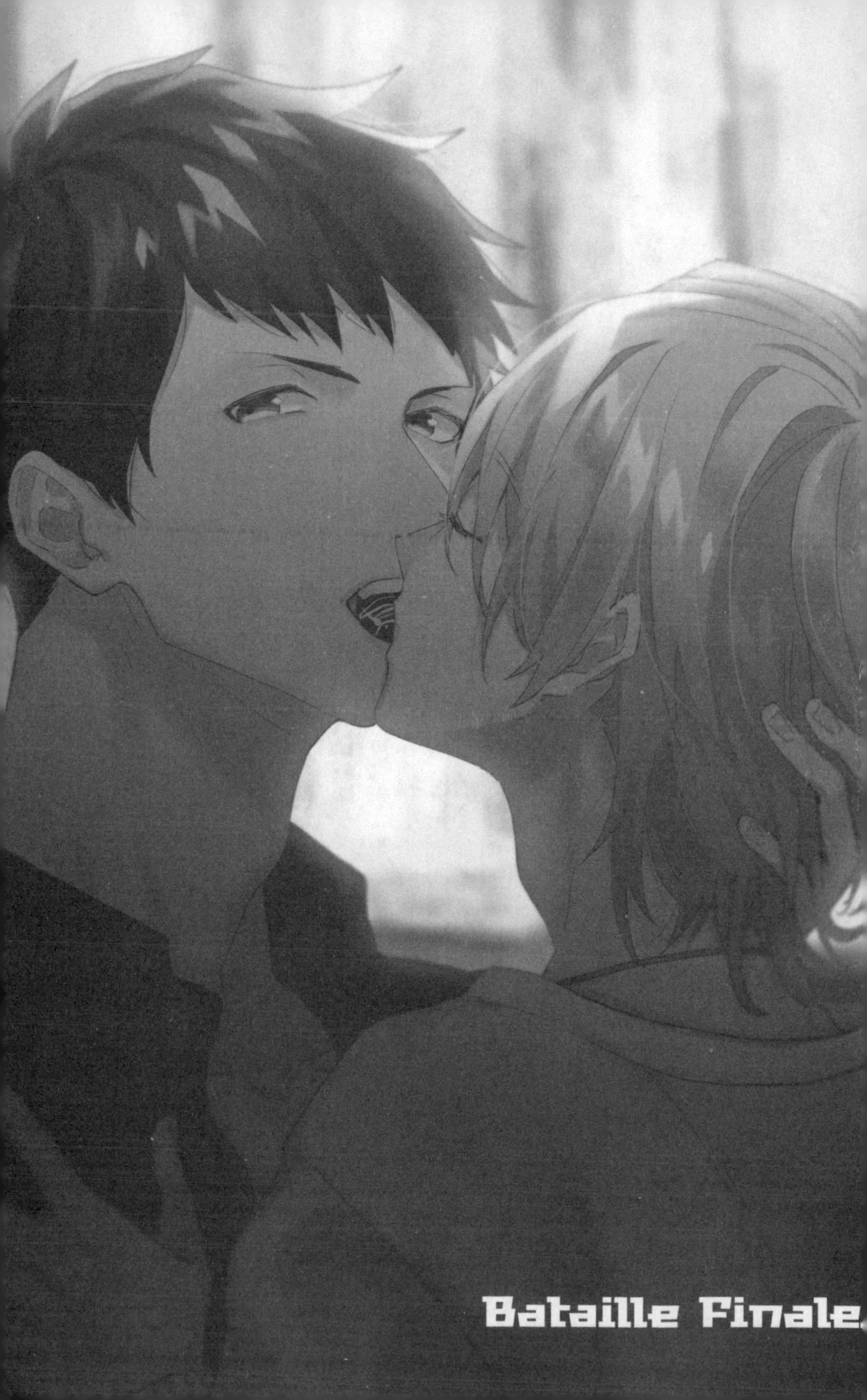
Bataille Finale.

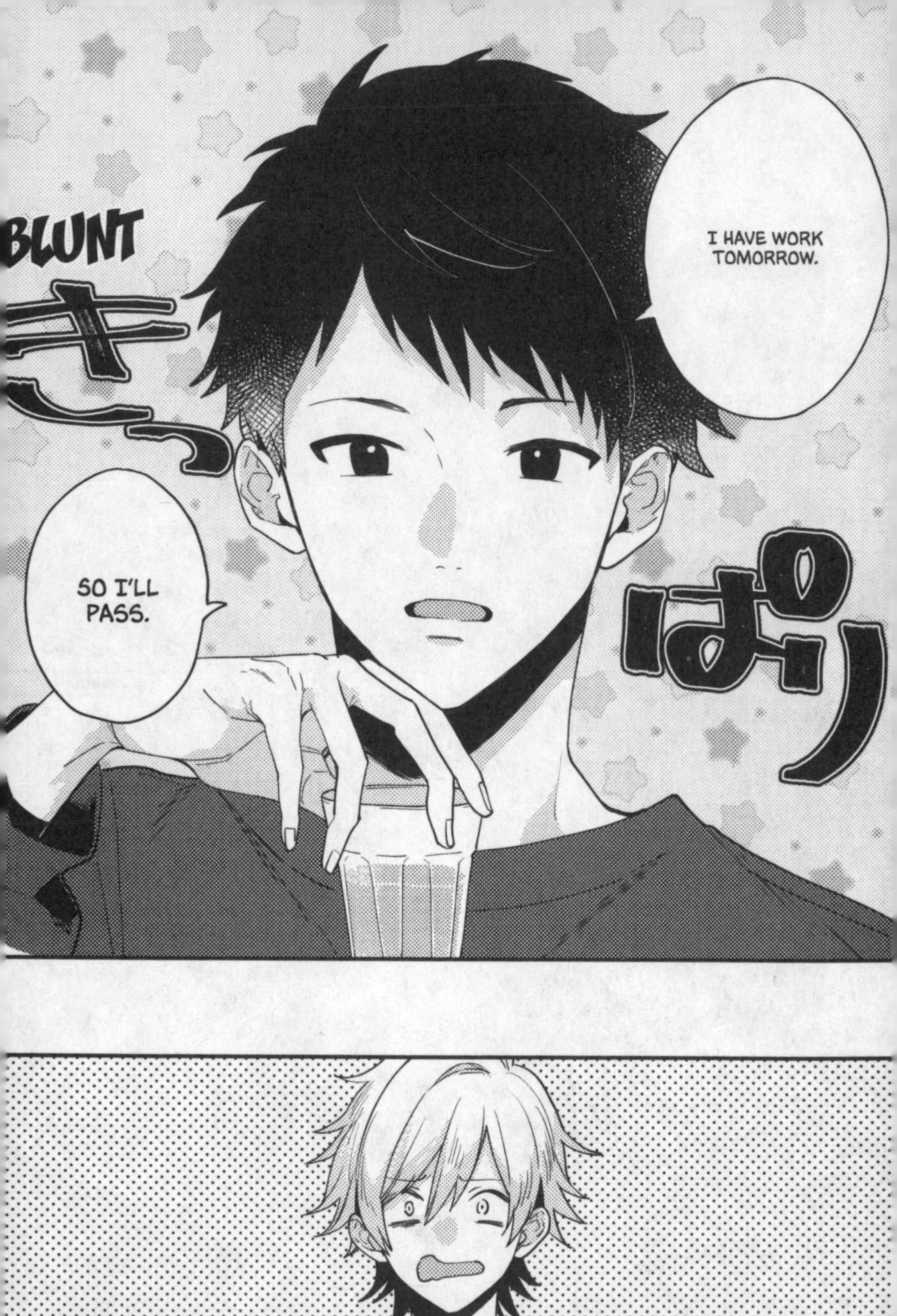
I HAVE WORK TOMORROW.
BLUNT
きっぱり
SO I'LL PASS.

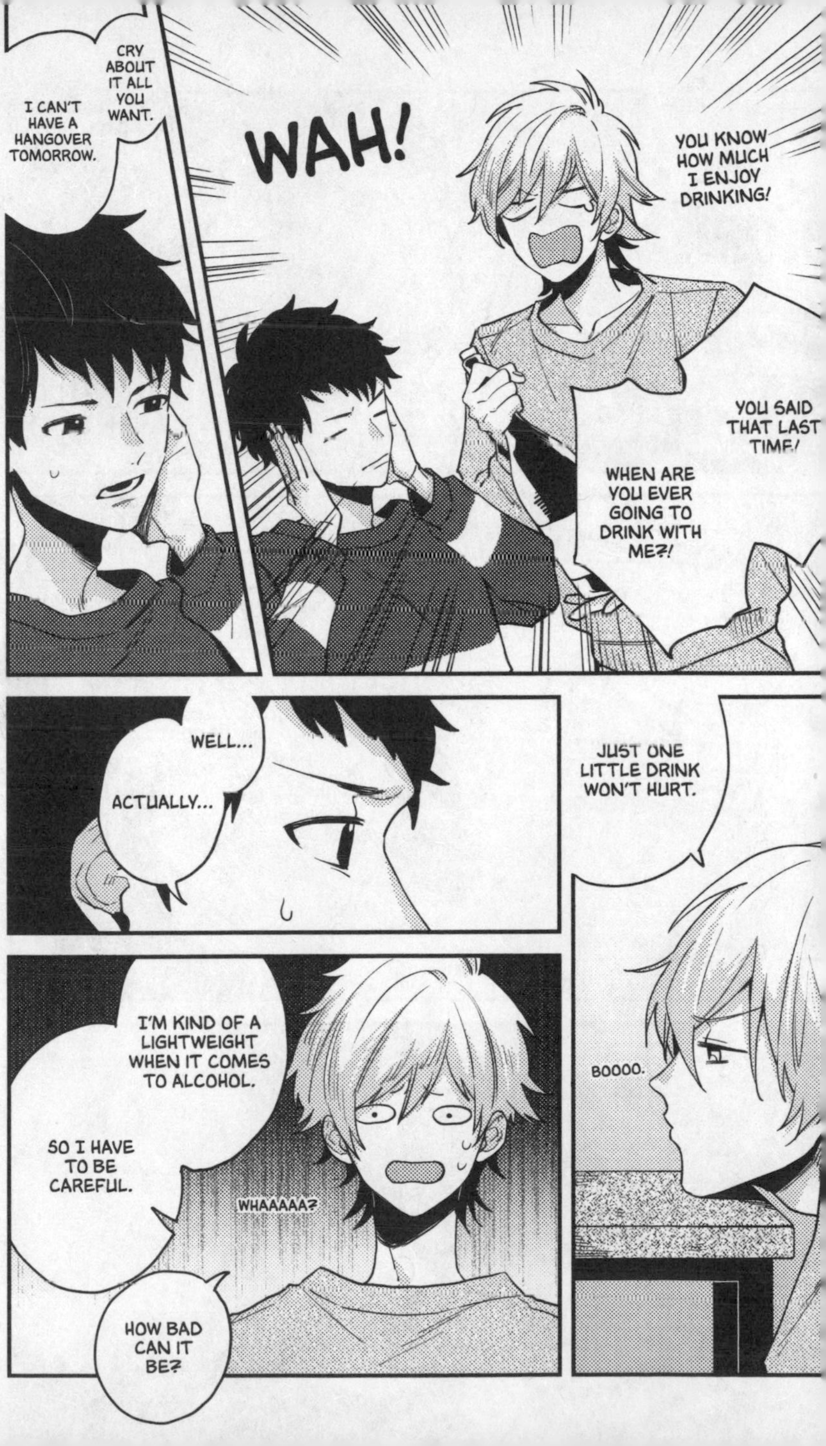
YOU KNOW HOW MUCH I ENJOY DRINKING!
WAH!
YOU SAID THAT LAST TIME!
WHEN ARE YOU EVER GOING TO DRINK WITH ME?!
CRY ABOUT IT ALL YOU WANT.
I CAN'T HAVE A HANGOVER TOMORROW.
JUST ONE LITTLE DRINK WON'T HURT.
BOOOO.
WELL...
ACTUALLY...
I'M KIND OF A LIGHTWEIGHT WHEN IT COMES TO ALCOHOL.
SO I HAVE TO BE CAREFUL.
WHAAAAA?
HOW BAD CAN IT BE?

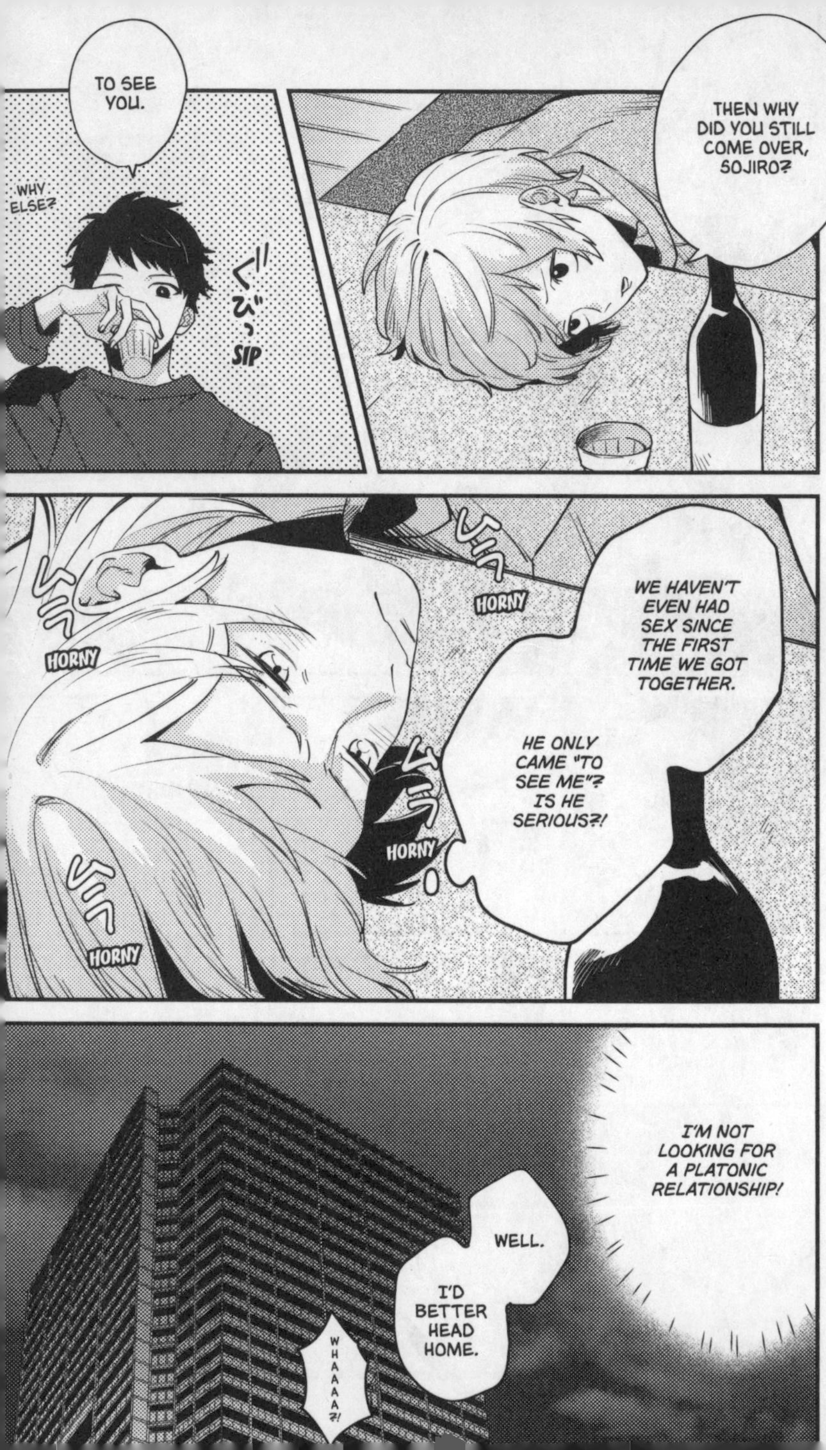
THEN WHY DID YOU STILL COME OVER, SOJIRO?
TO SEE YOU.
WHY ELSE?
SIP
HORNY
HORNY
WE HAVEN'T EVEN HAD SEX SINCE THE FIRST TIME WE GOT TOGETHER.
HE ONLY CAME "TO SEE ME"? IS HE SERIOUS?!
HORNY
HORNY
I'M NOT LOOKING FOR A PLATONIC RELATIONSHIP!
WELL.
I'D BETTER HEAD HOME.
WHAAAAA?!

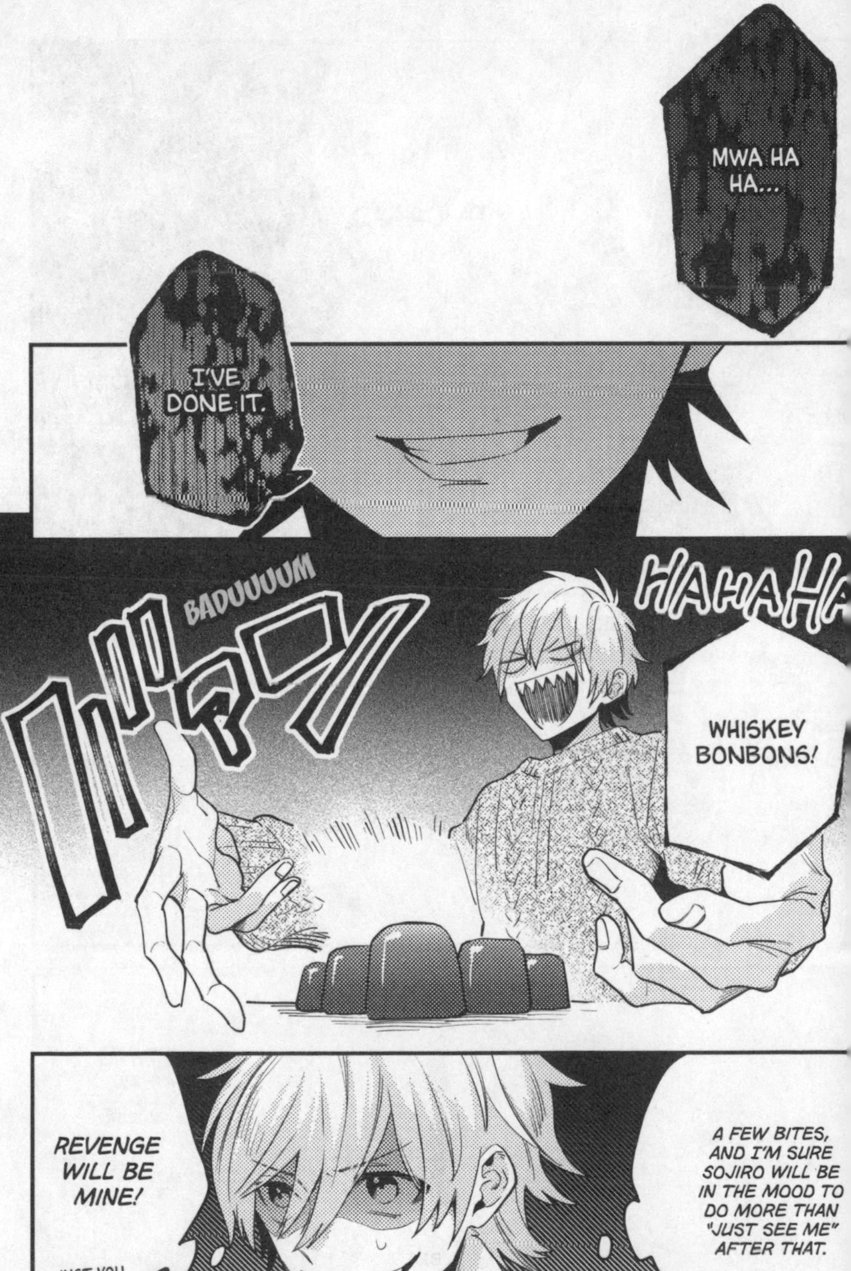
MWA HA HA...
I'VE DONE IT.
HAHAHA
WHISKEY BONBONS!
BADUUUUM
A FEW BITES, AND I'M SURE SOJIRO WILL BE IN THE MOOD TO DO MORE THAN "JUST SEE ME" AFTER THAT.
REVENGE WILL BE MINE!
JUST YOU WATCH.

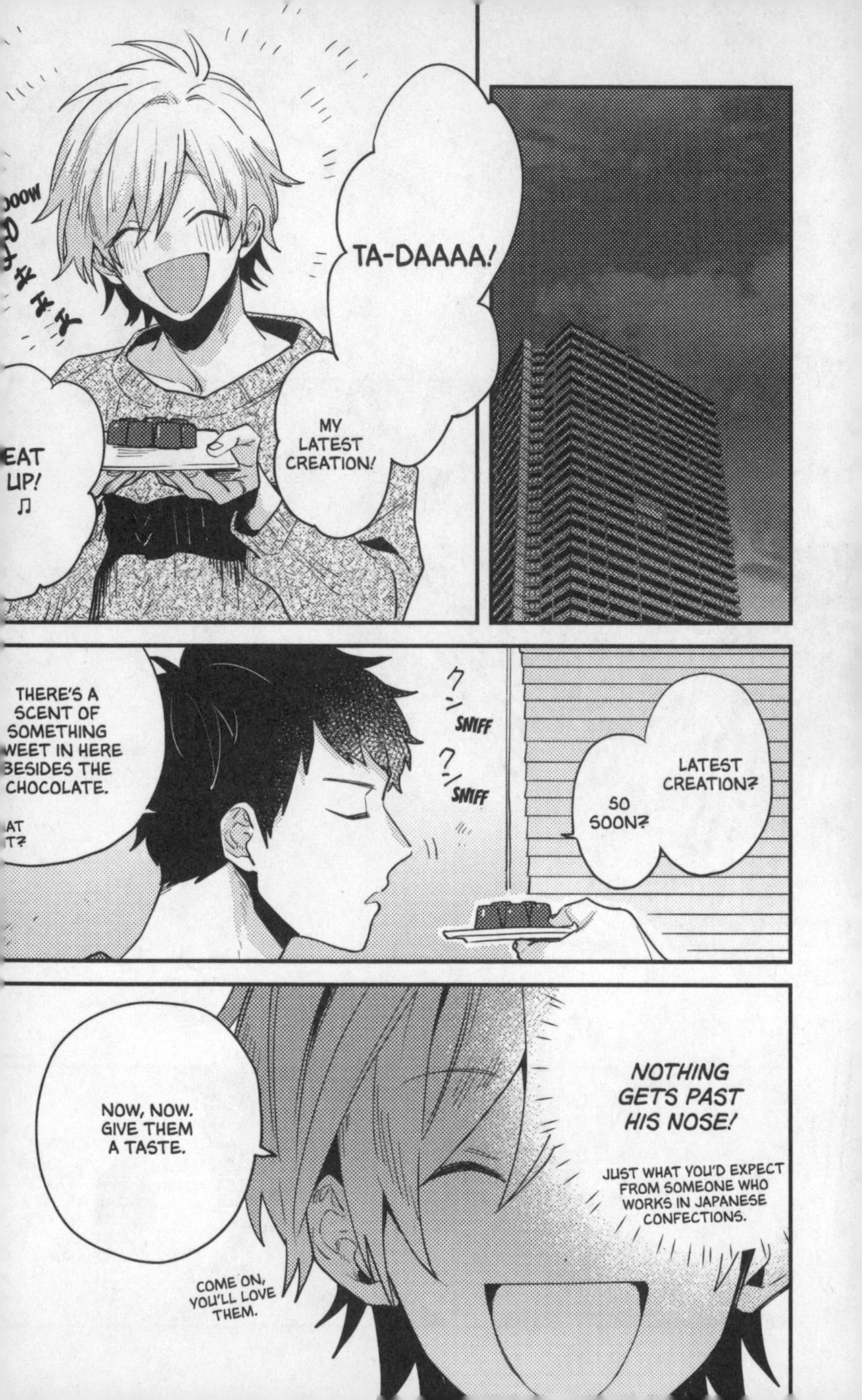
TA-DAAAA!
MY LATEST CREATION!
EAT UP! ♫
LATEST CREATION? SO SOON?
SNIFF
SNIFF
THERE'S A SCENT OF SOMETHING WEET IN HERE BESIDES THE CHOCOLATE.
NOTHING GETS PAST HIS NOSE!
JUST WHAT YOU'D EXPECT FROM SOMEONE WHO WORKS IN JAPANESE CONFECTIONS.
NOW, NOW. GIVE THEM A TASTE.
COME ON, YOU'LL LOVE THEM.

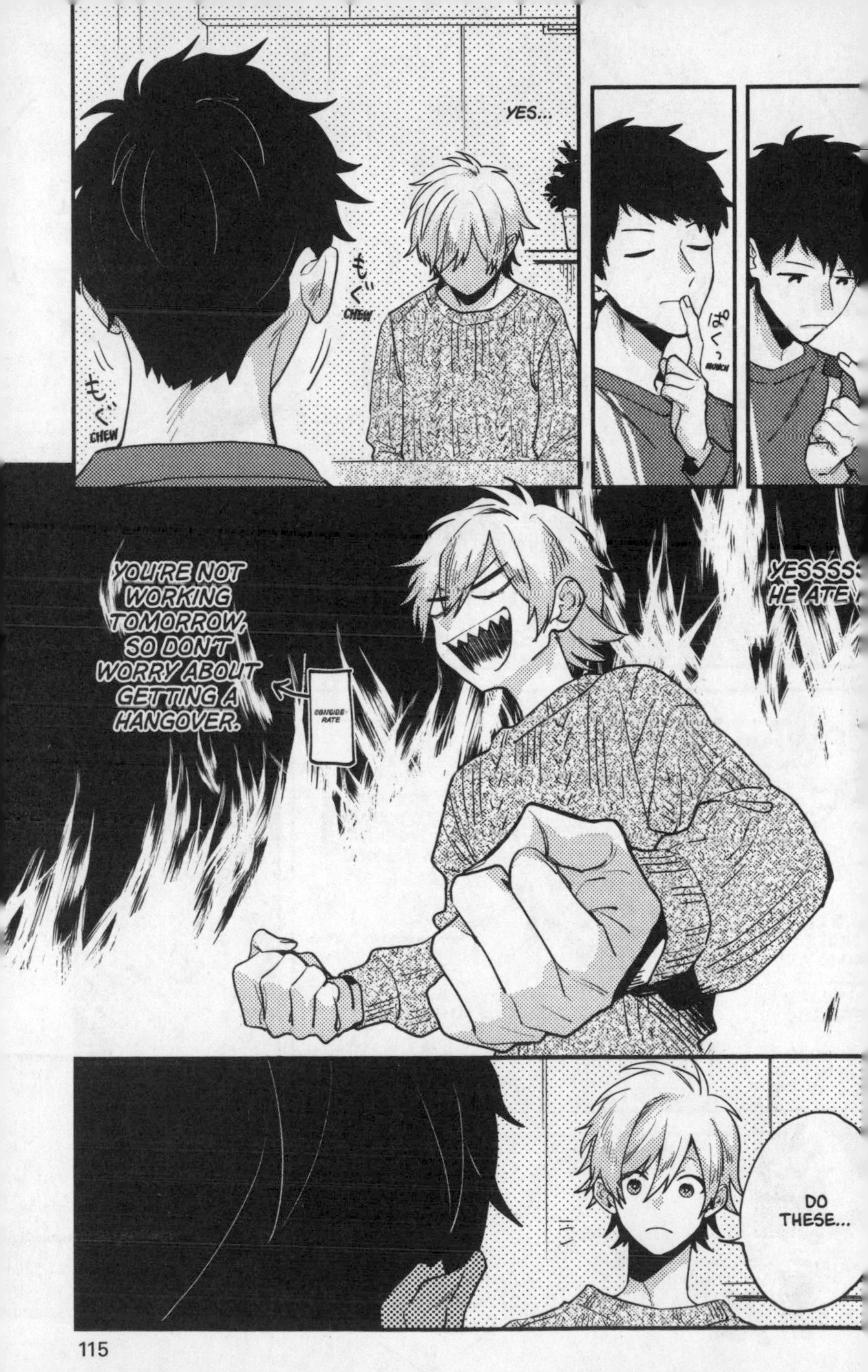
ぱくっ
MUNCH
YES...
もぐ
CHEW
もぐ
CHEW
YESSSS HE ATE
YOU'RE NOT WORKING TOMORROW, SO DON'T WORRY ABOUT GETTING A HANGOVER.
CONSIDE-RATE
DO THESE...

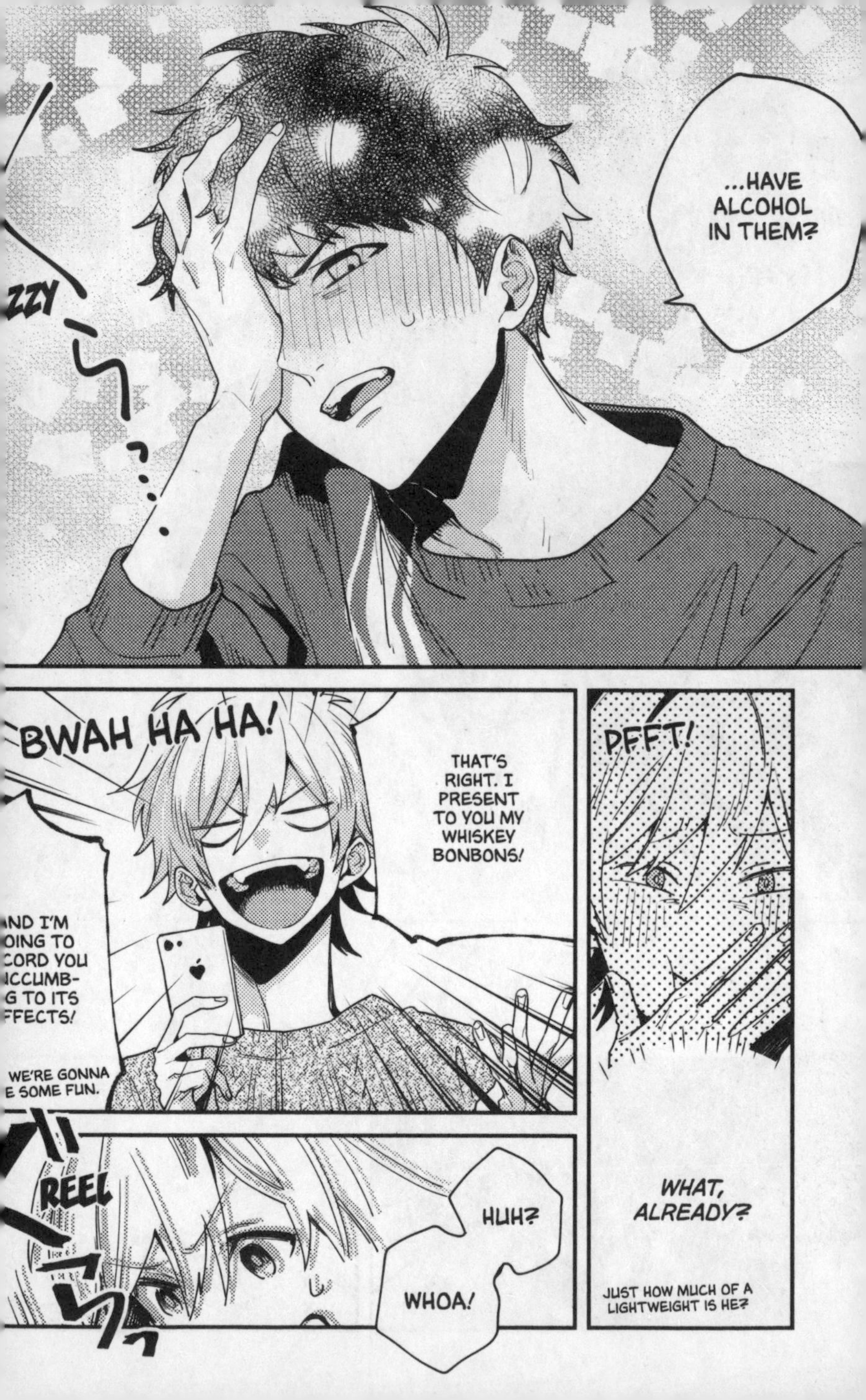

...HAVE ALCOHOL IN THEM?
ZZY
PFFT!
WHAT, ALREADY?
JUST HOW MUCH OF A LIGHTWEIGHT IS HE?
BWAH HA HA!
THAT'S RIGHT. I PRESENT TO YOU MY WHISKEY BONBONS!
ND I'M OING TO CORD YOU UCCUMB- G TO ITS FFECTS!
WE'RE GONNA E SOME FUN.
REEL
HUH?
WHOA!

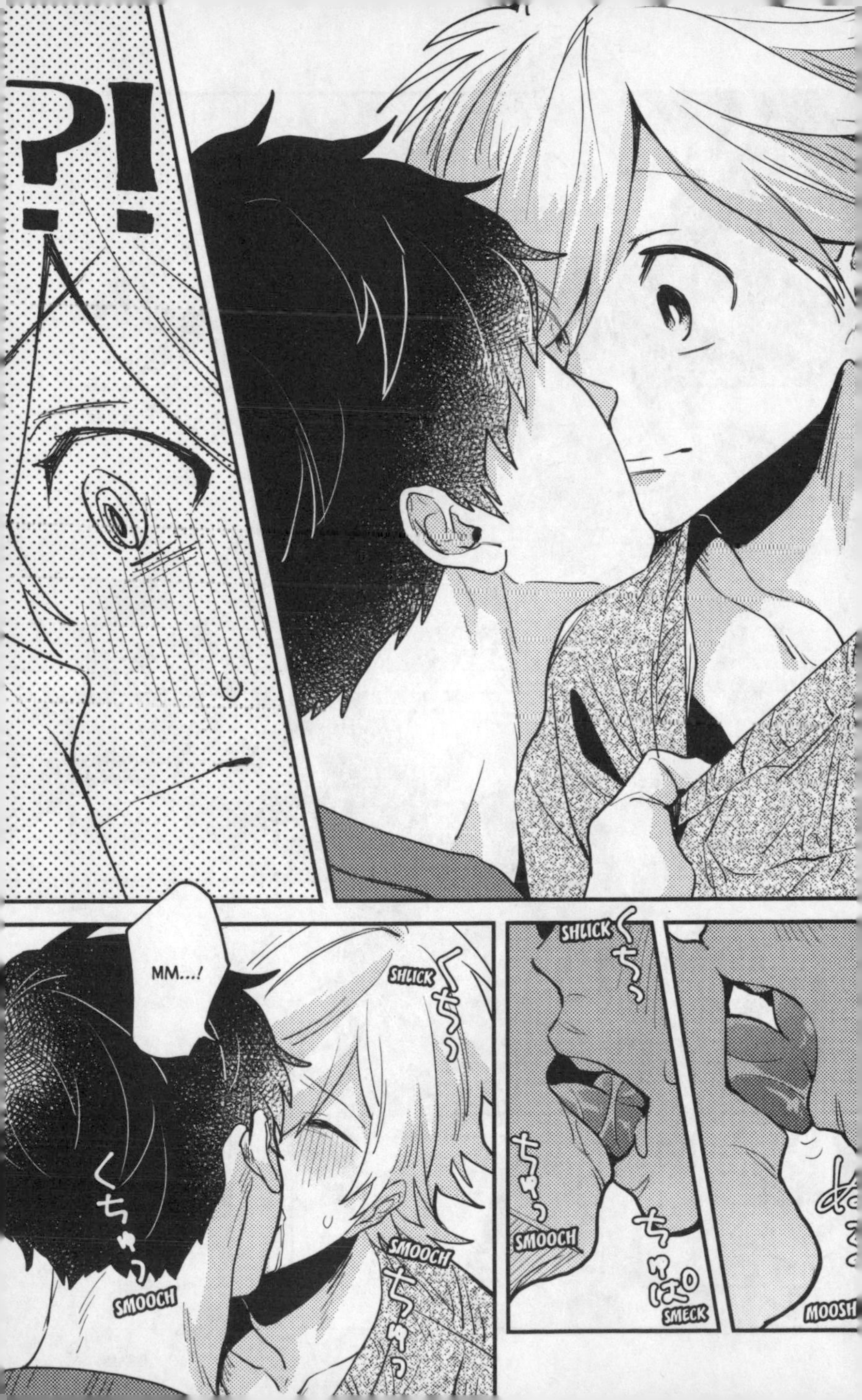
?!
MOOSH
SHLICK
くちっ
ちゅっ
SMOOCH
ちゅぱ
SMECK
MM...!
SHLICK
くちっ
SMOOCH
ちゅっ
くちゅっ
SMOOCH

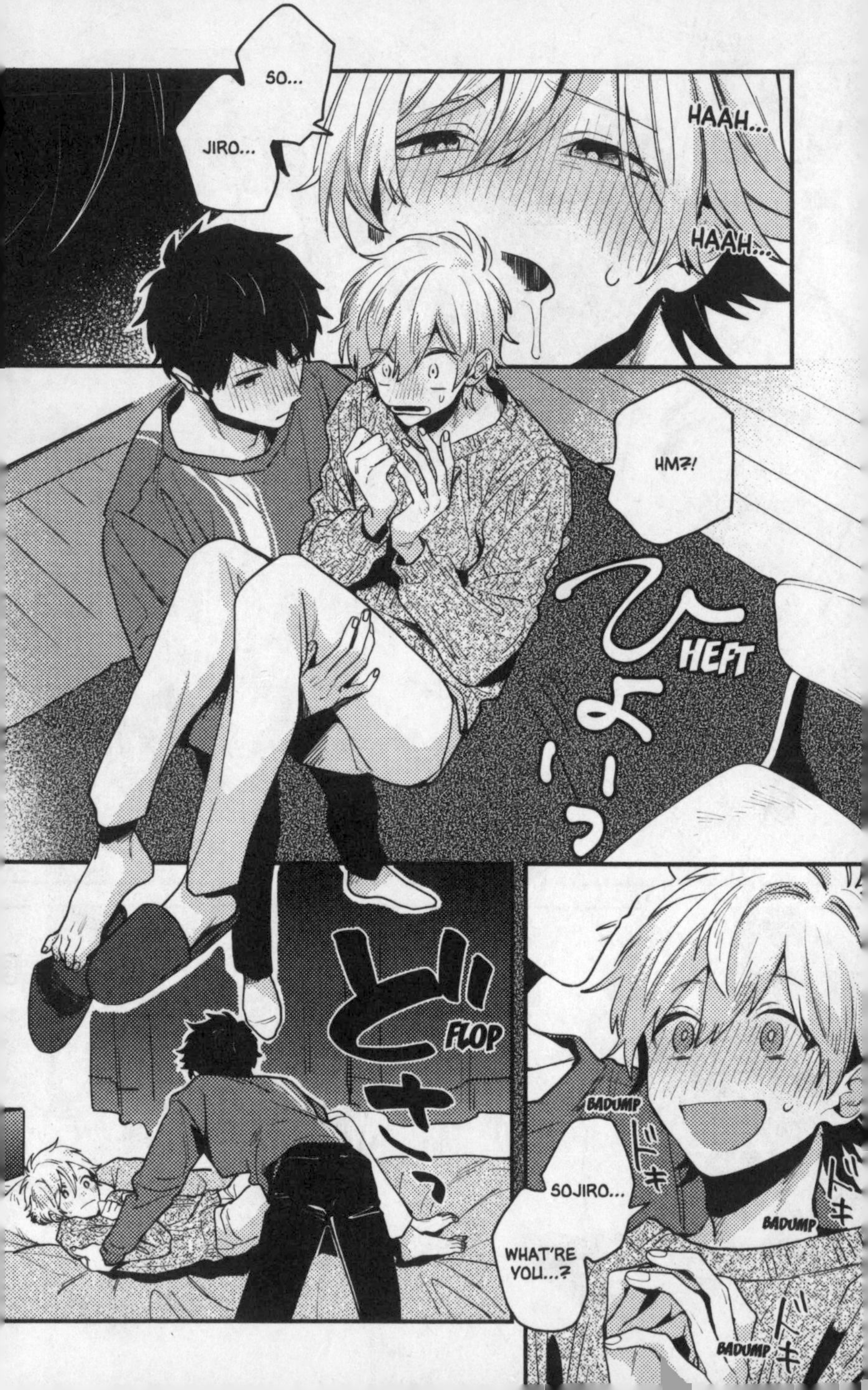
SO...
JIRO...
HAAH...
HAAH...
HM?!
ひょいっ
HEFT
SOJIRO...
WHAT'RE YOU...?
BADUMP ドキ
BADUMP ドキ
BADUMP ドキ
どさっ
FLOP

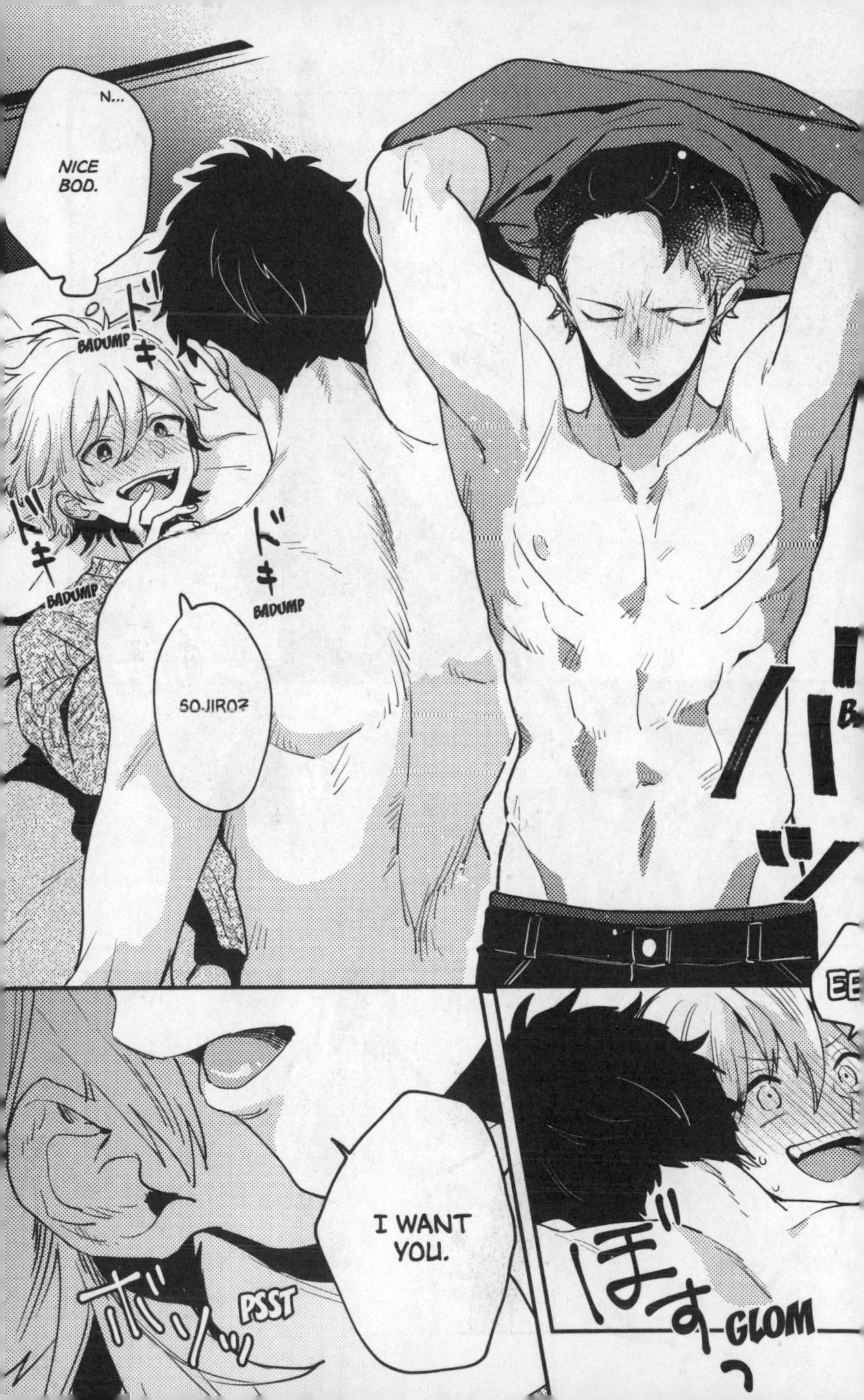
N...
NICE BOD.
ドキ
BADUMP
ドキ
BADUMP
SOJIRO?
ドキ
BADUMP
ぼす
GLOM
I WANT YOU.
PSST

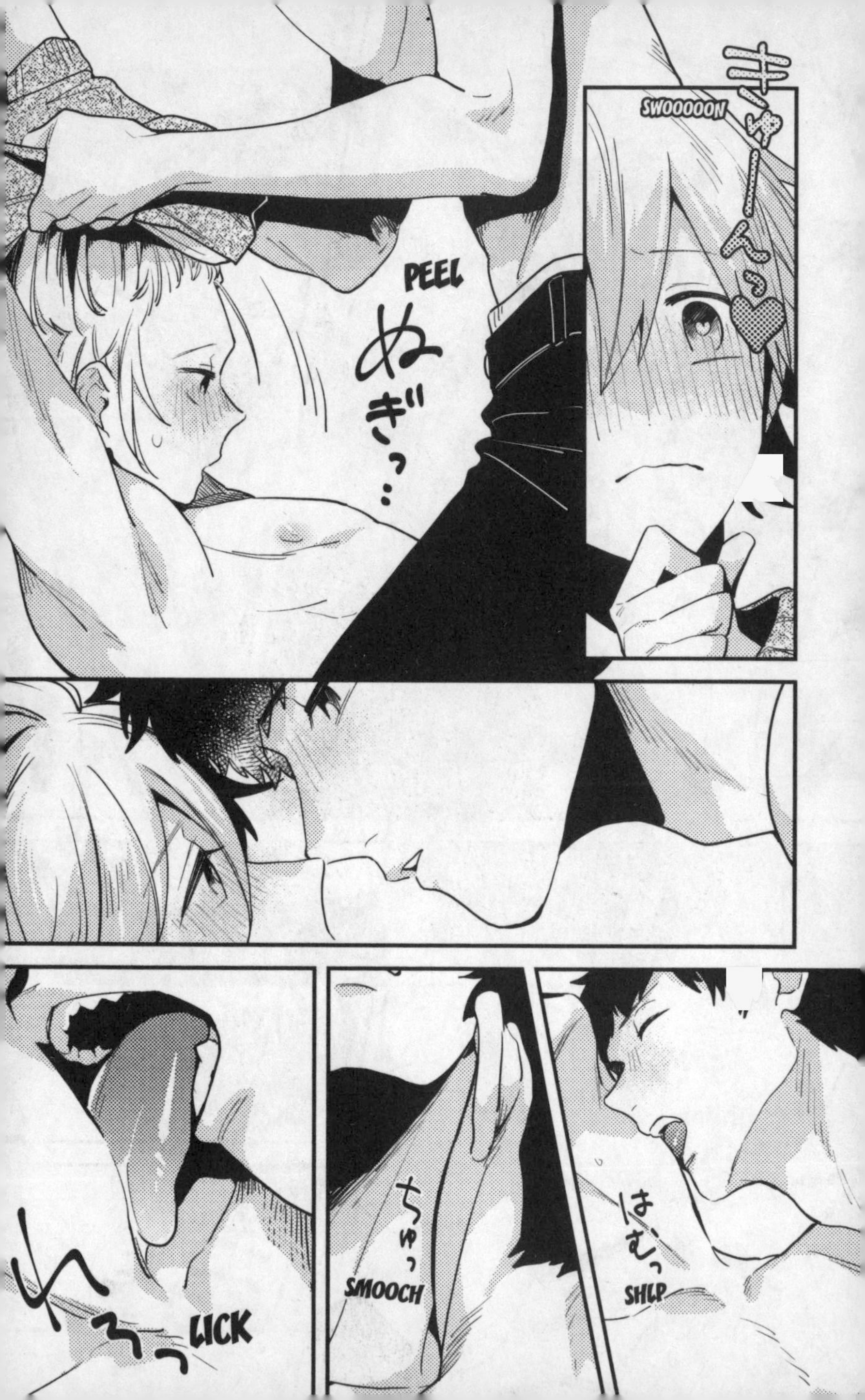
キューんっ♡
SWOOOOON
ぬぎっ
PEEL
はむっ
SHLP
ちゅっ
SMOOCH
れろっ
LICK

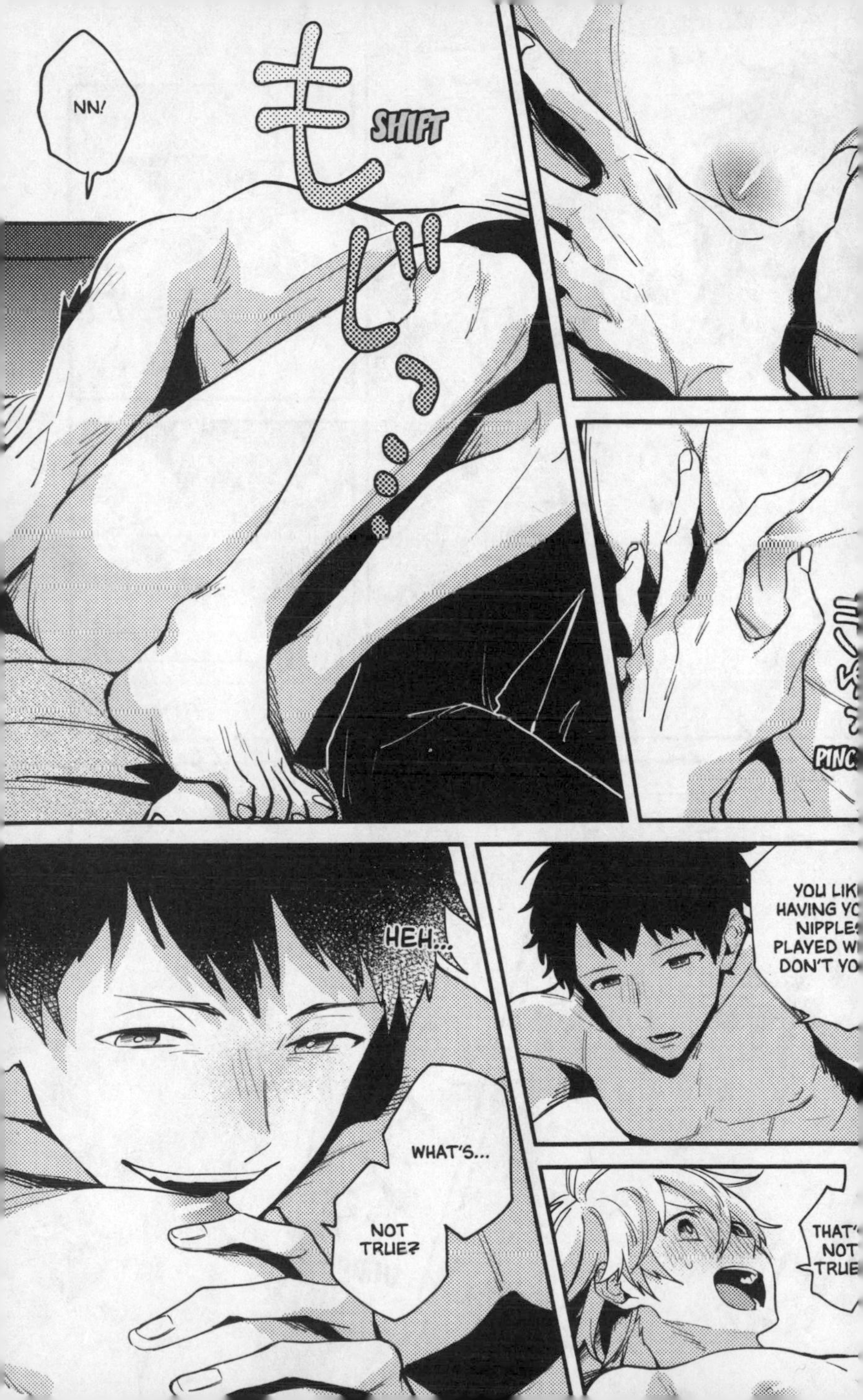
PINC
NN!
もじっ…
SHIFT
YOU LIK HAVING YO NIPPLES PLAYED W DON'T YO
THAT'S NOT TRUE
HEH...
WHAT'S...
NOT TRUE?

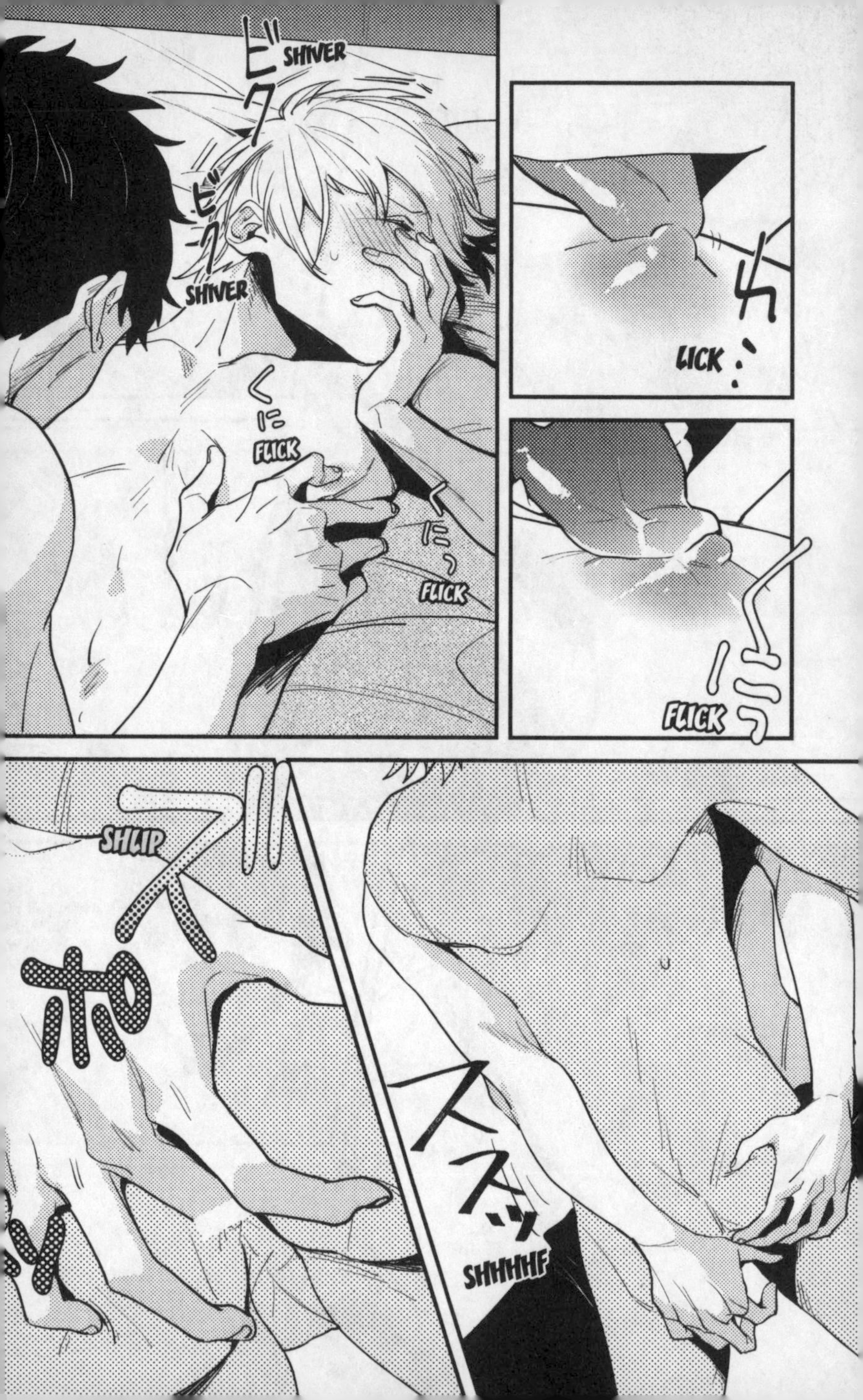
LICK
FLICK
SHIVER
SHIVER
FLICK
FLICK
SHHHHF
SHLIP

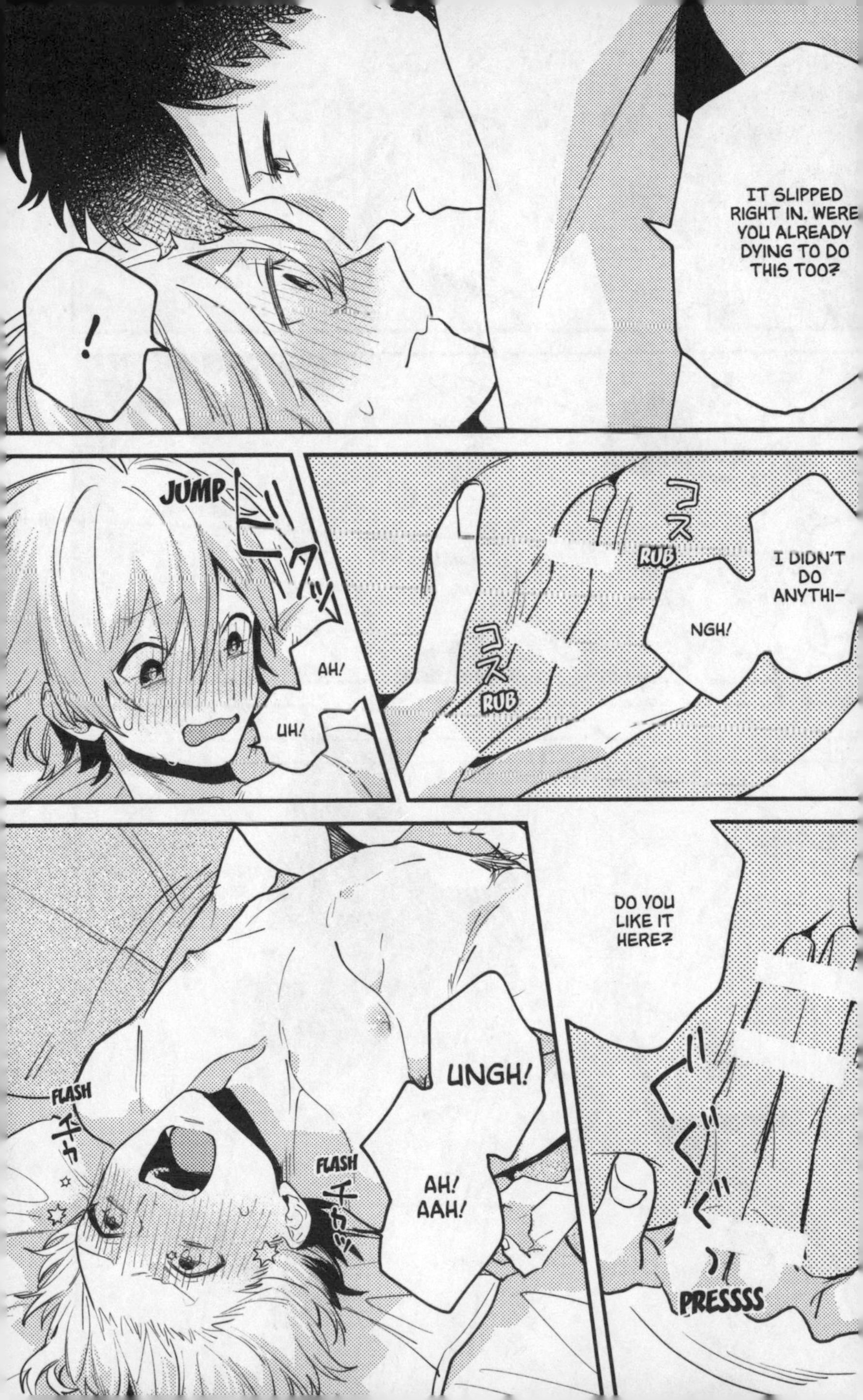

IT SLIPPED RIGHT IN. WERE YOU ALREADY DYING TO DO THIS TOO?
!
I DIDN'T DO ANYTHI–
NGH!
RUB
RUB
JUMP
AH!
UH!
DO YOU LIKE IT HERE?
PRESSSS
UNGH!
AH! AAH!
FLASH
FLASH

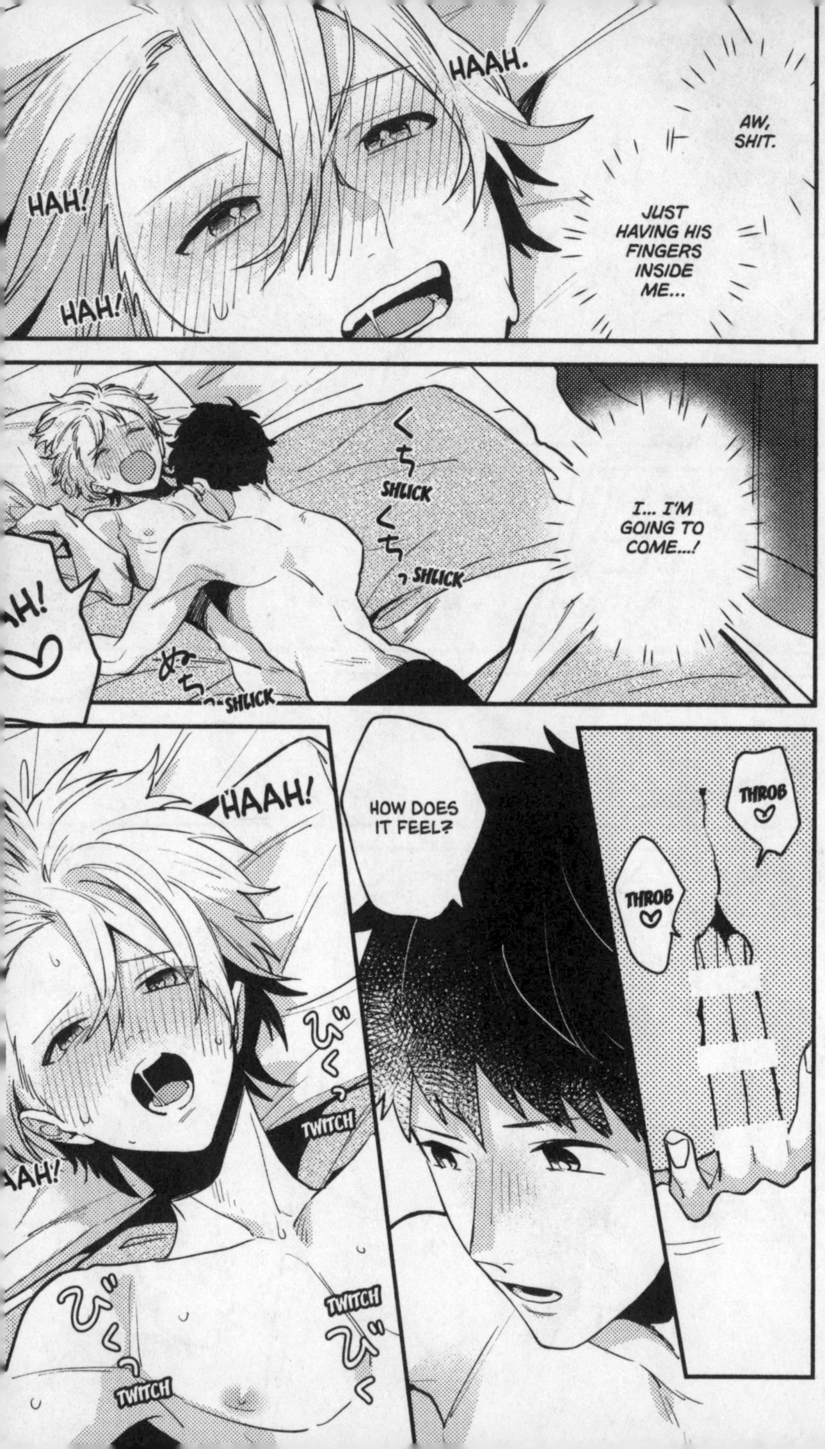
HAAH.
AW, SHIT.
JUST HAVING HIS FINGERS INSIDE ME...
HAH!
HAH!
I... I'M GOING TO COME...!
くち
SHLICK
くちっ
SHLICK
AH!
ぬちっ
SHLICK
THROB
THROB
HOW DOES IT FEEL?
HAAH!
びくっ
TWITCH
AAH!
TWITCH
びくっ
びくっ
TWITCH

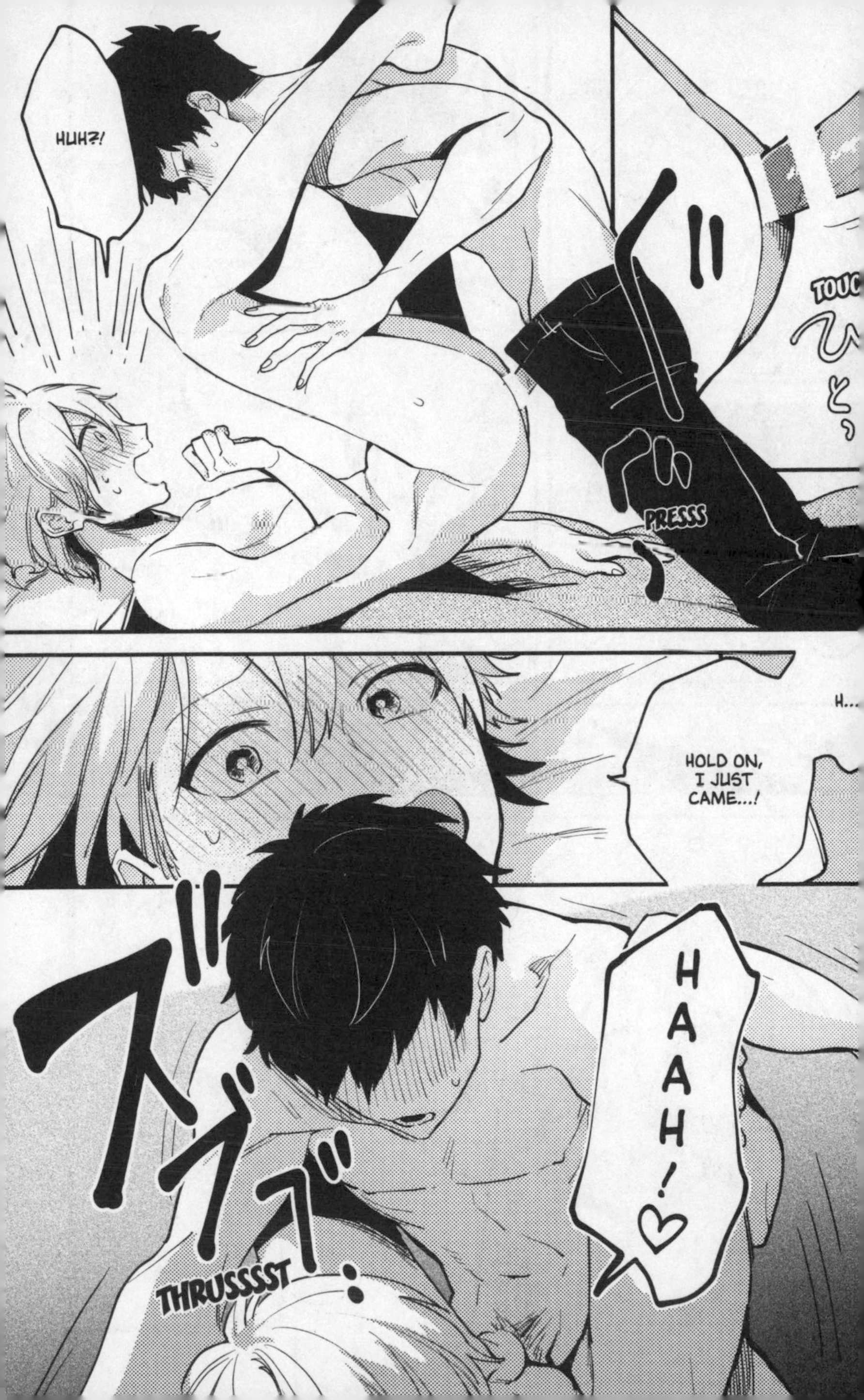
TOUC
PRESSS
HUH?!
H...
HOLD ON, I JUST CAME...!
HAAH!♡
THRUSSSST

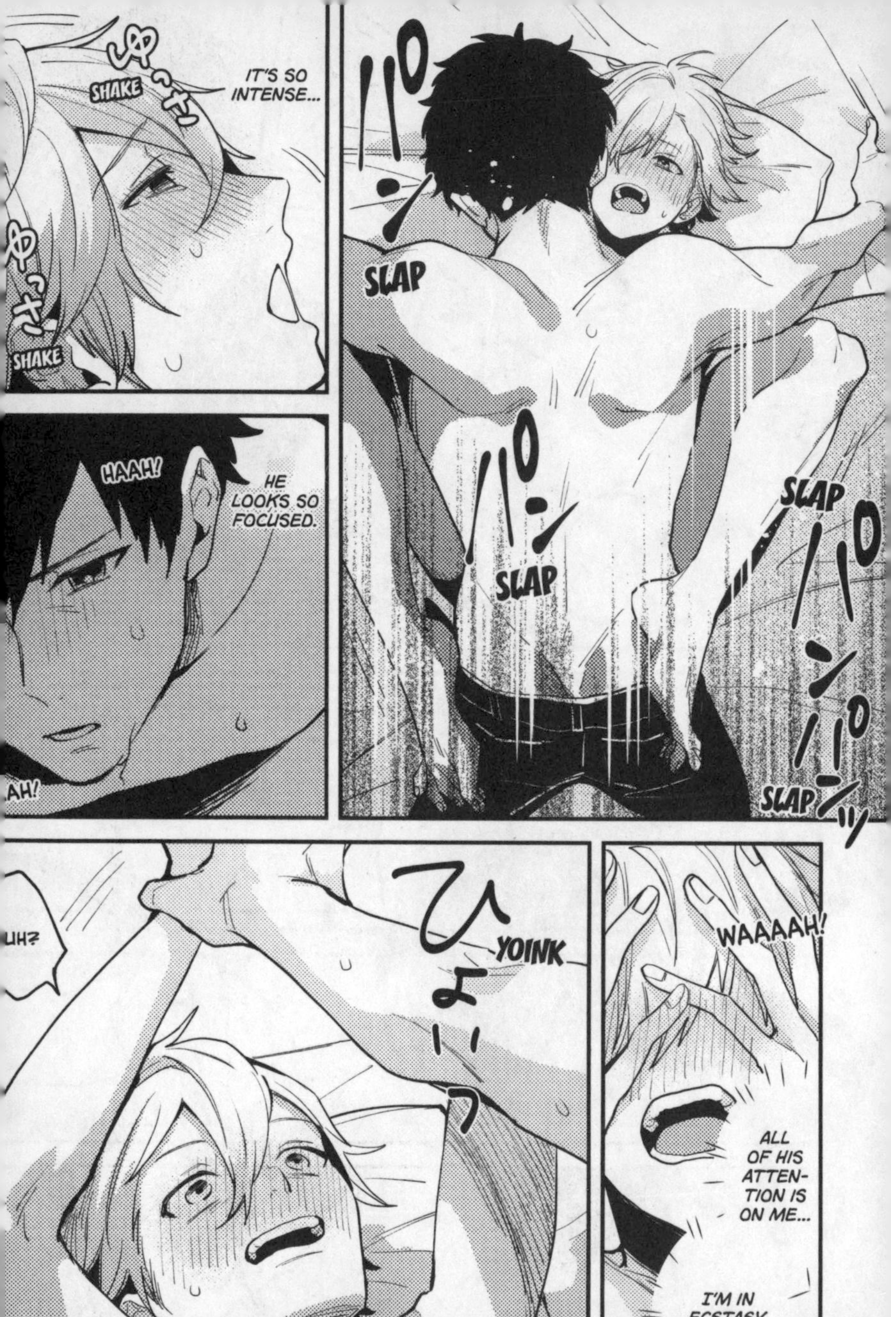
SLAP
SLAP
SLAP
SLAP
IT'S SO INTENSE...
SHAKE
SHAKE
HAAH!
HE LOOKS SO FOCUSED.
AH!
WAAAAH!
ALL OF HIS ATTENTION IS ON ME...
I'M IN ECSTASY.
ひょいっ
YOINK
UH?

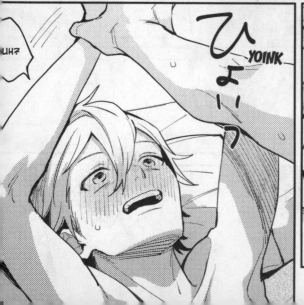

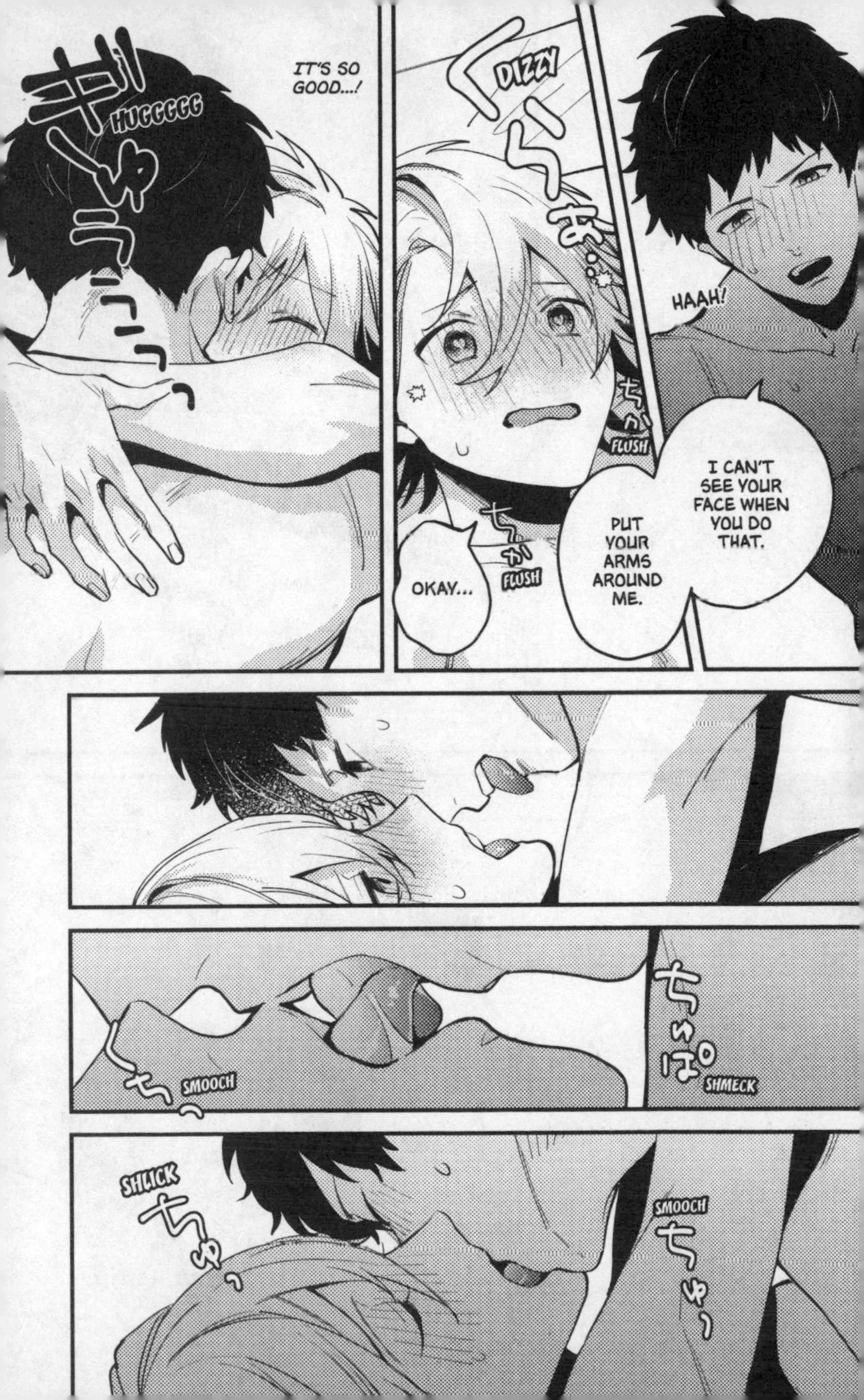
HAAH!
I CAN'T SEE YOUR FACE WHEN YOU DO THAT.
PUT YOUR ARMS AROUND ME.
DIZZY
FLUSH
FLUSH
OKAY...
HUGGGGG
IT'S SO GOOD...!
SHMECK
SMOOCH
SMOOCH
SHLICK

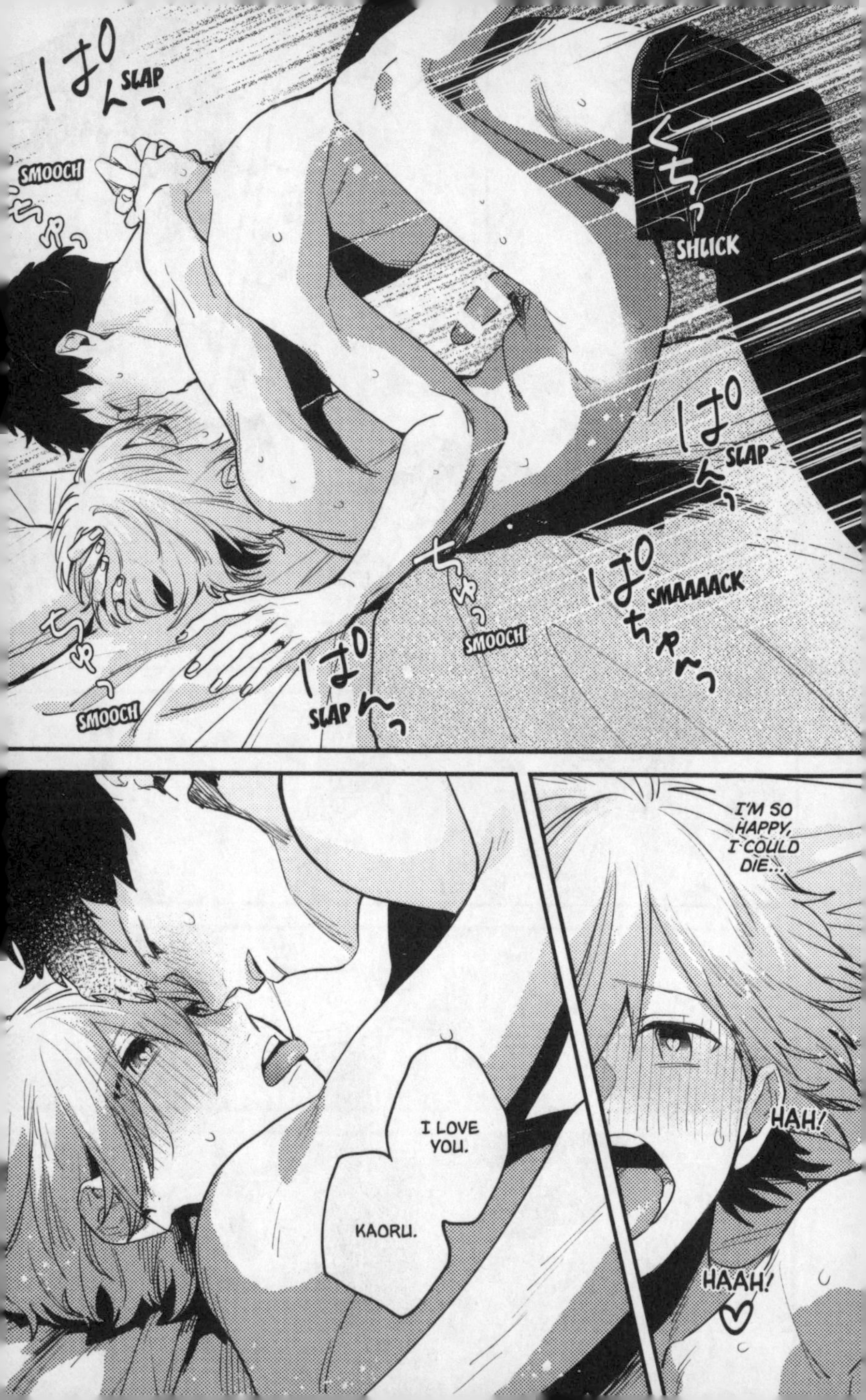
くちっ
SHLICK
ぱんっ
SLAP
ぱちゃんっ
SMAAAACK
ちゅっ
SMOOCH
ぱんっ
SLAP
ぱんっ
SLAP
ちゅっ
SMOOCH
ちゅっ
SMOOCH
I'M SO HAPPY, I COULD DIE...
HAH!
HAAH! ♡
I LOVE YOU.
KAORU.

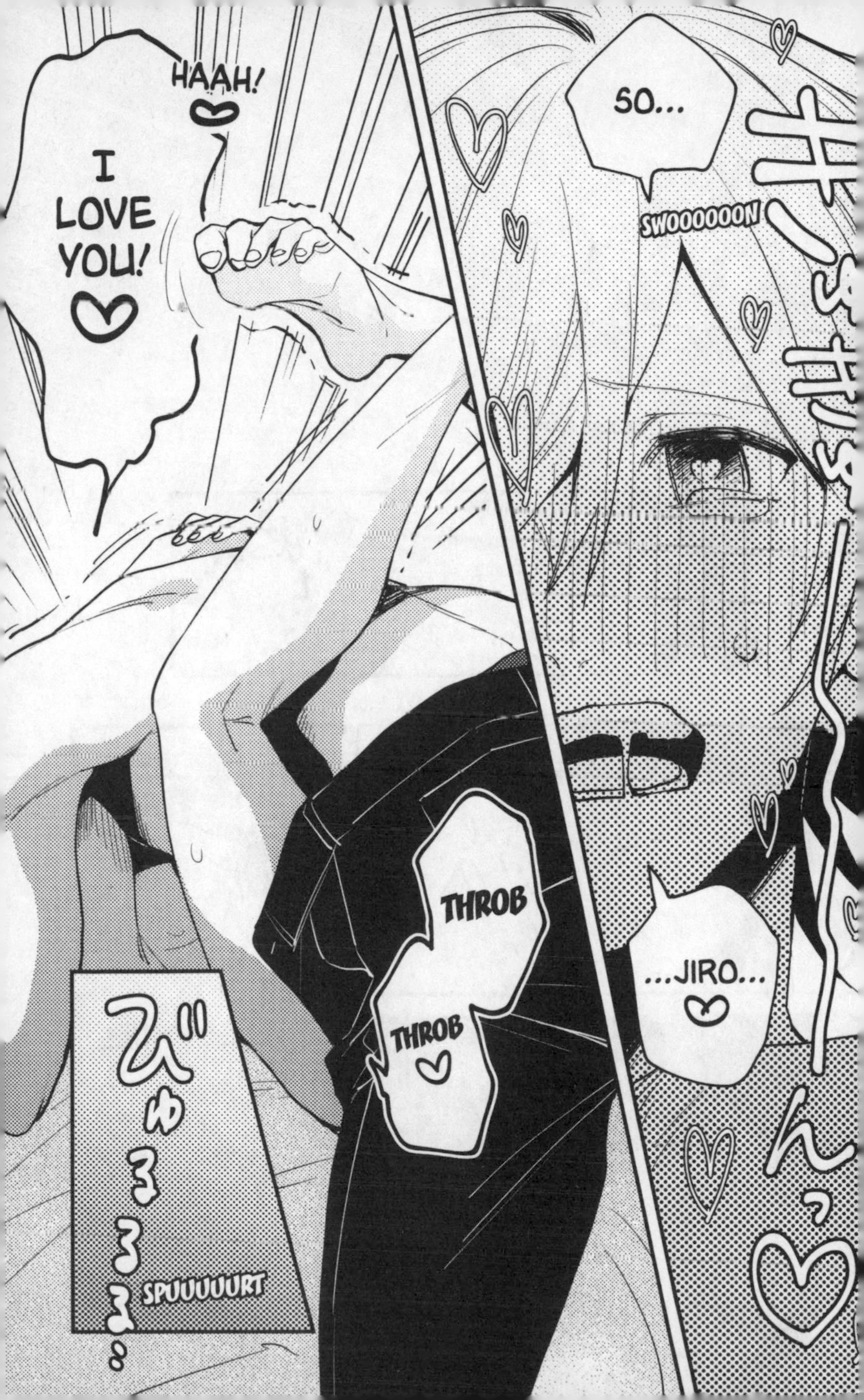
SO...
SWOOOOOON
...JIRO... ♡
THROB
THROB ♡
HAAH! ♡
I LOVE YOU! ♡
SPUUUUURT

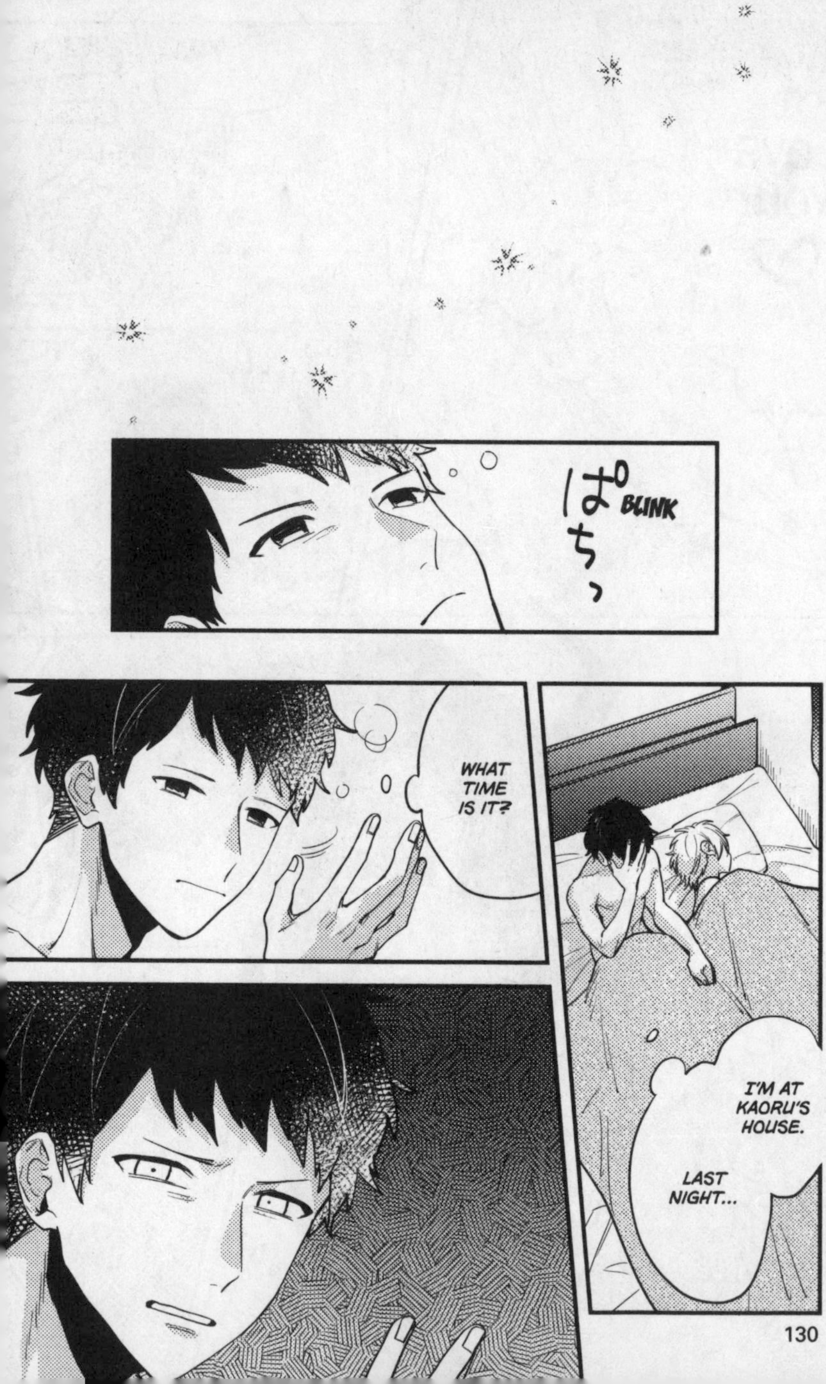
ぱちっ
BLINK
I'M AT KAORU'S HOUSE.
LAST NIGHT...
WHAT TIME IS IT?

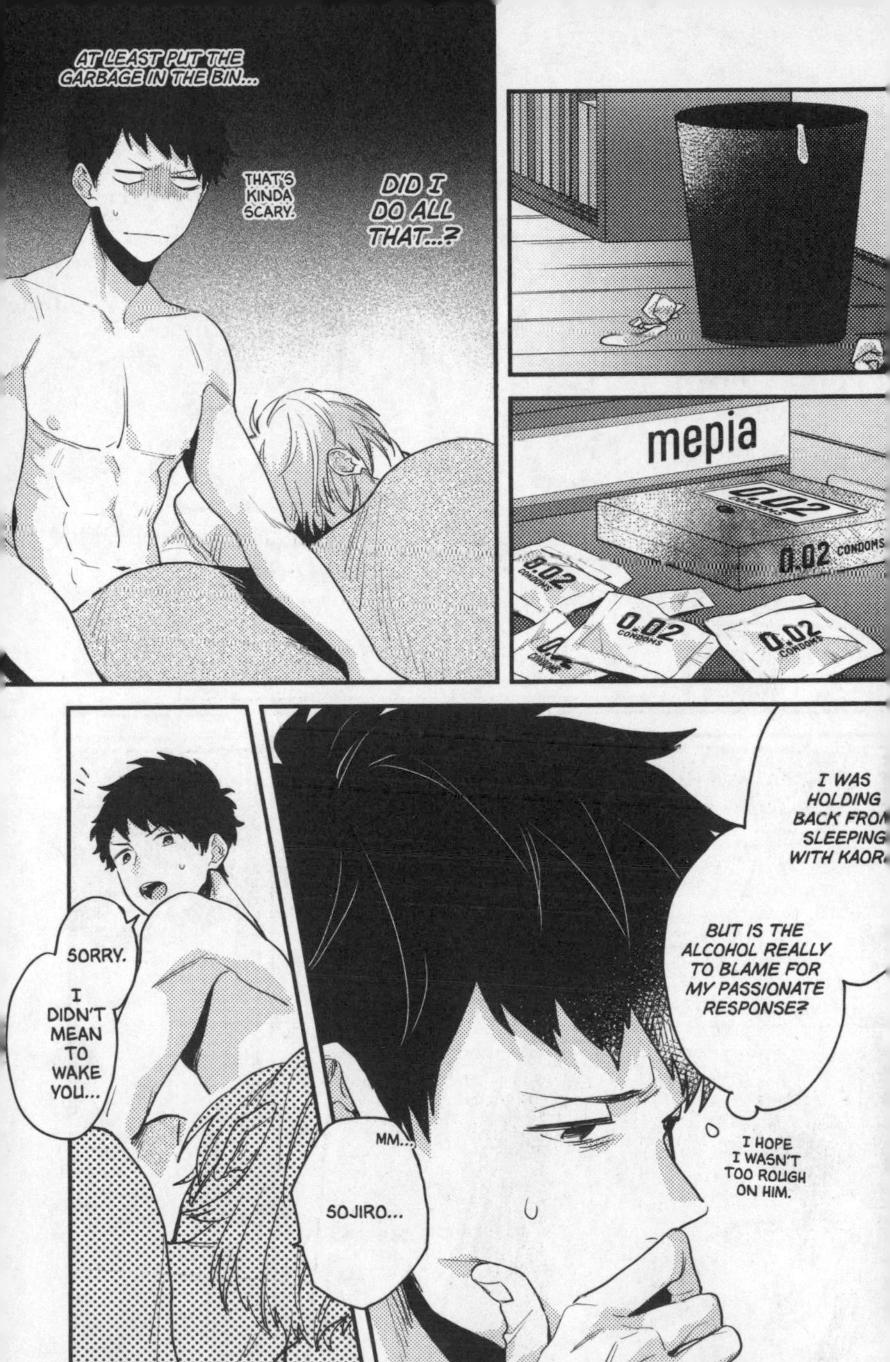
mepia
0.02 CONDOMS
AT LEAST PUT THE GARBAGE IN THE BIN...
DID I DO ALL THAT...?
THAT'S KINDA SCARY.
I WAS HOLDING BACK FRO SLEEPING WITH KAOR
BUT IS THE ALCOHOL REALLY TO BLAME FOR MY PASSIONATE RESPONSE?
I HOPE I WASN'T TOO ROUGH ON HIM.
MM...
SOJIRO...
SORRY.
I DIDN'T MEAN TO WAKE YOU...

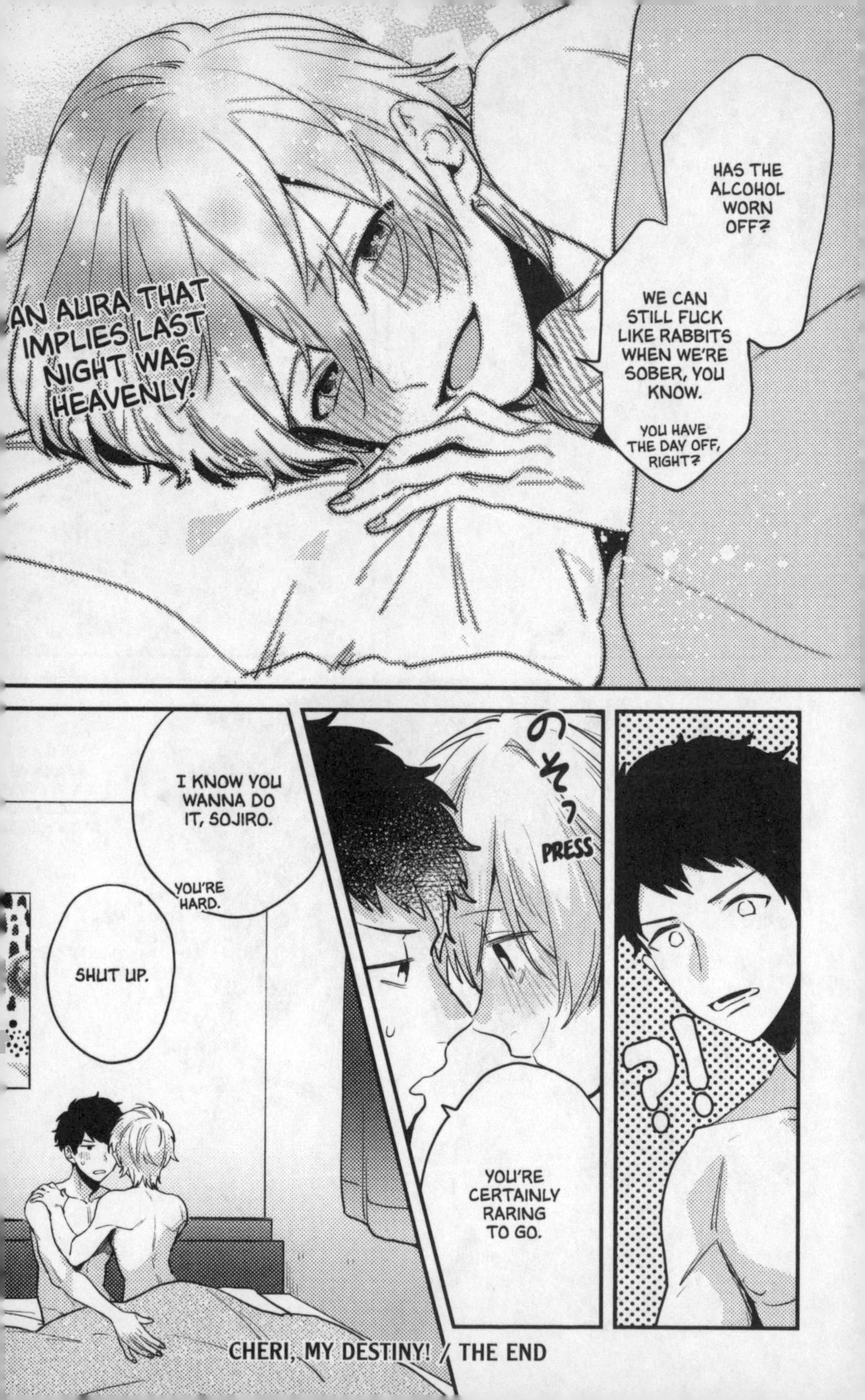
HAS THE ALCOHOL WORN OFF?
WE CAN STILL FUCK LIKE RABBITS WHEN WE'RE SOBER, YOU KNOW.
YOU HAVE THE DAY OFF, RIGHT?
AN AURA THAT IMPLIES LAST NIGHT WAS HEAVENLY!
PRESS
YOU'RE CERTAINLY RARING TO GO.
I KNOW YOU WANNA DO IT, SOJIRO.
YOU'RE HARD.
SHUT UP.

CHERI, MY DESTINY! / THE END

Chéri, my destiny!

Chéri, my destiny!

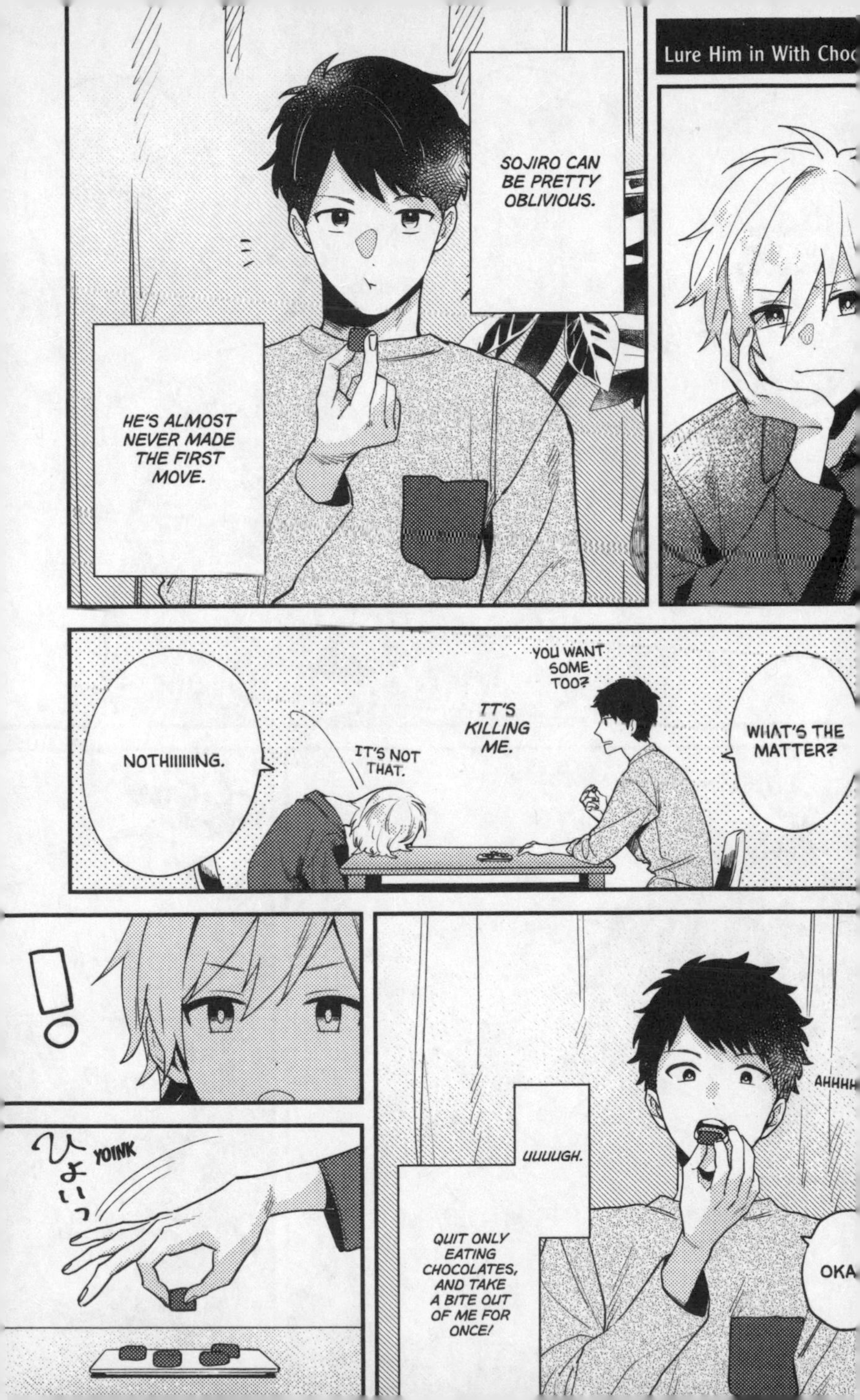
Lure Him in With Choc
SOJIRO CAN BE PRETTY OBLIVIOUS.
HE'S ALMOST NEVER MADE THE FIRST MOVE.
WHAT'S THE MATTER?
YOU WANT SOME TOO?
IT'S KILLING ME.
IT'S NOT THAT.
NOTHIIIIIING.
AHHHH
OKA
UUUUGH.
QUIT ONLY EATING CHOCOLATES, AND TAKE A BITE OUT OF ME FOR ONCE!
!
ひょいっ
YOINK

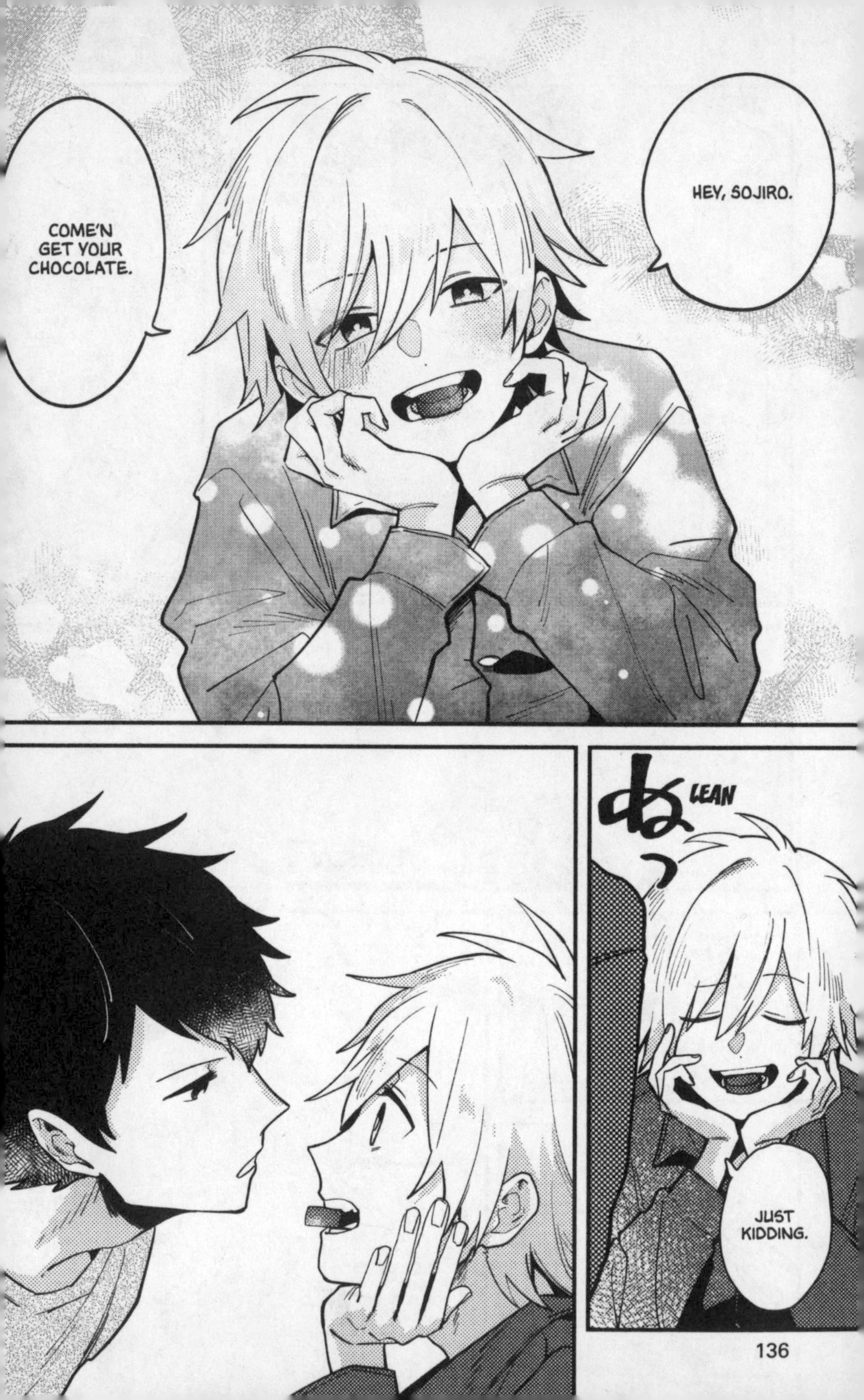
HEY, SOJIRO.
COME'N GET YOUR CHOCOLATE.
ぬっ
LEAN
JUST KIDDING.

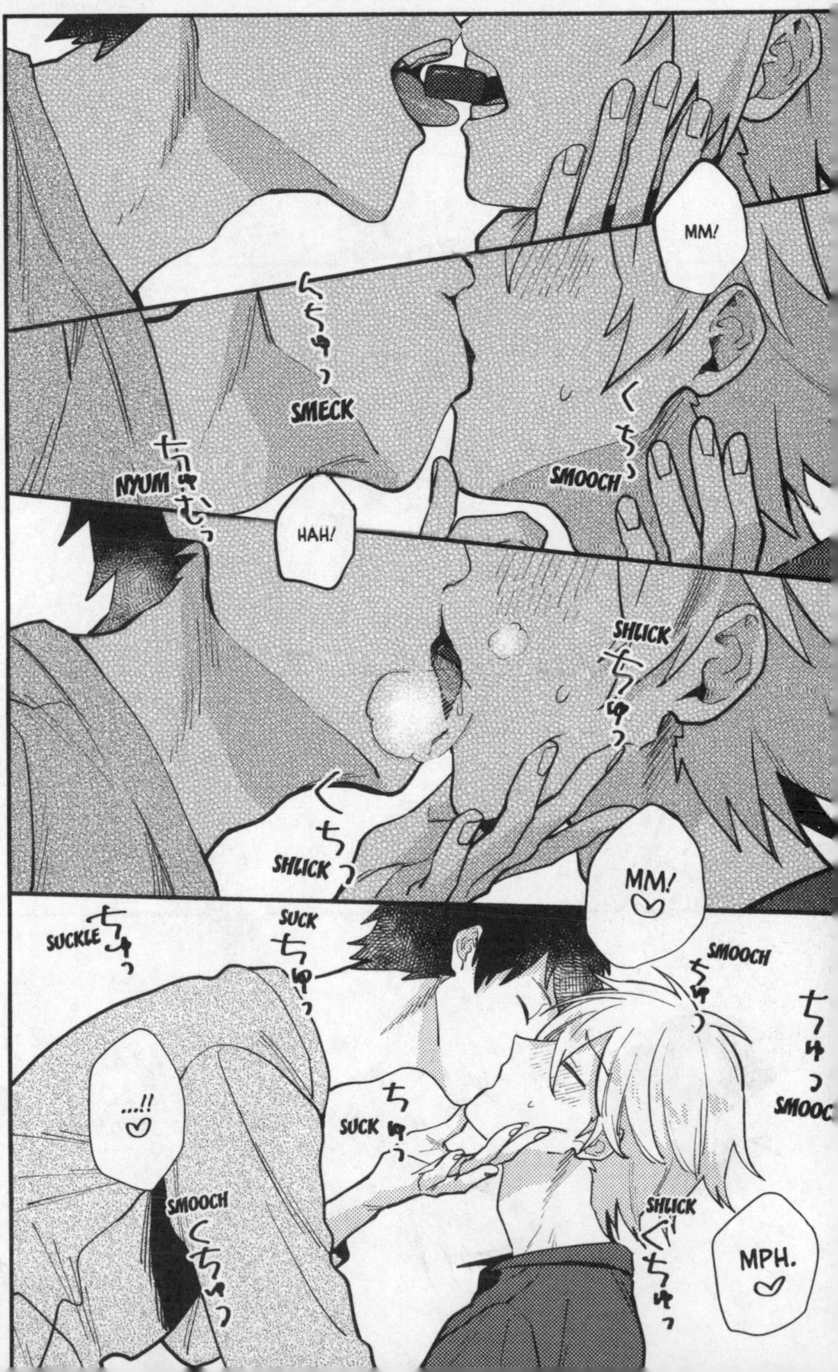
MM!
くちっ
SMOOCH
ちゅっ
SMECK
ちゅむっ
NYUM
HAH!
SHLICK
ちゅっ
MM! ♡
くちっ
SHLICK
ちゅっ
SMOOC
SMOOCH
ちゅっ
MPH. ♡
SHLICK
ぐちゅっ
SUCK
ちゅっ
SUCK
ちゅっ
SUCKLE
ちゅっ
...!! ♡
SMOOCH
くちゅっ

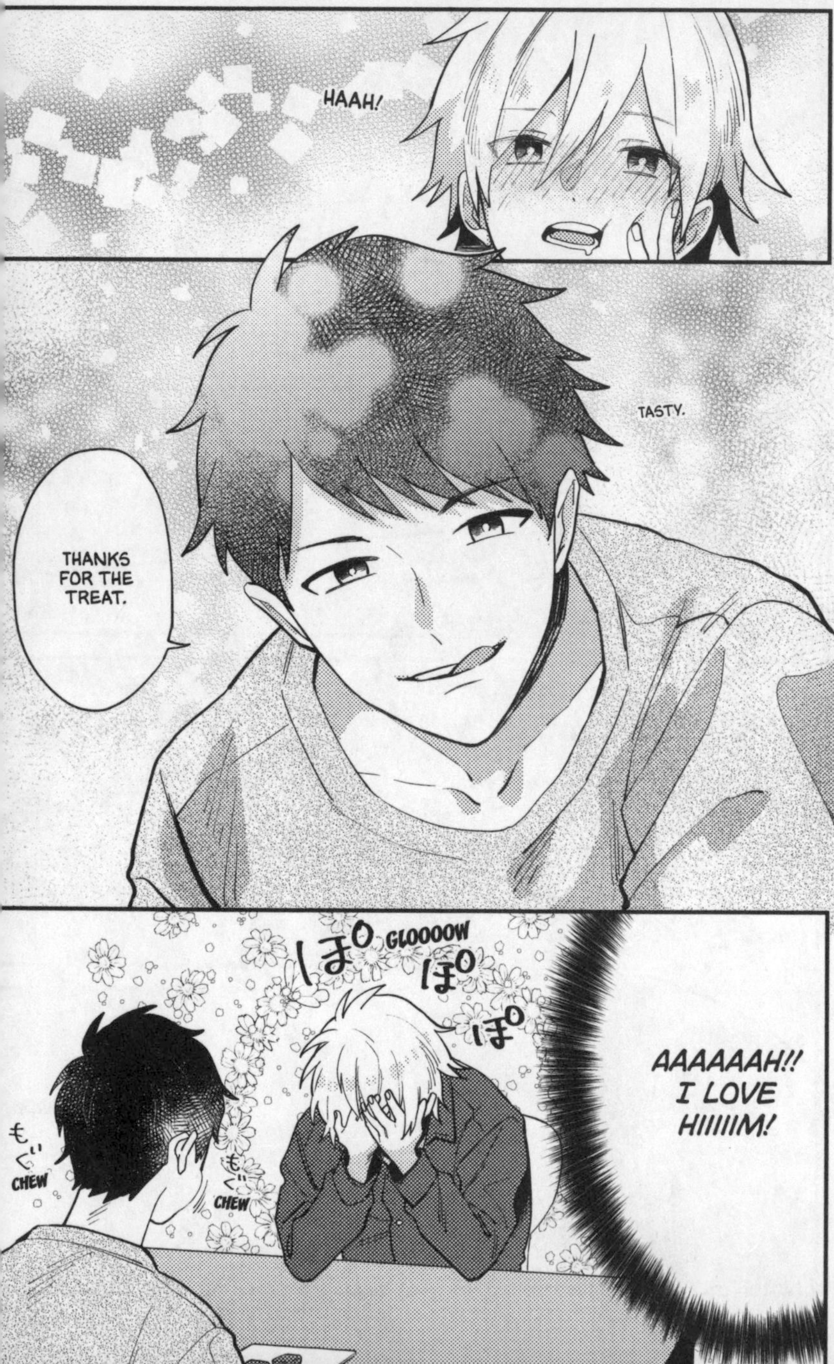
HAAH!
TASTY.
THANKS FOR THE TREAT.
AAAAAAH!! I LOVE HIIIIIM!
ぽ GLOOOOW ぽ ぽ
もぐ CHEW
もぐ CHEW

When You Say How You Feel...

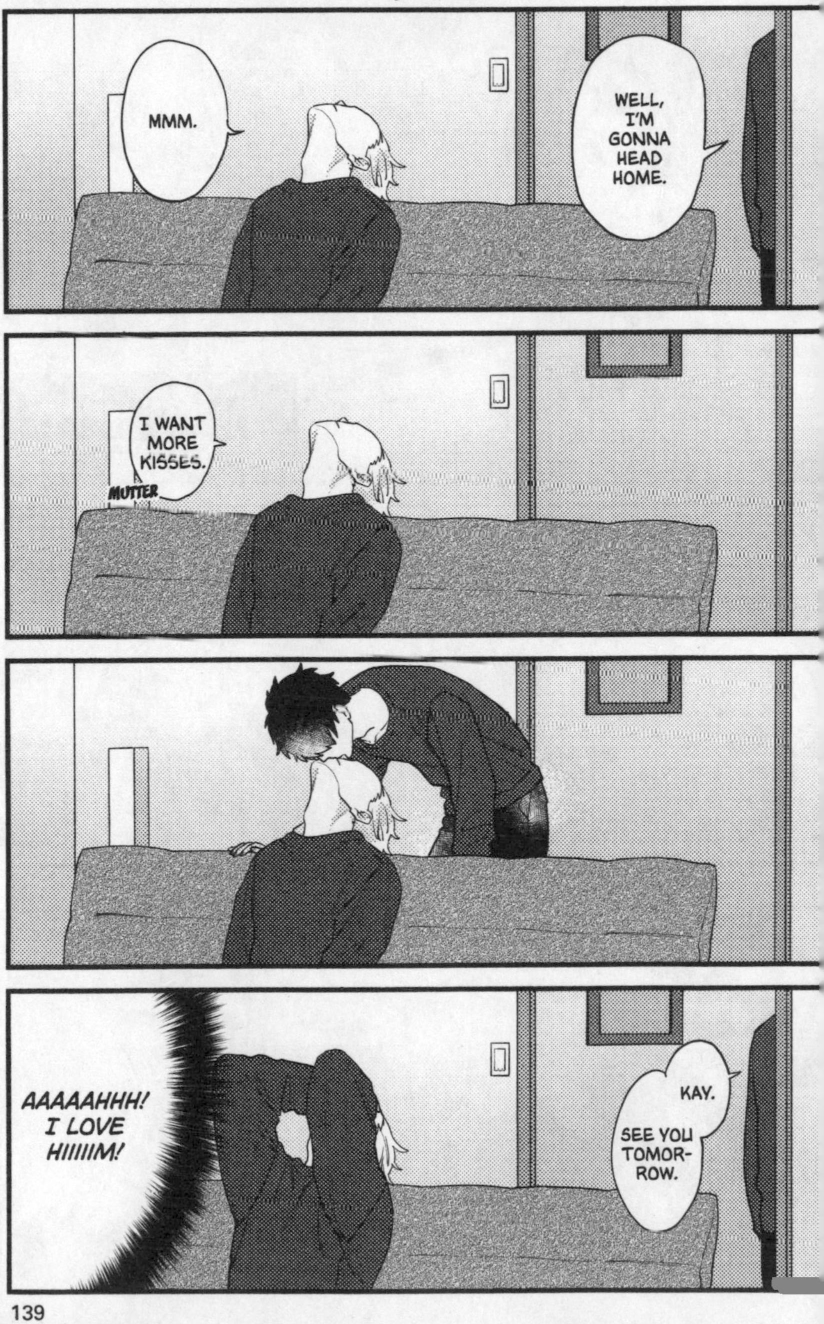
WELL, I'M GONNA HEAD HOME.
MMM.
I WANT MORE KISSES.
MUTTER
KAY.
SEE YOU TOMOR-ROW.
AAAAAHHH! I LOVE HIIIIIM!

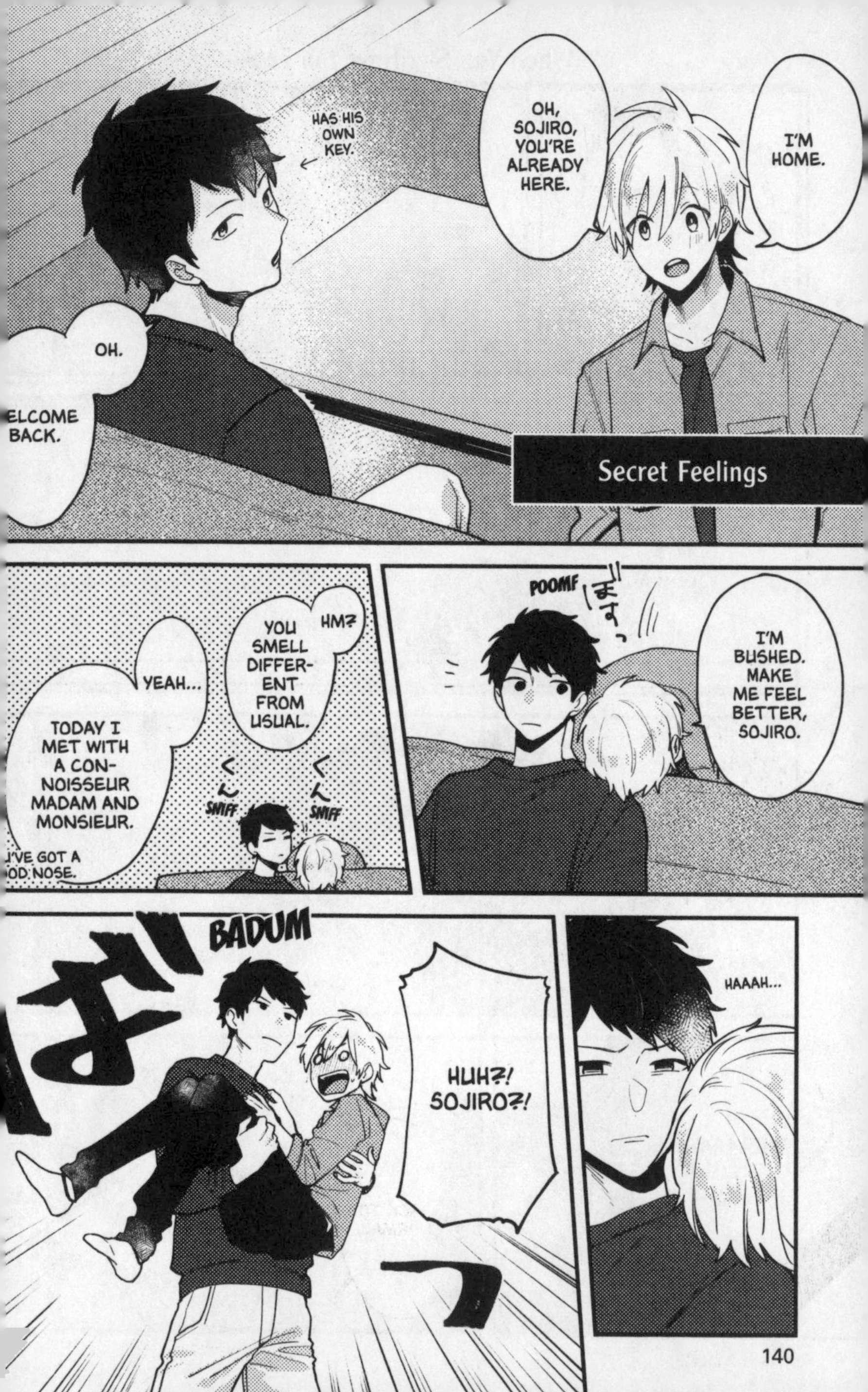

I'M HOME.
OH, SOJIRO, YOU'RE ALREADY HERE.
HAS HIS OWN KEY.
OH.
ELCOME BACK.
Secret Feelings
I'M BUSHED. MAKE ME FEEL BETTER, SOJIRO.
POOMF
ぼすっ
HM?
YOU SMELL DIFFER-ENT FROM USUAL.
くん
SNIFF
くん
SNIFF
YEAH...
TODAY I MET WITH A CON-NOISSEUR MADAM AND MONSIEUR.
U'VE GOT A OD NOSE.
HAAAH...
HUH?! SOJIRO?!
BADUM

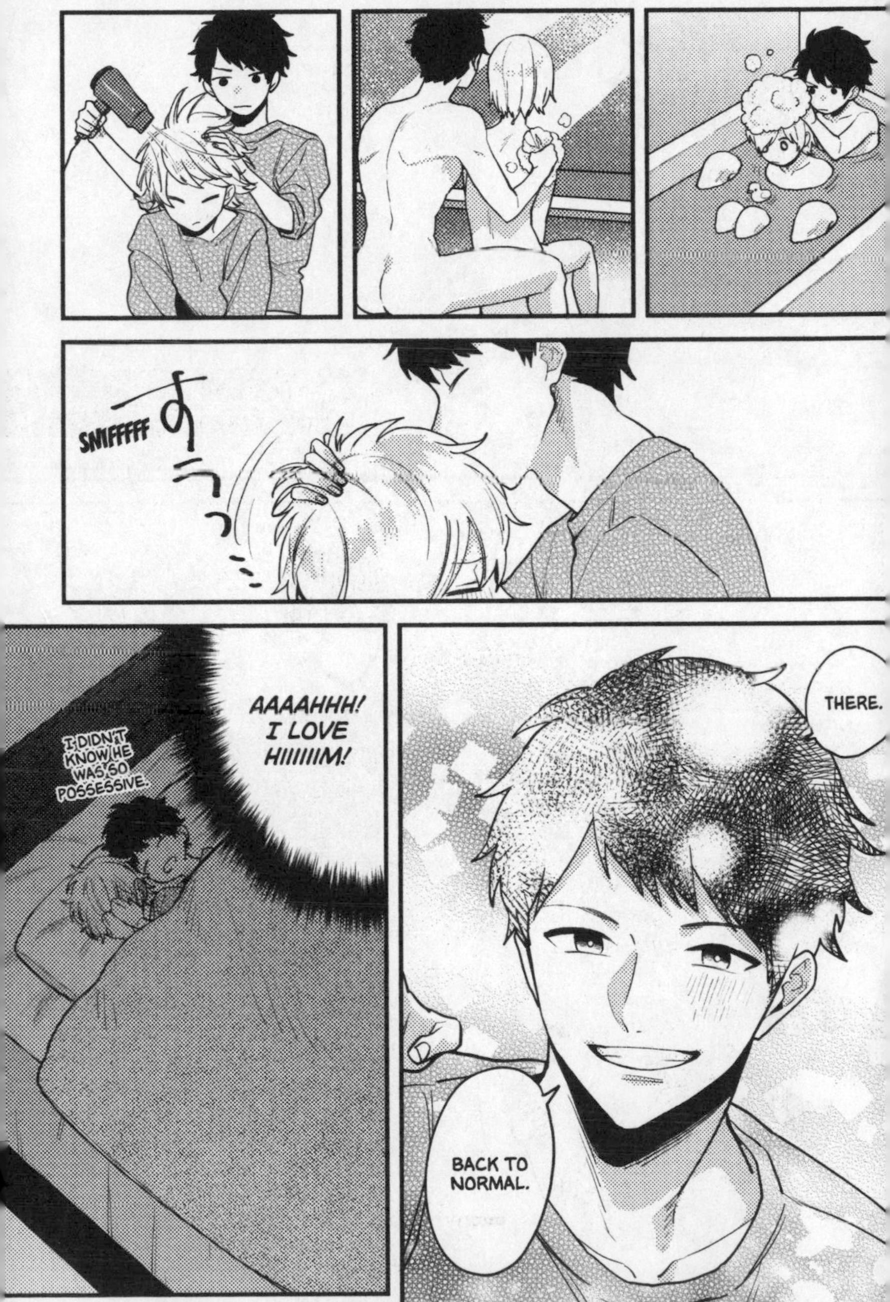
SNIFFFFF
すーっ
THERE.
BACK TO NORMAL.
AAAAHHH! I LOVE HIIIIIIM!
I DIDN'T KNOW HE WAS SO POSSESSIVE.

END

Chéri my defuting!

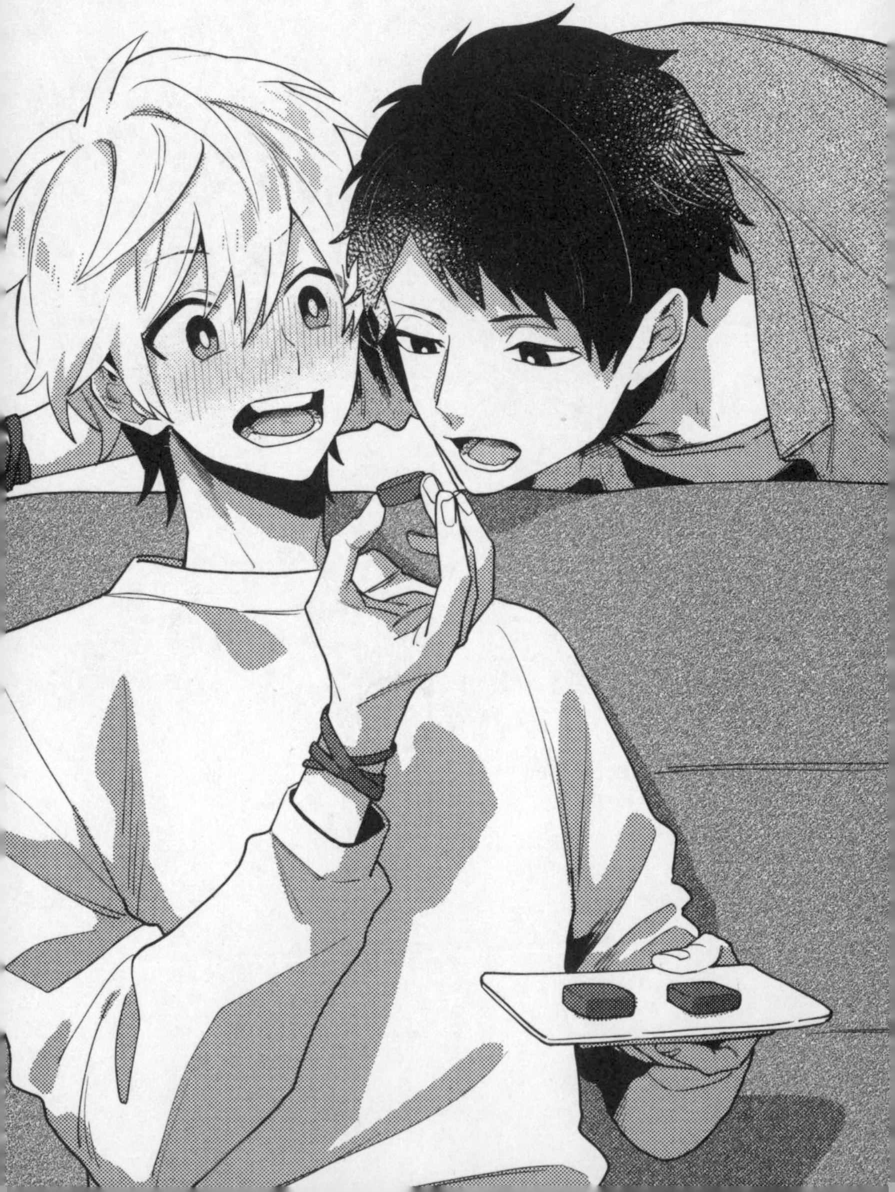

Hello. This is Okoge Mochino. And this is my second BL manga ever. Recently, I've been carrying around a head full of things I hadn't been able to draw, so I enjoyed getting to draw some of those things here. But man, I gotta say that BL, or rather manga overall, is hard!! There's so much I want to say, but I don't have enough space to express it all, so I have to give up on some of it. Still, all your fan letters gave me heaps of encouragement, so thank you very much! Those involved in the making of the book, such as the designer, everyone at the printing house, the editorial department, sales team, my editors H-san and K-san, and to all of you: thank you so much!

I look forward to seeing you again someday and somewhere!!

Okoge Mochino

KOIMONOGATARI

LOVE STORIES

1

TOHRU TAGURA

Tohru Tagura

KOIMONOGATARI: LOVE STORIES, VOLUME 1

§LOVE-x-LOVE§

When Yuiji accidentally overhears his classmate Yamato confessing to another friend that he's gay, his perspective shifts. Seeing Yamato in a new light, Yuiji does his best not to let prejudice color his view, but he still finds himself overthinking his classmates' interactions now. He especially notices the way Yamato looks at one particular boy: Yuiji's own best friend. Even though he tells himself he shouldn't get involved, Yuiji finds he just can't help it; watching Yamato's one-sided love draws him in a way he never expected. At first, it's empathy, knowing that the boy Yamato has his sights on is definitely straight and has no idea. But as his own friendship with Yamato develops and the two of them grow closer through a mutual study group, Yuiji comes to truly care about Yamato as a person, regardless of his sexuality. He only wants Yamato to be happy, and to be able to express his true self.

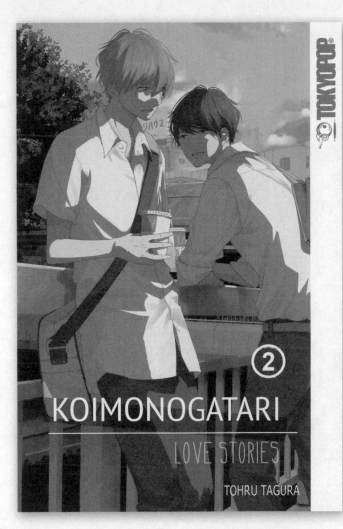

KOIMONOGATARI: LOVE STORIES, VOLUME 2
Tohru Tagura

KOIMONOGATARI

LOVE STORIES

TOHRU TAGURA

δLOVE-x-LOVEδ

When Yuiji accidentally finds out his classmate Yamato is gay and has a crush on his best friend, he doesn't know how to react at first. But after spending more time together, the two of them become close friends. While Yamato struggles with his sexuality, Yuiji supports him and keeps his secret, hoping that Yamato can find a way to accept himself and be happy. Meanwhile, Yuiji is having trouble feeling connected to his long-time girlfriend, realizing that although he still cares about her, the spark in their relationship has faded. Love is a complicated, messy thing — especially in high school, where hurtful rumors and intolerant classmates can make life unbearable. Yamato and Yuiji face their own individual struggles, but together, they learn one very important lesson: it's hard to search for romance if you don't love yourself first.

THE GOD AND THE FLIGHTLESS MESSENGER
Hagi

THE **God** & THE FLIGHTLESS **Messenger**

HAGI

§LOVE-x-LOVE§

A messenger's duty is to care for and protect the god they've been assigned to. In order to complete these tasks, such messengers require wings. Shin, however, can't fly. His tiny, useless wings make him the target of ridicule and scorn among the other messengers and have kept him from being able to serve a god... until now. Determined to prove himself as a capable messenger despite his flightlessness, Shin accepts his assignment to a mysterious being on one of the nearby mountains. At first, it seems an easy task to keep his charge safe and happy — especially when the deity in question is just a cute, fluffy ball of fur. But things aren't always what they seem. Recently, messengers flying over the strange god's mountain have been disappearing. Even as suspicion mounts against his deity, Shin just can't bring himself to think that such a gentle god could have a dark side. It's strange, but for some reason... the mysterious, fluffy being feels so familiar to him.

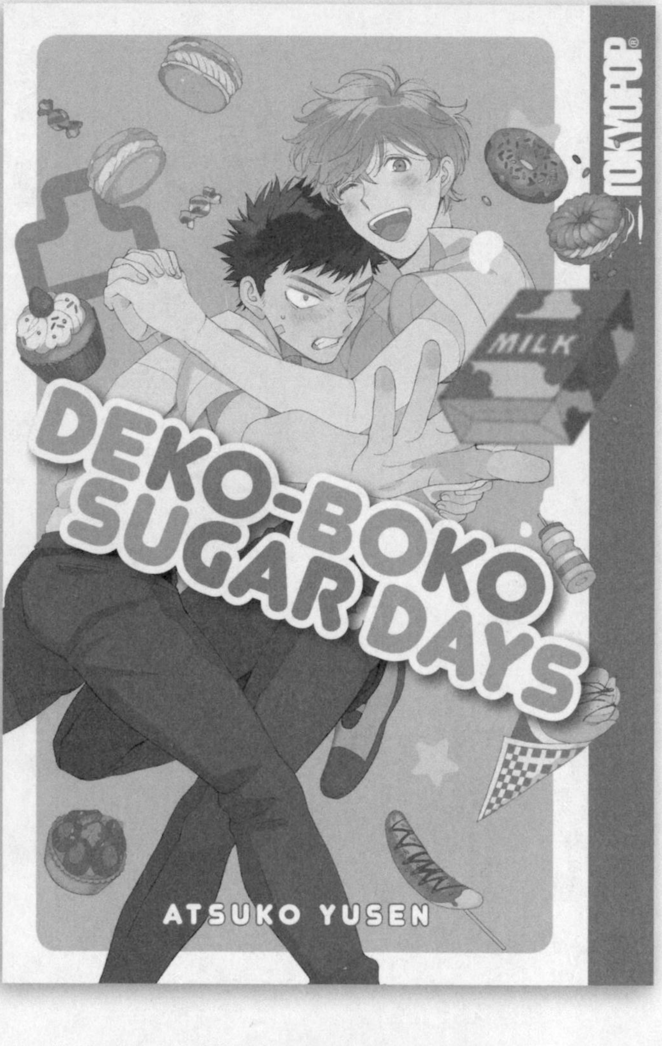
TOKYOPOP
MILK
DEKO-BOKO SUGAR DAYS
ATSUKO YUSEN

DEKOBOKO SUGAR DAYS

Atsuko Yusen

LOVE-x-LOVE MATURE 18+

Yuujirou Matsukaze has been close friends with Rui Hanamine since the two of them were children. Back then, Yuujirou was the one who stood up for and took care of his adorable, soft-hearted friend. But as it turns out, Yuujirou's childhood dreams end up growing a little too big to handle — or, rather, too tall! At over six feet in height, the cheerful and happy-go-lucky Rui towers over his would-be protector... and still has no idea Yuujirou's had a crush on him since they were kids!

TOKYOPOP

REPLAY

Saki Tsukahara

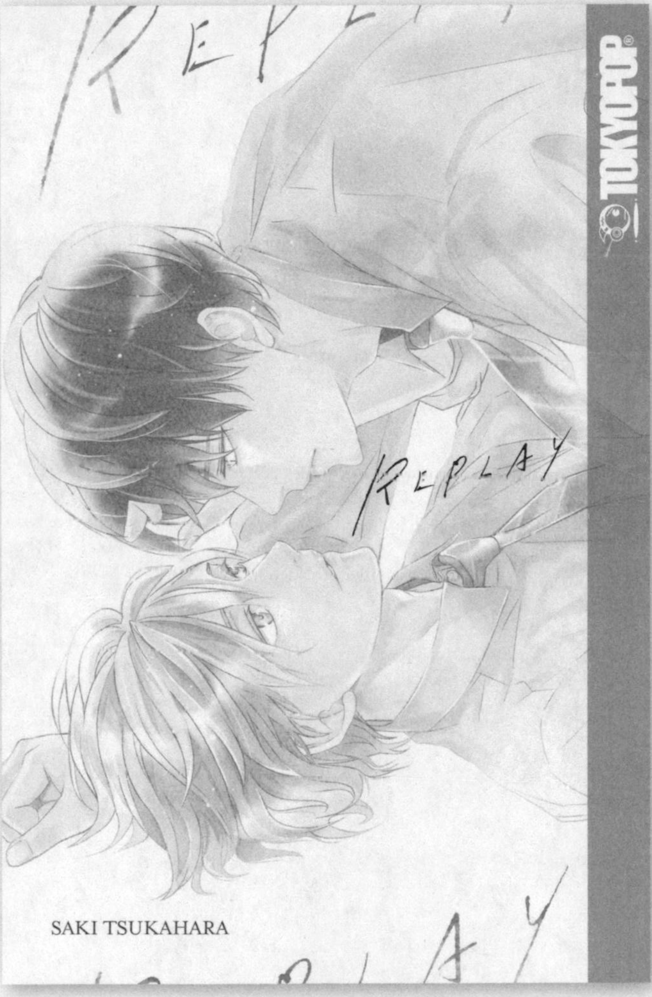
REPLAY
SAKI TSUKAHARA

MATURE 18+

LOVE x LOVE

TOKYOPOP

Yuta and Ritsu have been playing baseball together since they were children, but after being defeated in a local tournament over the summer, they must retire from the high school team to study for university entrance exams. Still, Yuta finds himself unable to give up his lingering attachment to baseball. The one person who can truly understand him is Ritsu, who has been acting worryingly distant since they quit the team. But there's something Yuta himself doesn't understand... Does he think of Ritsu as his partner in the way that a teammate would, or is the affection between them something stronger?

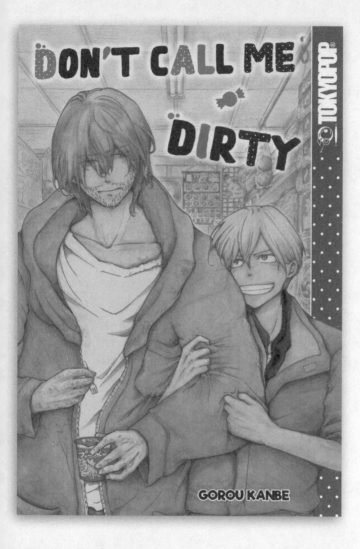

DON'T CALL ME DIRTY

Gorou Kanbe

♂LOVE-x-LOVE♂

After some time attempting a long-distance relationship, Shouji is crestfallen when he finds out his crush isn't gay. Having struggled with his sexuality for years, he tries to distract himself from the rejection, in part by helping out at the neighboring sweets shop — but when a young homeless man called Hama shows up at the store, Shouji finds himself curious to learn more about him. Attempting to make their way in a society that labels each of them as 'outcasts' and 'dirty,' the two men grow closer. Together, they begin to find they have more in common than either of them could have anticipated.

DON'T CALL ME DADDY

Gorou Kanbe

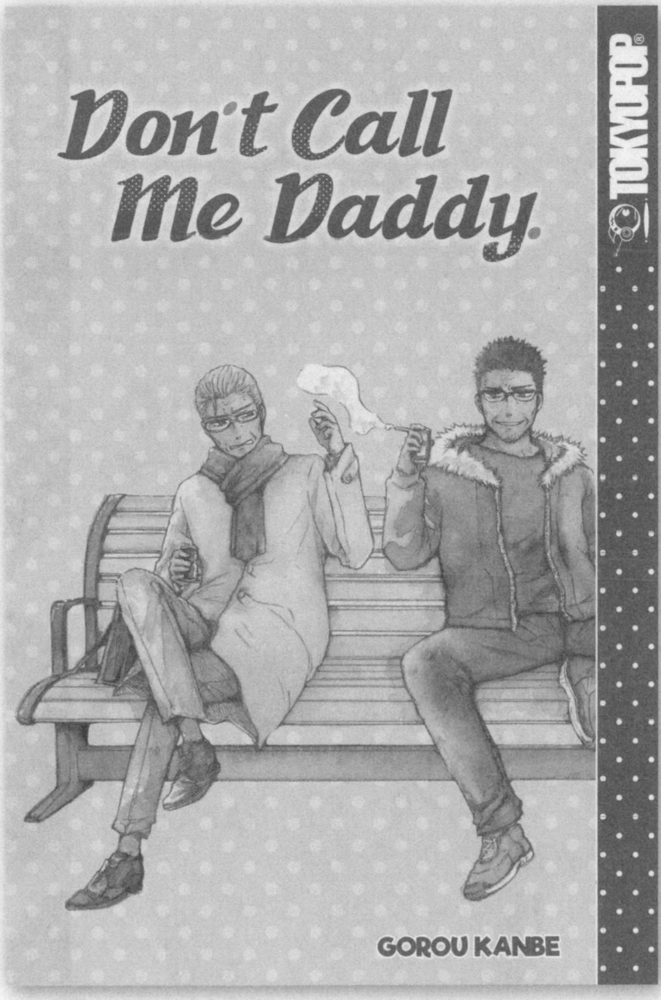
Don't Call Me Daddy
TOKYOPOP
GOROU KANBE

LOVE-x-LOVE

Long before the events of Don't Call Me Dirty, Hanao Kaji and Ryuuji Mita were close friends... When Ryuuji is left to raise his son Shouji as a single father, Hanao steps up to help him out. At first, their family life is happy and content, but Hanao's true feelings for Ryuuji become more and more difficult for him to ignore. The pressure of staying closeted eventually becomes too much to bear; Hanao leaves, choosing to run from his feelings and his fears of somehow "messing up" Shouji's life when he starts getting teased at school for having two dads. Years later, when he comes home to care for his aging father and ends up advising Shouji on his blossoming relationship with Hama, Hanao realizes it's time to face his own past... and his future.

TOKYOPOP

THE CAT PROPOSED

Dento Hayane

The Cat Proposed

Dento Hayane

δLOVE-x-LOVEδ

Matoi Souta is an overworked office worker tired of his life. Then, on his way home from a long day of work one day, he decides to watch a traditional Japanese play. But something strange happens. He could have sworn he saw one of the actors has cat ears. It turns out that the man is actually a bakeneko — a shapeshifting cat from Japanese folklore. And then, the cat speaks: "From now on, you will be my mate."

SERVANT & LORD

Lo & Lorinell Yu

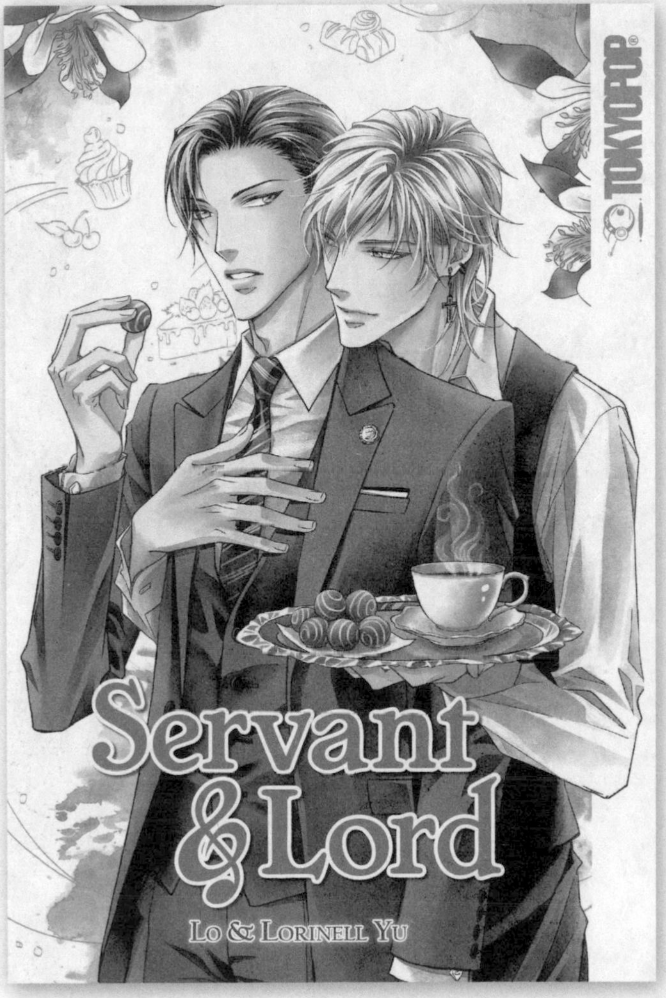
TOKYOPOP
Servant & Lord
Lo & Lorinell Yu

LOVE-x-LOVE

Christian has always admired handsome, talented composer Daniel. Their shared appreciation for music marked the beginning of a friendship between a willful boy and a sophisticated young man... But when tragedy strikes and circumstances twist around to put Daniel in the service of Christian's wealthy family, their bond is tried in unexpected ways. Years ago, the universal language of music drew them toward one another. Now, Christian has to hope it's still enough to bridge the gap between their vastly different lives.

TOKYOPOP

STAR COLLECTOR, VOLUME 1

Anna Backhausen & Sophie Schönhammer

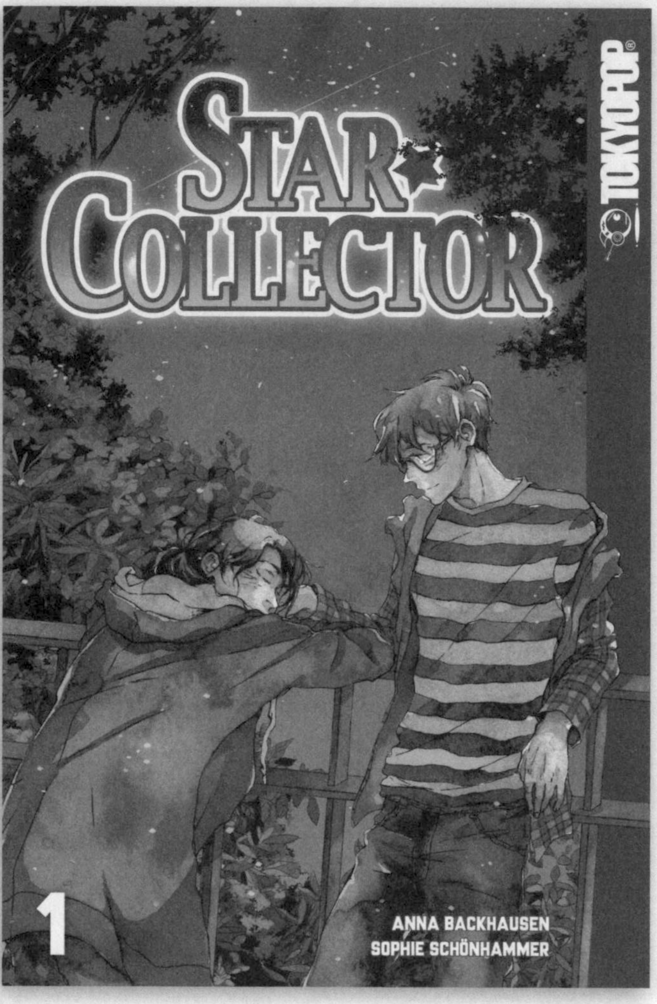
STAR COLLECTOR
TOKYOPOP
1
ANNA BACKHAUSEN
SOPHIE SCHÖNHAMMER

LOVE-x-LOVE

Fynn's favorite activities are skipping class, smoking, and lying around. So when he's told it's time to shape up and try doing something else for a change, he has no idea where to even start. Then, on a nighttime walk around his neighborhood, he sees a stranger with a telescope up on a hill: his name is Niko, and he loves to watch the stars. Intrigued, Flynn decides to find out more about this nerdy boy and what could be so interesting about the night sky that he loves so much.

TOKYOPOP

STAR COLLECTOR, VOLUME 2

Anna Backhausen & Sophie Schönhammer

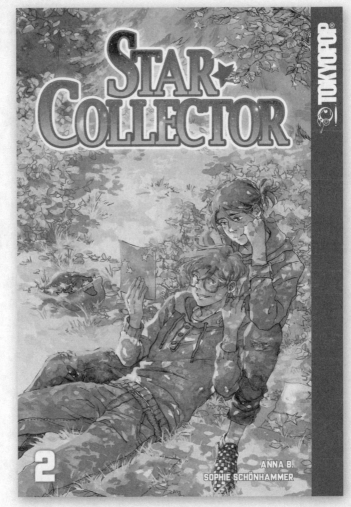

δLOVE-x-LOVEδ

Fynn's favorite activities are skipping class, smoking, and lying around. So when he's told it's time to shape up and try doing something else for a change, he has no idea where to even start. Then, on a nighttime walk around his neighborhood, he sees a stranger with a telescope up on a hill: his name is Niko, and he loves to watch the stars. Intrigued, Flynn decides to find out more about this nerdy boy and what could be so interesting about the night sky that he loves so much. This is the second and final volume of the Star Collector series.

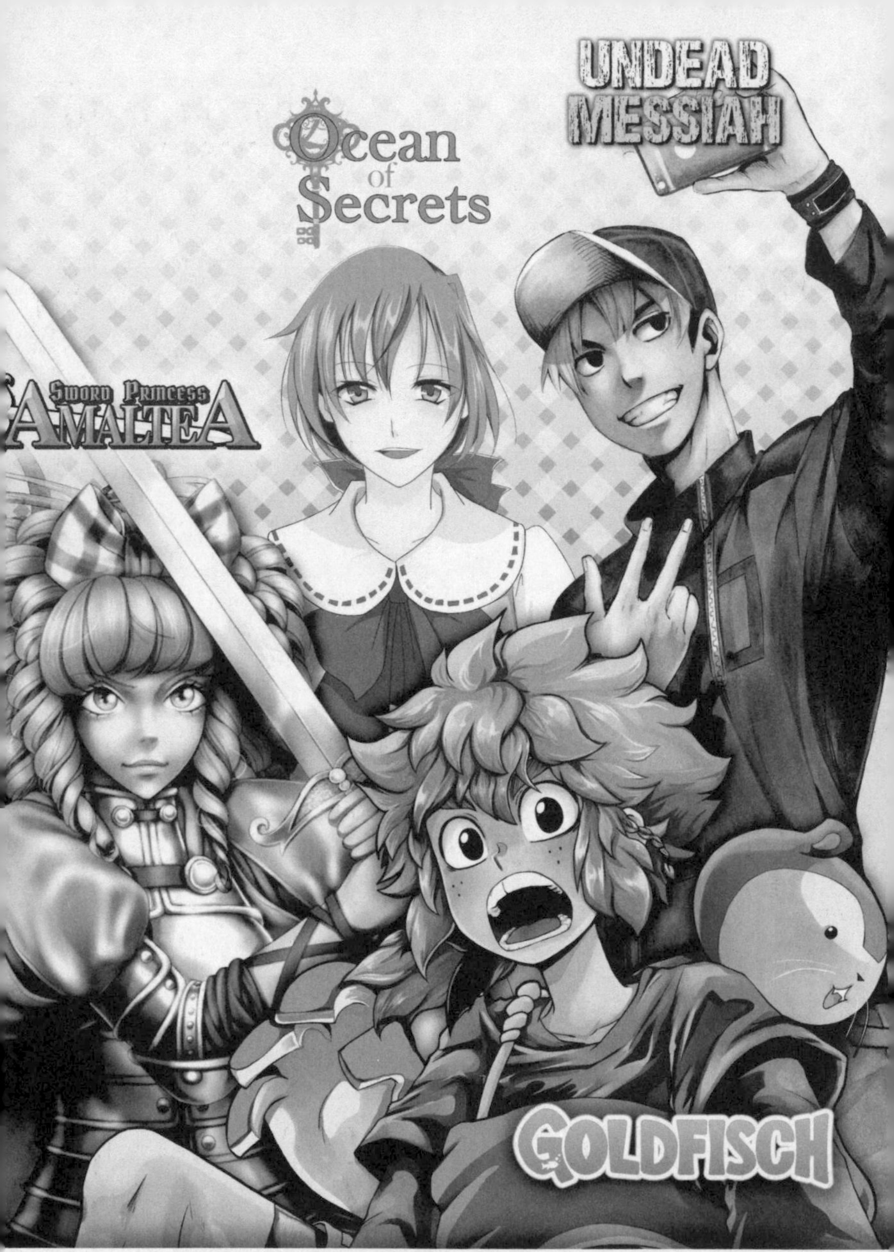
UNDEAD MESSIAH
Ocean of Secrets
SWORD PRINCESS AMALTEA
GOLDFISCH

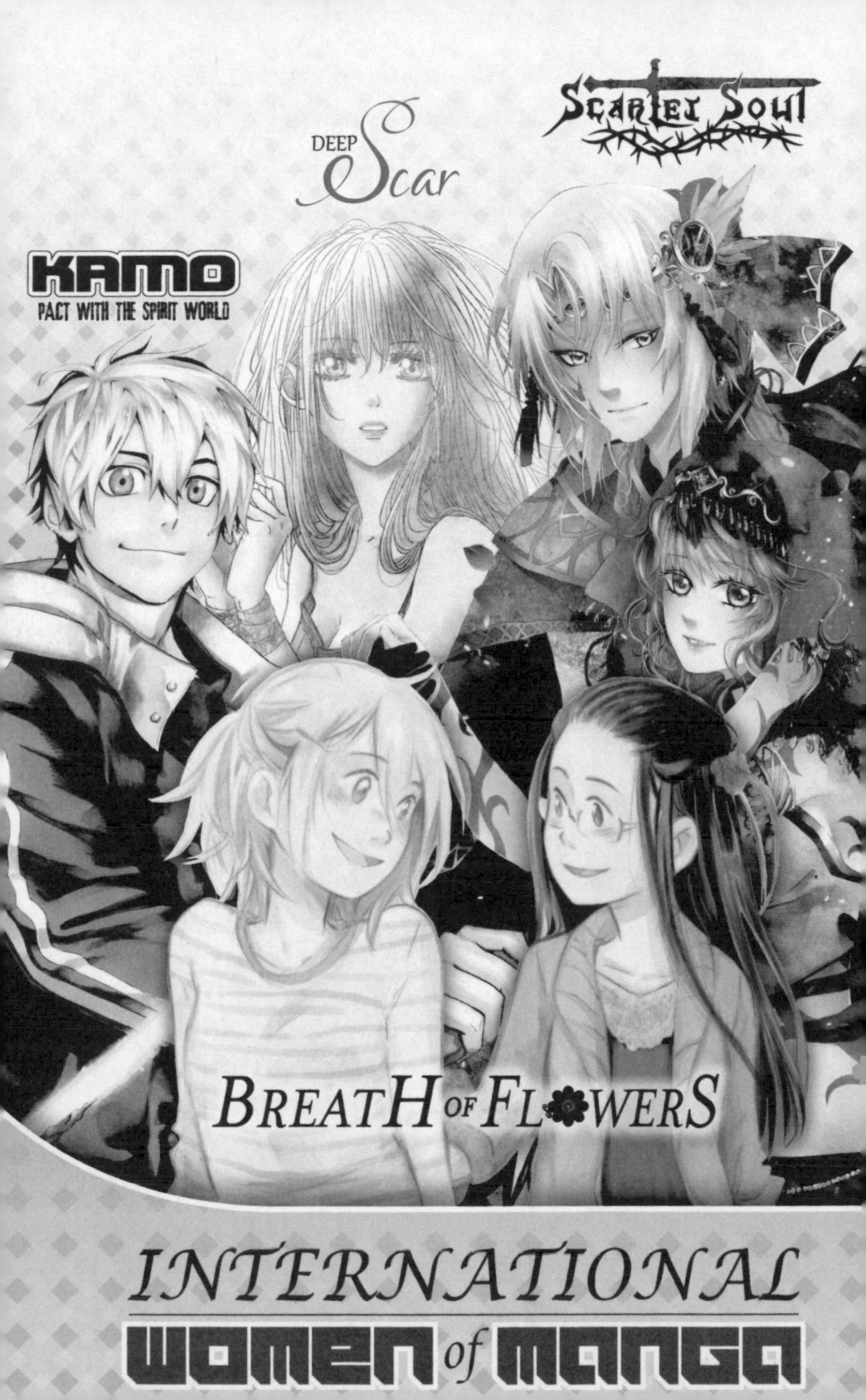
SCARLET SOUL
DEEP Scar
KAMO
PACT WITH THE SPIRIT WORLD
BREATH OF FLOWERS
INTERNATIONAL
WOMEN of MANGA

Chéri, My Destiny!
Manga by Okoge Mochino

Editor	-	Lena Atanassova
Marketing Associate	-	Kae Winters
Translator	-	Christine Dashiell
Copyeditor	-	Tina Tseng
Graphic Designer	-	Sol DeLeo
Editorial Associate	-	Janae Young
Licensing Liaison	-	Arika Yanaka
Retouching and Lettering	-	Vibrraant Publishing Studio
Editor-in-Chief & Publisher	-	Stu Levy

A  Manga

TOKYOPOP and 🐸 are trademarks or registered trademarks of TOKYOPOP Inc.

TOKYOPOP Inc.
5200 W. Century Blvd. Suite 705
Los Angeles, 90045

E-mail: info@TOKYOPOP.com
Come visit us online at www.TOKYOPOP.com

f www.facebook.com/TOKYOPOP
🐦 www.twitter.com/TOKYOPOP
𝓅 www.pinterest.com/TOKYOPOP
📷 www.instagram.com/TOKYOPOP

ISBN: 978-1-4278-6807-7
First TOKYOPOP Printing: May 2021
10 9 8 7 6 5 4 3 2 1
Printed in CANADA

STOP

THIS IS THE BACK OF THE BOOK!

How do you read manga-style? It's simple! Let's practice -- just start in the top right panel and follow the numbers below!

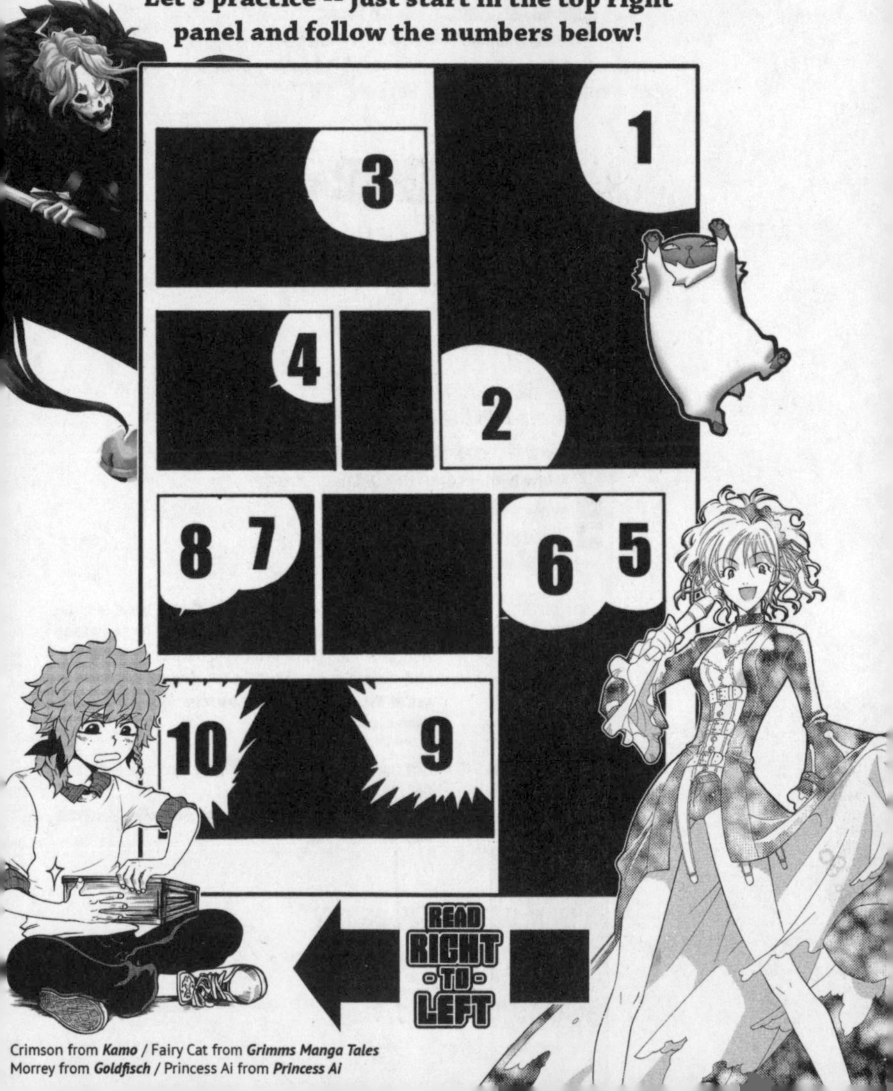
1
2
3
4
5
6
7
8
9
10
READ
RIGHT
-TO-
LEFT

Crimson from ***Kamo*** / Fairy Cat from ***Grimms Manga Tales***
Morrey from ***Goldfisch*** / Princess Ai from ***Princess Ai***